analysing ARCHITECTURE
THIRD EDITION, REVISED AND ENLARGED

'One would have no hesitation in recommending this book to new students: it introduces many ideas and references central to the study of architecture. The case studies are particularly informative. A student would find this a useful aid to identifying the many important issues seriously engaged with in Architecture.'

Lorraine Farrelly, *Architectural Design*

'The most lucid and readable introduction to architecture I have read.'

Professor Roger Stonehouse, Manchester School of Architecture

Clear and accessible, *analysing* ARCHITECTURE opens a fresh way to understanding architecture. It offers a unique 'notebook' of architectural strategies to present an engaging introduction to elements and concepts in architectural design. Beautifully illustrated throughout with the author's original drawings, examples are drawn from across the world and many periods of architectural history (from prehistoric times to the recent past) to illustrate analytical themes and to show how drawing can be used to study architecture. Since its first edition appeared in 1997, *analysing* ARCHITECTURE has established itself internationally as one of the key texts in architectural education.

This third edition includes a new chapter discussing the ways analysing examples cultivates a capacity for design. Original chapters have been expanded, new case studies added and the format rearranged for greater clarity. The bibliography of recommended supplementary reading has also been extended.

In *analysing* ARCHITECTURE, Simon Unwin clearly identifies the key elements of architecture and conceptual themes apparent in buildings and relevant to other works of architecture such as gardens and cities. He describes ideas for use in the active process of design. Breaking down the grammar of architecture into themes and moves, Unwin exposes its underlying patterns to reveal the organisational strategies that lie beneath the superficial appearances of buildings.

Exploring buildings as results of the interaction of people with the world around them, *analysing* ARCHITECTURE offers a definition of architecture as 'identification of place' and provides a greater understanding of architecture as a creative discipline. This book presents a powerful impetus for readers to develop their own capacities for architectural design. It will also be of use to all those with an interest in the human occupation of and involvement with space: anthropologists; archaeologists; film-makers; installation artists; planners; urban designers; politicians….

Simon Unwin is Professor of Architecture at the University of Dundee, Scotland. He has lived in Great Britain and Australia, and taught or lectured on his work in China, Israel, India, Sweden, Turkey and the United States. Its international relevance is indicated by *analysing* ARCHITECTURE's translation into Chinese, Japanese, Korean, Persian and Spanish and adoption for architecture courses around the world.

Some more reviews of *analysing* ARCHITECTURE (previous editions):

'Unwin chooses to look at the underlying elements of architecture rather than, as is more usual, at the famous names, styles, movements and chronology of the genre. This rejection of the conventional art-historical approach can lead to interesting conclusions… it is all presented cogently and convincingly through the medium of Unwin's own drawings.'

Hugh Pearman, *The Sunday Times*

'In clear, precise diagrams and thoughtful text, author Simon Unwin offers an engaging methodology for the study of architecture and aesthetic systems. Time-tested buildings from classical temples to traditional Japanese homes and early modernist masterpieces, are explored in this wide ranging, but focused study. Unwin demonstrates that while architectural styles change over time, the underlying principles that organize quality designs remain remarkably consistent. This book is a must for all architectural students interested in acquiring the visual skills needed to understand a wide variety of design methodologies.'

Diane78 (New York), *Amazon.com website*

'The text has been carefully written to avoid the use of jargon and it introduces architectural ideas in a straightforward fashion. This, I suspect, will give it a well-deserved market beyond that of architects and architectural students.'

Barry Russell, *Environments BY DESIGN*

'From the campsites of primitive man to the sophisticated structures of the late twentieth century, architecture as an essential function of human activity is explained clearly, and illustrated with the author's own excellent drawings. Highly recommended as a well-organized and readable introduction.'

medals@win-95.com, *Amazon.com website*

'This book establishes a systematic method in analyzing architecture. It explains how architectural elements are combined together to form designs that could relate an appropriate sense of "place" specific to the programme as well as the environment surrounding it. The book is well illustrated with diagrams and examples. An extremely useful introductory guide for those who want to learn more about the basics of architecture.'

nikana99@hotmail.com, *Amazon.com website*

'This is an excellent book, recommended to anyone seriously interested in architecture. Its starting point is Unwin's ability to draw well – to think through his hands, as it were. This is fundamental to architectural skill and Unwin has used it to "talk back to himself" and describe the architecture around him. He uses this skill to romp through a huge number and variety of buildings and architectural situations in order to describe architectural strategies. Unwin has at the heart of his book a definition and understanding of architecture that we thoroughly endorse: to be dealt with in terms of its conceptual organisation and intellectual structure. But he adds to this potentially dry definition an emotive overlay or parallel: architecture as the identification of place ("Place is to architecture as meaning is to language"). Thus he takes on the issue of why we value architecture.'

http://www.architecturelink.org.uk/GMoreSerious2.html

'*Analysing* **ARCHITECTURE** should become an essential part of all architectural education and an informative guide to the powerful analytical tool of architectural drawing.'

Howard Ray Lawrence, Pennsylvania State University

'Excellent in every way – a core book, along with *An Architecture Notebook*.'

Terry Robson, Teaching Fellow, University of Bath, UK

'I think this is an excellent book and I will continue to recommend it to my students.'

Professor Donald Hanlon, University of Wisconsin-Milwaukee, US

'Probably the best introductory book on architecture.'

Andrew Higgott, Lecturer in Architecture, University of East London, UK

Architecture Notebooks *by Simon Unwin:*

An Architecture Notebook: Wall
Doorway

  www.routledge.com/textbooks/9780415489287/

analysing *ARCHITECTURE*

THIRD EDITION, REVISED AND ENLARGED

Simon Unwin

Routledge
Taylor & Francis Group

London and New York

First published 2009 by Routledge
2 Park Square, Milton Park, Abingdon, Oxon, OX14 4RN

Simultaneously published in the USA and Canada by Routledge
270 Madison Avenue, New York, NY10016

Routledge is an imprint of the Taylor & Francis Group, an informa business

First edition © 1997 Simon Unwin

Second edition © 2003 Simon Unwin

This third edition © 2009 Simon Unwin

Designed and typeset in Adobe Garamond Pro by Simon Unwin

Printed and bound in Great Britain by The Cromwell Press, Trowbridge, Wiltshire

British Library Cataloguing in Publication Data
A catalogue record for this book is available from the British Library

Library of Congress Cataloging-in-Publication Data
A catalog record for this book has been requested

ISBN10 0-415-48927-X (hbk)
ISBN10 0-415-48928-8 (pbk)
ISBN10 0-203-88090-0 (ebk)

ISBN13 978-0-415-48927-0 (hbk)
ISBN13 978-0-415-48928-7 (pbk)
ISBN13 978-0-203-88090-6 (ebk)

for Gill

CONTENTS

check PORLIO.

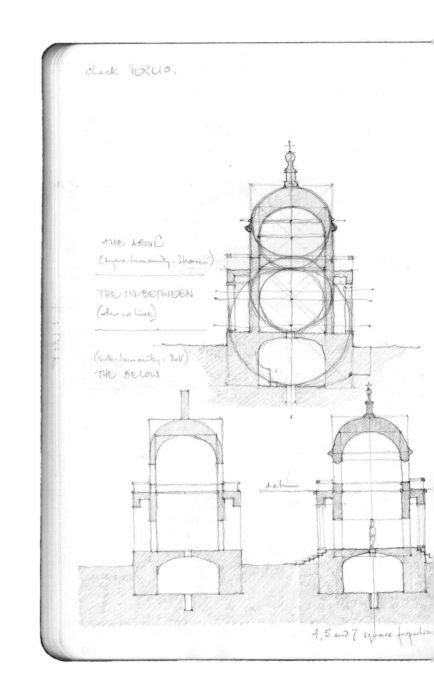

THE ABOVE
(supra-humanity. 'Heaven')

THE IN-BETWEEN
(where we live)

(sub-humanity. 'hell')
THE BELOW

datum

4, 5 and 7 square proportion

Tempietto , S Pietro in Montorio, Rome   4. April 2008
Bramante 1502   drawn 9 April 2008
very approximate proportions of courtyard.

123

analysing **ARCHITECTURE**

'The search is what everyone would undertake if he were not stuck in the everydayness of his own life. To be aware of the possibility of the search is to be on to something. Not to be on to something is to be in despair.'

Walker Percy – *The Moviegoer*, quoted in Lawrence Weschler – *Seeing is Forgetting the Name of the Thing One Sees: a Life of Contemporary Artist Robert Irwin*, 1982.

PREFACE TO THE THIRD EDITION

There was a spin-doctor character* in a BBC political comedy called 'The Thick of It' (2007) who once said firmly into the face of an underling, 'Don't ever, EVER call me a bully!… I'm SO much worse!' Well, I've heard people call architecture a 'visual art' and it makes me want to reply, 'Don't ever, EVER call architecture a visual art! It's SO much more!'

Architecture is the most wonderfully rich art form. Perhaps too rich. Perhaps it is the jealousy of other art forms that has led to it being 'brought down a peg or two' and consigned to being considered (as suggested in my *Preface to the Second Edition*) as merely a visual or sculptural art, or a media sensation. Perhaps architecture is richer than even architects can cope with. Certainly, to describe (and worse, to conceive) architecture as merely a visual or sculptural art form is seriously to diminish its role in framing just about everything we do in setting the spatial matrix of life. Architecture has the potential to establish and influence relationships, elicit emotional responses, even to affect how we behave and who we think we are. Architects who are able to inform their work with more than a small fraction of architecture's full potential are few.

In all human culture, even for people who live in open landscapes, architecture is as ubiquitous as (perhaps even more so than) language. (Just think of the huge variety of architectural forms covered by the word 'window', infinitely more subtle in their variations than can be encompassed even by 'oriel', 'bay', 'leaded', 'picture', 'stained glass', 'plate-glass', 'small-paned', 'Diocletian', 'Venetian'….) Architecture is the practical, poetic and philosophical art by which we organise and give form to space; it is the medium by which we make sense of our world spatially and physically. Through history and now, it has often involved building complex and expensive structures, but equally it might involve no more than drawing a circle on a beach, sweeping an area of ground clear of scrub for a ceremony; or even as little (or much) as identifying distinctive landscape features with mythical beings and events. It may be difficult to comprehend but architecture nevertheless deals with the inescapable settings of our lives, and deserves the effort required (particularly of those who wish to do it professionally) to understand how it works and how its powers can be used.

In its third edition, this book is approaching three hundred pages in length, but still it is possible to deal with architecture's richness as an art in little more than an introductory way. (This is partly because of space, but also because I am still learning.) Additional examples, especially from the most recent past, have been included and new case studies added. There is a new website associated with the book, discussing how to use a notebook to study architecture: **www.routledge.com/textbooks/9780415489287/**. (The bibliography

* *The character was Malcolm Tucker, played by Peter Capaldi. 'The Thick of It' was devised and directed by Armando Iannucci, and written by Jesse Armstrong, Simon Blackwell and Tony Roche.*

3

of recommended supplementary reading has also been extended, and the index revised.) But the purpose of the book remains: to understand the workings of the common language of architecture that has been developed since we human beings (and animals for that matter) began to make places by which to situate ourselves, our activities and belongings within the world in which we find ourselves. To do this it is necessary to include examples from ancient as well as contemporary times, primitive as well as sophisticated situations, and from as wide a geographical spread as possible. (The translation of previous editions into Chinese, Japanese, Korean, Persian and Spanish, as well the use of *analysing* ARCHITECTURE in architecture courses around the world, seems to justify and validate this approach.)

Perhaps most significantly, this new edition of *analysing* ARCHITECTURE offers a discussion of the ways in which studying the work of others cultivates, informs and stimulates the capacity for design. This is an aspect of the development of an ability to do architecture that is clearly evident in architects (great and mediocre) through the centuries but which is sometimes acknowledged only reluctantly by student architects inclined to believe that their own originality and greatness will prosper best by insulating their creative genius from 'corruption' by the ideas and accomplishments of others; and anyway, they do not want to be accused of copying. But it was not 'copying' when Le Corbusier, probably the most inventive of twentieth-century architects, drew on his extensive travels through Greece, Italy and Turkey to develop architectural ideas informed by his analysis of monasteries, ancient villas and troglodyte houses. It is not 'copying' either when Zaha Hadid seeks to subvert orthodoxy by distorting the regular orthogonal geometries by which buildings have been ordered since time immemorial. Both evolutionary development and contradictory revolution depend on understanding what has gone before.

Simon Unwin, September 2008

PREFACE TO THE SECOND EDITION

Since it was published in 1997, *analysing* ARCHITECTURE has established itself as one of the set texts for student architects. I am gratified that the book has been found to be useful, and thank all those who have written with supportive comments.

Preparation of this second edition has involved both expansion and clarification. I have expanded most of the chapters by including a few additional examples, and in some cases written additional sections dealing with new themes. I have divided the previously over-long chapter on *Geometry in Architecture* into two separate chapters on *Geometries of Being* and *Ideal Geometry*. I have also added some more case studies at the end of the book, broadening the range of examples covered. In various places I have added quotations from novels, mostly descriptions of places, as reminders that the core of architecture is about producing practical and poetic settings for life.

I have revised the whole of the text, clarifying arguments and ideas where I have felt necessary. Mostly these revisions have been in the form of minor adjustments, the insertion of a better word or an explanatory sentence here and there. The places where I have felt the need for more substantial clarification have been in the chapters on *Architecture as Identification of Place* and *Temples and Cottages*.

The aim of the second edition remains the same as in the first, to offer the beginnings of a framework for the analytical understanding of the workings of architecture. In this edition however, in response to some observations by readers, I have laid greater stress on the suggestion that the acquisition of an analytical understanding of the workings of architecture is not meant as an academic exercise that is sufficient to itself, but should be seen as a foundation and stimulus for the creative activity of design. This book is fundamentally about ideas, and ideas are the 'stock in trade' of architects. It deals with architecture as an activity, as a matter of conception before perception. It is for people who are engaged in the challenge of *doing* architecture, not just looking at it. The aim is to try to understand how architecture works and what it can do; to identify what William Richard Lethaby called its 'powers' (see the quotation on p. 8).

The method adopted is teleological, in that it analyses products of architecture to expose the intellectual processes underlying them. This book does not promote a particular process for design. Rather it seeks to expose the 'meta-language' of architecture, the workings of which are apparent in examples from across the world and from all times. The task is one of description, not of prescription. *Analysing* ARCHITECTURE is not about how architecture should be done but about how it has been done, and is intended as a stimulus to thinking about how it might be done. This 'might' originates as much from contradiction as from emulation or imitation. One can find direction by contrariness, as children often demonstrate. It is a noble aim to try the opposite of what has been tried by others, even though the results might turn out to be desolate.

Part of the original purpose of this book was as a reminder that architectural design is about a great deal more than visual appearance. I used to complain about what I saw as the diminishment of architecture to criteria that focus on style and visual impact. Like Le Corbusier in *Towards a New Architecture*, I would complain about 'eyes which do not see'. I was overawed by the realisation that architecture is fundamentally about place; that place-making, or even just place-choosing, comes well before (and can be more consequential than) the sculptured appearance of buildings. I was also fascinated by the idea of architecture as a philosophical discipline that works not in words but through the organisation of the physical world. The mind tries to *makes sense* of the world through philosophy, usually expressed in words; but it also *makes sense* of the world physically through architecture. Architecture, in that it sets the matrix within which lives are lived, is philosophical at a fundamental, though non-verbal, level.

I am still driven by these interests, though now I have become reconciled to the power of image, to the inescapable fact that most architecture is promoted through photographs in architectural magazines, and that visual appearance is the basis on which many in architecture (critics as well as architects themselves) make their living. Superficiality rules, to a large extent. This may always be so but it nevertheless remains important for architects to understand the underlying workings of what they do, as a basis for striving towards the highest levels of intellectual and poetic aspiration. That is what this book is about.

Simon Unwin, January 2003

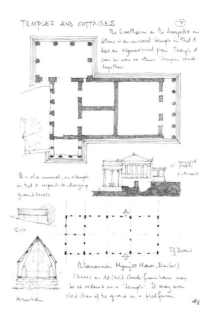

INTRODUCTION

'Modern builders need a classification of architectural factors irrespective of time and country, a classification by essential variation…. In architecture more than anywhere we are the slaves of names and categories, and so long as the whole field of past architectural experiment is presented to us accidentally only under historical schedules, designing architecture is likely to be conceived as scholarship rather than as the adaptation of its accumulated powers to immediate needs….'

W.R. Lethaby – *Architecture*, 1911, pp. 8-9.

INTRODUCTION

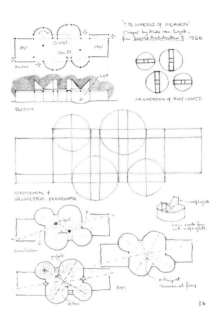

A notebook, in which you can analyse the work of other architects, is an essential accoutrement to learning how to do architecture.

Architecture is an adventure that is best explored through the challenge of doing it. But as in any creative discipline, the adventure of architecture can be informed by looking at what others have done and, through analysing their work, trying to understand the ways they have met the challenges. Look in the notebooks of any great architect and you will see a magpie acquiring ideas from wherever they may be found, playing with them and taking possession of them.

For some years I have used a notebook to analyse works of architecture. I find this exercise useful as an architect and it helps focus my teaching. My simple premise is that one's capacity for doing architecture can be developed by studying how it has been done by others. In this way one becomes aware of what Lethaby called 'the accumulated powers' of architecture and, by looking at how other architects have used them, see how they might be exploited and developed in one's own design.

The form of this book

The following chapters illustrate some of the themes that have emerged in my notebooks. They offer observations on architecture, its elements, the conditions that affect it and attitudes that might be adopted in doing it.

After a more detailed discussion of *How Analysis Helps Design*, the second chapter offers a working definition of architecture, as *Identification of Place*. This is put forward as the primary concern and burden of architecture as an activity. Realisation that the fundamental motivation of architecture is to identify (recognise, amplify, create the identity of) places where things happen has been the key that has allowed me access into the related areas explored in this book. As a theme it underpins everything that follows.

The subsequent chapters identify the *Basic* and *Modifying Elements of Architecture*, considerations that may be taken into account when doing it, and some common strategies for organising space. Each chapter deals with a specific theme; some deal with a number of sub-themes under a more general heading. These themes and sub-themes are like analytical filters or frames of reference. Each focuses on a particular aspect of the complexity of architecture: *Elements Doing More Than One Thing*; *Using Things That Are There*; *Primitive Place Types*; *Architecture as Making Frames*; *Temples and Cottages*; *Geometries of Being*; *Ideal Geometry*. After that there are four chapters that explore some of the fundamental strategies in organising space: relations between *Space and Structure*; *Parallel Walls*; *Stratification*; and *Transition, Hierarchy, Heart*.

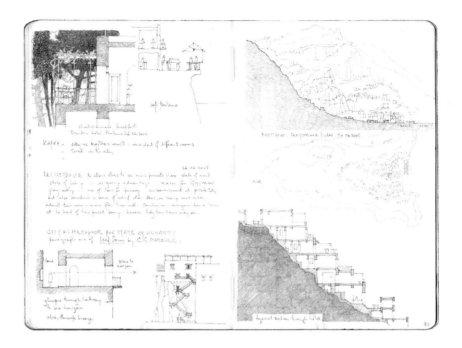

In your notebook you can record the places you visit…

In all the chapters there is an intimate connection between text and drawings. Some of the drawings are diagrams of particular elements or ideas but many are of examples that illustrate the themes being discussed. Examples are usually presented in plan or section, where their underlying ideas and conceptual strategies are often most clearly evident. Plans and sections tend to be the abstractions through which architects primarily design. They are often also the most appropriate medium for analysis.

Examples have been taken from many different times, cultures, climates and regions of the world. I have provided references to periodicals or other books where more information and photographs of the examples may be found.

The examples are dealt with as illustrating what might be termed the 'meta-language' (or 'common language') of architecture rather than the orthodox stylistic classifications of architectural history – 'Classical', 'Gothic', 'Modern', 'Queen Anne', 'Arts and Crafts' and so on. The examples in this book are grouped according to their underlying ideas and strategies rather than by style or period. Thus an ancient Greek temple might be discussed alongside a Gothic cathedral or a twentieth-century Finnish cemetery chapel because all employ the 'parallel-wall' strategy; or a Modern library might be discussed alongside a Victorian Gothic tower because both illustrate 'stratification'.

Some works have been selected as appropriate examples in more than one of the chapters, illustrating a different theme in each. Any work of architecture may of course be examined through any or all of the analytical filters, though this will not necessarily produce interesting revelations in all instances. Towards the end of the book there are some *Case Studies* which show how a fuller analysis of particular works can be achieved by examining them under a number of themes.

Analysing creative work is different from analysing natural phenomena (a geological

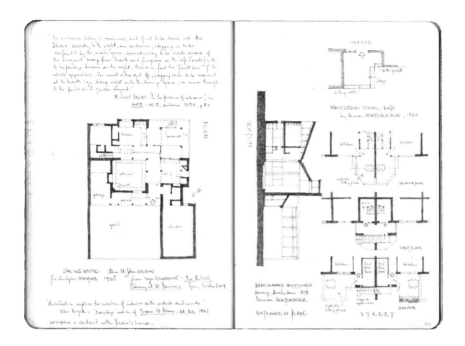

formation, a region's flora, the workings of the digestive tract of a rabbit…). In analysing works of architecture, which are products of creative minds, one has to be sensible to the intellectual agenda inherent in the examples studied and be prepared to find and acknowledge ideas and strategies that may be original or used in new ways. Through time architects have invented, discovered and experimented with new ideas: there was once a time, in the very distant past, when that ubiquitous architectural element, the wall, had not yet been invented; there is evidence (in archaeological remains) of the gradual discovery of and experimentation with the powers of axial symmetry in organising space; and so on. The meta-language of architecture (just like the language we speak and write) has evolved over thousands of years and will continue to develop in the future.

… and study the works of architecture you encounter in books and journals.

The poetic potential of architecture

The poetic potential of architecture is, I think, evident throughout this book. If poetry is a condensation of experience of life, then architecture is an exercise in poetry, essentially. But it can be seen that some works of architecture achieve more: they seem to provide a transcendent poetry, a level of meaning and significance that overlays the immediate presentation of place and which is to be interpreted, as a complement to sensual perception and experience, for appreciation by the intellect and sensibility. Sometimes this poetry is susceptible to analysis; sometimes it defies analysis and remains ineffable. The overall aim of the exercise is to explore architecture without prejudice and to allow the framework for analysis to expand as more themes are identified. I started by wanting to understand how architecture works so I could do it myself and help others come to their own understanding of how it might be done.

I try to be as open as possible to as many different dimensions of architecture as present themselves to me. I am not interested in restrictive, partial or prescriptive definitions of architecture nor in promulgating a manifesto for how it *should* be done. I do not want to get entangled in semantics or etymology, nor to distort my understanding of the subject by inappropriate use of metaphor. So I work from examples. I study examples that are generally accepted as 'works of architecture' (as well as some that are not usually accepted as such but which may possess some claim to be so) and distil from them the underlying ideas and strategies they manifest and sometimes share. This is an open-ended exploration that goes hand in hand with design.

All is presented as a stimulus for you to try analysing examples for yourself, and to play with the ideas and strategies you find in your own design. What one discovers for oneself – by searching, recording, analysing, reflecting, experimenting – can be more consequential than what one is told or reads in this or any other book.

A notebook also provides space for assimilating, through drawing, the sensual and qualitative subtleties of the places you find yourself: light and shade; reflection; texture; mood; layering; views; geometry.

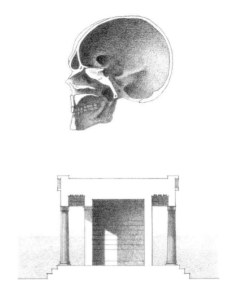

HOW ANALYSIS HELPS DESIGN

'Writers have to start out as readers,
and before they put pen to paper, even
the most disaffected of them will have
internalized the norms and forms
of the tradition from which they
wish to secede.'

Seamus Heaney – *The Redress of Poetry*,
1995, p. 6.

HOW ANALYSIS HELPS DESIGN

I found it difficult learning to do architecture. Many people do. Initially it can be like asking your brain to do something for which it has no frame of reference. The learning skills developed in school, mainly using words and numbers, do not prepare the brain for the particular challenges of architectural design. And yet, at the same time, it feels as if the skill of architectural design is one that is innate; and that the traditional focus in school on subjects that are studied through language and mathematics allows it to atrophy, submerging it beneath so much knowledge. The trick in beginning to do architecture is to wake up that innate skill; to revive that childhood fascination with making campfires in the woods, digging pits to sit in on the beach, making dens under tables and up trees.

Some years ago I organised a small exhibition of drawings produced by the Royal Commission for Ancient and Historic Monuments in Wales. They had been working for some years preparing an inventory of vernacular buildings in Wales and had made many clear and beautiful drawings of cottages, houses, barns etc. from different parts of the country.* Most were plans and sections but some were three-dimensional. They recorded spatial organisation as well as construction. To do these drawings they had measured many examples. I remember a conversation with the archaeologists working on this inventory. I said something along the lines of, 'You have measured and drawn all these hundreds of houses, surely now you would find it easy to design one. And, what is more, you could design according to the subtle differences between the regions.' They agreed. It made me realise that by immersing themselves in examples, and by reproducing those examples through drawing, they had learnt the 'language' and the regional 'dialects' of architecture in Wales; and that they could now 'speak' them fluently.

The importance to me of this realisation was less to do with perpetuating the vernacular architecture of Wales and more to do with the power of the process through which the Royal Commission archaeologists had taken themselves. I realised that this process could work for students learning to do architecture more generally. Certainly this is a powerful technique for anyone concerned to keep alive the regional or national traditions of architecture in any part of the world. But, more importantly, it helps too in learning the fundamental 'common language' of architecture; the underlying language on which all architecture – regional or international – draws.

I began studying that common language myself by analysing examples through drawing. And the (interim) result is the present book with its thematic chapters on some of the different aspects (the 'parts' – as in the 'parts of speech') of architecture. But no one ever learnt to speak any language just by reading a book. The book might help in

* *Many of these drawings can be seen in:* Peter Smith – *Houses of the Welsh Countryside*, 1975.

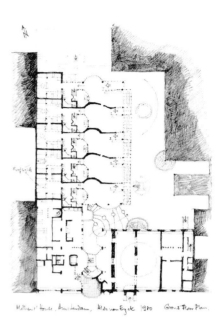

providing focus and a frame of reference but what is really required is commitment to practise. The person who wishes to learn a language must listen, read, analyse and try it repeatedly for themselves, making mistakes and getting feedback from those who can already speak and write it. This takes time and effort. As the poet Seamus Heaney says (see the quotation at the beginning of this chapter), 'writers have to start out as readers'. It is the same with architecture. Architects have to start out as 'readers', of books, yes, but more importantly and usefully, of other architect's designs. I am the person who has gained most from the production of the present book; for in studying all the buildings it illustrates (and more) and in analysing them through drawing, I have developed my fluency in the common language of architecture. It is up to you to do the same for yourself.

Analysing the work of other architects through drawing has helped me learn the common language of architecture.

Using this book

It will be useful then, before beginning properly, to offer some thoughts on how best to use and relate to this book. Some readers will have picked it up just because they are interested in how architecture works. But others, perhaps most, will be reading it because they are facing the challenges of design. These are two facets to our relationship with most subjects: the passive and the active; the analytical and the propositional; acquiring understanding and applying it in practice. Both facets are beneficial and potentially pleasurable but are most productive when operating in tandem. For example…

Two of our most dependable aesthetic and intellectual pleasures derive from (a sometimes grudging) admiration for the intelligence, wit and imagination of other people's minds as evident in their work, and from an abiding fascination with interplays between order and irregularity. We are surrounded by interplays between order and irregularity in the products and workings of nature: the rhythms of the days, seasons, years set against the variety of what they bring; the perfect scientific straightness of sunbeams through a chaos of almost identical leaves; the relentless breakers on the beach that are always similar but have never, since the ocean began moving, twice been exactly the same; the underlying standard forms of a billion trees, fish, human faces… with each individual subtly different from the rest. We enjoy the interplay between order and irregularity in our own creations too: in poems, dance, songs with their layers of rhythm and narrative, choreographic or melodic line; in a thousand similar aircraft, each with its own particular differences, each carrying a different set of passengers on a different route around the world; in a million identical iPods each filled with different tunes; in the vocabulary of a language set against

The world is full of interplays between order and irregularity, standard forms and variations upon them.

the apparently infinite variety of things that can be said with its standard stock of words; in the squares of a chessboard on which billions of different games of chess might be played. There are many examples.

We enjoy observing and being impressed by the imagination and wit of other minds evident in their creative work: the plots and twists of the stories and plays they have written; the ingenuity of the experiments they have contrived; the emotional journeys of the symphonies they have composed; the sophistication of the contraptions they have invented; the composition of great paintings; the brilliance of jokes well constructed and delivered, or magic tricks cleverly devised and dexterously performed. All these we appreciate intuitively; but we appreciate more if we understand them. That is one of the purposes of structured analysis: to understand examples in a consistent and thoughtful way; to share in and celebrate the vicarious achievements of creative minds.

But there is another, less dependable but potentially even more satisfying, pleasure – the one that attaches to our personal creativity, our own ability to make something that never existed before. In this each of us is, even when we collaborate with others, essentially alone and could do with some help. To move from passive to active, spectator to performer – from being a person who appreciates, enjoys, criticises, listens to, lives in, purchases, laughs at – (even at the level of a connoisseur) to one who *creates,* is exciting but difficult. To laugh at a joke is one thing; to write a joke that makes someone else laugh is quite another. To live in a house is one thing; to plan a house that is practically satisfying and aesthetically pleasing for someone else to live in is quite another. To criticise a new proposal for an art gallery as monstrous is one thing; to design a new art gallery that commands public attention is quite another. The question is how to mitigate the loneliness of the creating mind; how to find support and information, material that will help with the unrelenting demand for ideas; how to meet the demand for propositions, for design, for architecture.

Analysis and experiment

As observed by Seamus Heaney, and as is illustrated by the case of the archaeologists of the Royal Commission in Wales, the most successful way to begin to tackle the difficulty of being active in any creative discipline is to become curious and analytical about the work of others. Songwriters listen to and study other people's songs; poets and novelists borrow devices from other people's poems and stories; lawyers base their arguments on legal precedent; the designers of Formula 1 racing cars evolve their designs from previous versions and scrutinise the cars of competitors for ideas; military strategists endlessly study how battles have gone in the past, to come up with ideas about how to fight them in the future, as a matter of life and death. All take analysis – understanding and evaluating what has gone before – as the foundation for creative action.

The word 'analysis' comes from the Greek αναλυση (*analyein*), which means 'to break apart' or 'to unloose'. To analyse something is to release, to unloose, to expose for assimilation its constituents and workings – its powers. The purpose of analysing architecture, as any other creative discipline, is to understand its underlying constituents and workings, so that their powers may be assimilated and acquired. Architectural analysis need not be a purely academic pursuit, done for its own sake, though that can be informative and entertaining. Analysis is most useful when it provides an understanding of what is possible and develops a framework of ideas for the imagination to work with.

This book is specifically intended to help with the challenge of architectural design, which can seem obscure and perturbing. It does not, however, present a method or formula for design (like a recipe for beef stew). Rather, it offers an approach to acquiring (or perhaps, since it is arguably innate in everyone, *developing*) the capacity for architectural design. A comparison has already been made with language. When each of us was a child no one gave us a method or formula for learning language or for deciding what to say with it; we did this by listening and trying, thinking and judging; developing these capacities for ourselves in active intercourse with other people and in relation to our surroundings. It can be the same beginning to learn how to do architecture. Our capacity for architectural design is helped by engaging with and analysing what others have done (just like as a child we listened avidly to what our parents said and weighed up how it related to what was happening).

But just reading this book, or even learning by heart everything it says, would not in itself help anyone develop their innate capacity for architecture. Analysis is not sufficient in itself; it only really becomes productive when it is allied with exploration and experiment, playing with ideas through creative work; just as a child not only listens to and analyses what its parents are saying but imitates them too, playing with language. This emphasis on experiment, on trying things for one's self, is crucial. Like all those trees or iPods, each of us grows in our abilities in a slightly different way, fills our gigabytes of memory with different 'tunes', reconfiguring the ideas we find into our own narratives and propositions.

The frame of reference provided in the present book is offered in the belief and knowledge that the more we play with the ideas and strategies we encounter, pushing sometimes at their limits, contradicting sometimes their dictums, the more able and versatile we become as architects. So, for example, when you have read the chapter entitled *Parallel Walls,* try experimenting with parallel walls for yourself – using drawings and models or just with your two hands, or even by making a real place with windbreaks or driftwood on a beach. Acknowledge the parallel walls of the building in which you find yourself now, reading this book; consider what they are doing, spatially as well as structurally. Assess this strategy for organising space, defining a place. Experience the partial enclosure provided by your two walls on the beach; sense their power – the power you have exercised through building them. Consider how they make you feel when you stand between them, and when you are outside them. Stand on the axis they establish, looking from inside out and from outside in, and through to the landscape and ocean beyond. Observe the focus they create on a distant but specific point on the horizon. Reflect on how the regularity and axis of these two geometrically arranged walls interplay with the irregularity of the landscape around. Think how they might constitute a theme on which many variations are possible. Reflect too on how the space between the walls might itself be organised, how this standard form might variously be developed into a house, a temple or even a prison. Assimilate and exploit these powers for yourself. In doing so they will become part of your personal repertoire of potential responses to the design challenges you will face.

And do not worry that the 'parallel wall' strategy (to continue with the same example) is in some way unoriginal; it was just as unoriginal for the Greek architects who built classical temples two and a half thousand years ago as it was for the master masons of medieval cathedrals, and the twentieth-century architects of modernist and postmodernist houses. The parallel wall strategy is, in any case, not the only strategy for organising space; but it is a common one that has been used by architects for thousands of years, since the building of Troy, the Egyptian temples, ancient burial chambers and beyond. It would be as well if you, as a professional architect, understood and could, when you felt it appropriate, use its powers effectively rather than ignoring it because you feel it is 'unoriginal'. That would be like deciding never to use the standard sentence construction of subject-verb-object ('the boy hit the ball') because it has been used often and is somehow unoriginal! And anyway, as I have already suggested, even subversion depends on understanding what you want to subvert. As Seamus Heaney suggests, 'even the most disaffected' of us will, by studying the work of others, 'have internalized the norms and forms of the tradition from which (we) wish to secede'.

Do something similar after reading each of the other chapters. When you have read the chapter on *Temples and Cottages*, try designing some 'aloof' or 'submissive' architecture; places that transcend their conditions and others that respond to them. Adopt different attitudes towards the people you envisage using them – be a 'dictator' assuming that people will behave as you want them to, or an 'enabler' helping people to do as they wish – and see how your differing attitudes alter the character of what you produce. Or, when you have read the chapters on *Architecture as Identification of Place* and *Basic Elements of Architecture*, experiment with how small compositions of a few basic elements can identify places with different properties and relationships.

Your primary medium for doing these exercises will be the one you will use most when designing, and which is used throughout this book – drawing. Drawing, even if it is merely drawing boundary lines on the beach, is the primary medium for architectural design. But you might also build models or even make real places when you can. Enjoy the experience of changing the world, if only a small part of it. Your aim is to become fluent in this common language of architecture so that you can 'speak' and 'write' it with the same ease as your mother tongue.

Architectural ideas

Architectural design depends on ideas. The purpose of analysing the work of others is not only to acquire the common language of architecture, it is also to stimulate ideas for what you might do with it (what you might 'say' with it).

The only way to define an architectural idea is by giving examples, and even then one risks limiting something that should perhaps be open to continual reinvention. The simplest ideas are perhaps the easiest to grasp. Your two parallel walls on the beach constitute the realisation of an idea. (As it happens, I gave you that idea, but I did not invent it.) Other ideas, both architectural in a rudimentary way, would be: to plant a piece of driftwood – a tree trunk perhaps – vertically in the sand, making a marker that can be seen for miles around; or to draw that circle around a small area of beach, defining it and making a boundary between outside and in.

In all three cases you would have taken an idea (each of them now delivered to you by me; ideally, you should have some ideas of your own!) and then put some effort into giving it form in the real world, i.e. building it. In all three cases too you can see how such simple ideas have informed much bigger works of architecture: the two parallel walls could become a house or temple; the stake in the ground could become a church spire or a sky-scraper, both 'markers' that can be seen for miles around; and the circle in the sand could become the wall around a church graveyard or the defensive battlements of a fortress or a medieval city.

Towards the other end of the scale architectural ideas become more sophisticated. Some of these are illustrated in the following pages. One would be the idea that architecture can define a route. In his design for the Villa Savoye (which you will find in the following pages), Le Corbusier designed the house as a *promenade architecturale*, a route that takes the visitor from the entrance under an overhanging first floor, up a ramp to the living room and enclosed terrace, and then up another ramp to the roof under the sky. Another would be the idea that space might be managed more subtly, more fluidly, by a loose composition of plane walls, platforms, roofs and columns than by a more rigid arrangement of box-like rooms. Mies van der Rohe's Barcelona Pavilion (which you will also find in the following pages) is a case in point. Other architects, such as Daniel Libeskind and Zaha Hadid, have developed the idea of distorting rectangular geometries. Ushida Findlay have produced buildings with the form and space of sea shells, whilst Frank Gehry, in his design for the Guggenheim Museum in Bilbao, had the idea of astonishing everyone with an enormous sculptural form constructed of curved sheets of titanium cladding.

But architectural ideas can be less about form and more about attitude and approach. For example, opportunism or even chance is an idea that can be applied in architecture: responding to or exploiting fortuitous occurrences, things that happen or are there already. If an oak tree sprouts from an acorn dropped by a squirrel passing through your garden you can either decide to uproot it or to keep it; if you keep it, it becomes an important architectural element in your garden, even though you did not decide where it should be or even to plant it, only to keep it once it arrived. Through history, the foundation of temples, churches, graves etc. has been decided by such aleatoric means. In relation to topography – the lie of the land – you can either decide to use a slope beneficially or problematically, or try to obviate it by levelling it out. You might just have the idea of building on the pinnacle of a rocky crag or within a deep crevice (examples of both of which you will find in the following pages). No architectural project is free of contextual constraints; and many productive ideas come from understanding them and responding to them.

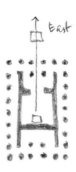

The idea of a Greek temple.

One thing is clear: in present times there is a high demand for architectural ideas. Reputations stand or fall not only on the ability to get commissions (which is difficult in itself) but on the originality of ideas generated (sometimes irrespective of their appropriateness to the task in hand). This was not always so. In classical Greek culture, the temples in which the gods were accommodated generally adhered to one small clutch of architectural ideas. There were many variations on the theme but – like aeroplanes that have different particulars but follow the same basic form (fuselage with wings, tailplane and cockpit) – each had: an enclosed chamber (with parallel side walls) containing an effigy of the god; a doorway establishing an axis stretching past an external altar and out into the world; and a screen of columns all around the outside (supporting a pitched roof) or just in front and at the rear. (You will find this form illustrated a few times in the pages that follow.) In the past, Greek architects were satisfied with this clutch of consistent architectural ideas to sustain their temple building through centuries. It was more or less the same in the times of prehistoric burial chambers (a few standing stones with a large capstone balanced on top); of the great cathedrals in Europe (an altar at the focus of a cruciform plan); and of the great mosques of the Moorish empire (a 'doorway' or *mihrab*, indicating the direction of worship towards Mecca, alongside a pulpit – *minbar* – all sheltered under an impressive composition of arches and huge domes). Nowadays it seems that every new building needs its own new idea.

The idea of a cathedral.

Whatever the cultural situation in which we find ourselves, ideas can be found in many places, and then made our own by processes of amendment, variation, contradiction. The evidence exists that the approach advocated in the present book is the one adopted by some of the most successful architects in history. Le Corbusier for example famously went on a series of journeys around Europe and into the Middle East. His many sketchbooks record his adventures and the buildings he encountered. Looking through them one can

The idea of a mosque.

see possible sources for some of the ideas he used in his own work. For example, there are plan drawings and perspectives of some of the houses in the preserved Roman city of Pompeii, with their atria and peristyle gardens defined by free-standing columns. It is not beyond plausibility that in drawing these spaces, ideas took root that became the 'pilotis' (free standing columns) in Le Corbusier's great house designs of the 1920s. Nor is it impossible that his experience of the horizontal route through a Roman villa, from the entrance to the reception room deep at the back, developed into the vertical route – the *promenade architecturale* – that was one of the core ideas of his Villa Savoye. There are many similar instances (some of which are illustrated in the following pages) where the ideas manifest in the work of great architects may be traced back to their travels, and their experiences and analyses of the buildings they encountered.

The role of drawing

I have already mentioned that the primary medium for analysing examples, for acquiring and practising the common language of architecture, for playing with ideas, is drawing. For architects, drawing is a non-negotiable essential skill. An architect who does not draw is like a politician who does not speak. Both need a medium through which to develop and express ideas (their own, or those they have borrowed from elsewhere).

Nowadays a great deal of architecture-related drawing is done on computers, but still the timeless simplicity of a pencil and blank sheet of paper is attractive. To a large extent the language of architecture is the language of drawing. And if, as in the case of people in prehistory, you find yourself with no pencil and no paper, you can always draw your ideas with a stick in the dirt. And if you draw them big enough – like a child with leaves in the playground – they just about become works of architecture in themselves.

It might seem counter-intuitive, but there is no clear boundary between drawing and architecture. Drawing is the crucible of architecture. It is where the creative architectural mind grapples with ideas and their relationship to the task in hand, whether that task is to make a house, a temple, an art gallery or a city. As such it is also the most appropriate forum where the analytical and critical mind can meet up with the creative mind. The architecture of others is best explored, analysed and understood through drawing. One learns a lot more about, for example, the Villa Savoye or the Barcelona Pavilion (or any other work of architecture) by drawing its plans and sections than just by looking at them or visiting the buildings (though the latter is of course important too). The plans and

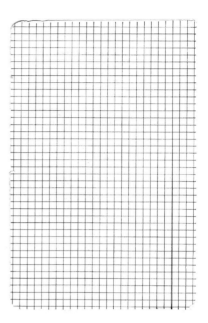

A piece of squared paper is a useful addition to a notebook. You should be able to see it through a page so that you can use it as a guide for drawing the plans and sections of buildings, and for making notes.

sections are particularly important because, since architecture is primarily a spatial art, that is where spatial ideas are most clearly apparent. And by redrawing the plans and sections of existing buildings (like the Welsh archaeologists or like a child imitating what its parents say) somehow one's own proficiency and fluency increase.

So the most important accoutrement to the present book (apart from a curious mind) will be a good plain paper notebook, one that you will be able to carry around with you wherever you go and will find pleasure in using. You will also need a pencil (arguably better than a pen because you can rub it out and make changes) and, I would suggest, a sheet of quarter inch or five millimetre squared paper, strong enough to be seen through the pages of your notebook. This may seem a superfluous suggestion, but it is a key one. Just as there are billions of games that can be played on a chess board, so too have there been thousands and millions of buildings that have been conceived and built according to a rectangular (orthogonal) architecture, and even those that appear not to have been are often found to have been designed on the implicit graph-paper of computer draughting programmes. These issues are discussed in more detail in the chapters on *Geometries of Being* and *Ideal Geometry* but for the moment take my word for it that a sheet of squared paper will be useful. It represents the order, the underlying musical beat, against which many architectural 'melodies' have been played.*

* Further discussion of how to use a notebook to study architecture, together with illustrations from my own notebooks, can be found at the *analysing* **ARCHITECTURE** website:

www.routledge.com/textbooks/9780415489287/

Children under a tree have, in the most primitive way, made an architectural decision by choosing it as a place to sit. This is architecture at its most rudimentary.

ARCHITECTURE AS IDENTIFICATION OF PLACE

'Architecture has its own realm. It has a special physical relationship with life. I do not think of it primarily as either a message or a symbol, but as an envelope and background for life which goes on in and around it, a sensitive container for the rhythm of footsteps on the floor, for the concentration of work, for the silence of sleep.'

Peter Zumthor – 'A way of looking at things' (1988), in *Thinking Architecture*, 1998, p. 13.

ARCHITECTURE AS
IDENTIFICATION OF PLACE

Before we can get on to looking at some of the conceptual strategies of architecture in detail, it is necessary to lay out some ground work with regard to the nature of architecture and its purpose. Before we can get on to the 'how?', we need to look briefly at the 'what?' and 'why?': 'what is architecture?' and 'why do we do it?'.

Despite the huge literature on architecture, its definition and purpose have never been settled. These are issues about which there is a great deal of confusion and debate, which is strange considering that architecture as a human activity is literally older than the Pyramids. The question 'what is one doing when one is doing architecture?' appears simple, but it is not an easy one to answer.

Various ways of framing an answer to this question seem to have contributed to the confusion. Some of these relate to comparison of architecture with other forms of art. Is architecture merely sculpture – the three-dimensional composition of forms in space? Is it the application of aesthetic considerations to the form of buildings – the art of making buildings beautiful? Is it the decoration of buildings? Is it the introduction of poetic meaning into buildings? Is it the ordering of buildings according to some intellectual system – classicism, functionalism, postmodernism?

One might answer 'yes' to all these questions, but none seems to constitute the rudimentary explanation of architecture that we need. All of them seem to allude to a special characteristic or a 'superstructural' concern, but they all seem to miss a central point that one suspects should be more obvious. What is needed for the purposes of this book is a much more basic and accessible understanding of the nature of architecture, one that allows those who engage in it to know what they are doing.

Perhaps the broadest definition of architecture is that often found in dictionaries: 'architecture is the design of buildings'. One cannot contradict this definition but it does not help very much either; in a way it actually diminishes the conception of architecture by limiting it to 'the design of buildings'. Although it is not necessary to do so, one tends to think of 'a building' as an object (like a vase or a cigarette lighter); but architecture involves rather more than the design of objects.

A more useful way of understanding architecture can be gleaned, ironically, from the way the word is used in regard to other art forms, music in particular. In musicology the 'architecture' of a symphony can be said to be the conceptual organisation of its parts into a whole, its intellectual structure. It is strange that the word is rarely used in this sense with regard to architecture itself. In this book this is adopted as the root definition of architecture. Here, the architecture of a building, a group of buildings, a city, a garden… is considered

The architectural actions of a prehistoric family making its dwelling place can be replicated and updated in a beach camp. The fire is the focus, and also a place to cook. A windshield protects the fire from too much breeze, and as a wall begins to give some privacy. There is a place where the fuel for the fire is kept, and the back of the car acts as a food store. There are places to sit, and if one were to stay overnight, one would need a bed. These are the basic 'places' of a house; they come before walls and a roof.

to be its *conceptual organisation*, its *intellectual structure*. This is a definition of architecture that is applicable to all kinds of examples, from simple rustic buildings, through grand public edifices, to formal urban settings.

Though this is a useful way of understanding architecture as an activity, it does not address the question of purpose – the 'why' of architecture. This appears to be another difficult 'big' question, but again there is an answer at the rudimentary level that is useful in establishing something of what one is striving to achieve when one is doing architecture. In looking for this answer, simply suggesting that the purpose of architecture is 'to design buildings' is again an unsatisfactory dead end; partly because one suspects that architecture involves rather more than that, and partly because it merely transfers the problem of understanding from the word *architecture* to the word *building*. The route to an answer lies in forgetting altogether, for the moment, about the word *building*, and thinking about how architecture began in the distant primeval past.

Imagine a prehistoric family making its way through a landscape unaffected by human activity. They decide to stop, and as the evening draws on they light a fire. By doing so, whether they intend to stay there permanently or just for one night, they have established a *place*. The fireplace is for the time being the centre of their lives. As they go about the business of living they make more places, subsidiary to the fire: a place to store fuel; a place to sit; a place to sleep; perhaps they surround these places with a fence; perhaps they shelter their sleeping place with a canopy of leaves. From their choice of the site onwards they have begun the evolution of the house; they have begun to organise the world around them into places they use for a variety of purposes. They have begun to do architecture.

The idea that *identification of place* lies at the generative core of architecture can be explored and illustrated further. In doing this one can think of architecture, not as a language, but as being in some ways like one. *Place is to architecture*, it may be said, *as meaning is to language*. Meaning is the essential burden of language; place is the essential burden of architecture. Learning to do architecture can seem to be like learning to use language.

The inside of this Welsh farmhouse can be compared with the beach camp on the previous page. The places of the beach camp have been transposed into a container, which is the house itself. Although such images can feed our romantic ideas of the past, the architecture itself was, before it became anything else, a product of life.

Like language architecture has its patterns and arrangements, in different combinations and compositions as circumstances suggest. Significantly, architecture relates directly to the things we do; it changes and evolves as new, or reinterpreted, ways of identifying places are invented or refined.

Perhaps most important, thinking of architecture as identification of place accommodates the idea that architecture is participated in by more than the individual. In any one example (a building for instance) there will be places proposed by the designer and places created by adoption by the users (these may or may not match). Unlike a painting or a sculpture, which may be said to be the intellectual property of one mind, architecture depends upon contributions from many. The idea of architecture as identification of place asserts the indispensable part played in architecture by the user as well as the designer. And for the designer who will listen, it suggests that places proposed should accord with places used, even if it takes time for this to happen.

So-called 'traditional' architecture is full of places that, through familiarity and use, accord well with users' perceptions and expectations. The illustration on this page shows the interior of a Welsh farmhouse (the upper floor has been cut through to show some of the upstairs room). The places that are evident can be compared directly with those in the beach camp shown on the opposite page. The fire remains the focus and a place to cook, though there is now also an oven – the small arched opening in the side wall of the fireplace. The 'cupboard' to the left of the picture is actually a box-bed. There is another bed upstairs, positioned to enjoy the warm air rising from the fire. Under that bed there is a place for storing and curing meat. There is a settle to the right of the fire (and a mat for the cat). In this example, unlike the beach camp, all these places are accommodated within a container – the walls

Reference for Welsh farmhouses:
Royal Commission on Ancient and Historical Monuments in Wales – *Glamorgan: Farmhouses and Cottages,* 1988.

and roof of the house as a whole (which itself, seen from the outside, becomes an identifier of place in a different way). Although nobody is shown in the drawing, every one of the places mentioned is perceived in terms of how it relates to use, occupation, meaning. One projects people, or oneself, into the room: under the blankets of the bed, cooking on the fire, chatting by the fireside. Such places are not abstractions such as one finds in other arts; they are an enmeshed part of the real world. At its rudimentary level architecture deals not in abstractions but with life as it is lived, and its fundamental power is to identify place.

Place is the *sine qua non* of architecture. We relate to the world through the mediation of place. Situating ourselves is an *a priori* requisite of our existence. Simply to be is to be in a specific place at a specific time. We are constantly placing ourselves: we have a sense of where we are and of other places around us; we weigh up where we might go next. We feel comfortable when we are settled in a place: in bed; in an armchair; at home. We feel uncomfortable when we find ourselves in the wrong place (at the wrong time): in a field during a thunderstorm; embarrassingly exposed at some social event; lost in an unfamiliar city. In our lives we either establish places for ourselves or have them established for us. We are constantly playing the game of situating ourselves in relation to things, to people, to forces of nature. Whether simple or complex, places accommodate us, the things we do, and our possessions; they provide the frames in which we exist and act. When they work, they make sense of the world for us; or we make sense of the world, in a physical and psychological sense, through them. Those who organise the world (or a part of it) into places for others have a profound responsibility.

We make sense of our surroundings by organising them into places. Places mediate between us and the world. We recognise a chair as a place to sit…

Conditions of architecture

In trying to understand the powers of architecture one must also be aware of the conditions within which they are applied. Though its limits cannot be set, and should perhaps always be under review, architecture is not a free art of the mind. Discounting for the moment those architectural projects that are designed as conceptual or polemic statements never intended to be realised, the processes of architecture are applied in (or on) a real world with real characteristics: gravity, the ground and the sky, solid and space, climates, the progress of time, and so on. Works of architecture are constructed with real materials with their own innate characteristics and capacities.

Also, architecture is operated by and for people, who have needs and desires, beliefs and aspirations; who have aesthetic sensibilities that are affected by warmth, touch, odour,

… and a pulpit as a place to stand and preach.

sound, as well as by visual stimuli; who do things and whose activities have practical requirements; who see meaning and significance in the world around them.

Such is no more than a reminder of the simple and basic conditions under which we all live and with which architecture must contend or harmonise. There are, however, other general themes that condition the operation of architecture. Just as the languages of the world have their common characteristics – a vocabulary, grammatical structures, etc. – so too architecture has its elements, patterns and structures (both physical and intellectual).

Though not as open to flights of imagination as other arts, architecture has fewer limits. Painting does not have to take gravity into account; music is mainly aural. Architecture is however not constrained by the limits of a frame; nor is it confined to one sense. Since ancient times architecture has been considered the 'mother' of the arts. While music, painting and sculpture exist in a way separate from life in a transcendent special zone, architecture incorporates life. People and their activities are an indispensable component of architecture, not merely as spectators to be entertained but as contributors and participants. Painters, sculptors, composers of music may complain about how their viewers or audience never see or hear their art in quite the same way as it was conceived, or that it is interpreted or displayed in ways that affect its innate character. But they do have control over the essence of their work and that essence is, in a way, hermetically sealed within the object: the musical score, the covers of a book or the picture frame. By contrast even the essence of architecture is penetrated by the people whose activities it accommodates.

Architecture has also been compared with film-making – an art form that incorporates people, place and action through time. But even in film the director is in control of the essence of the art object through the control of plot, sets, camera angles, script etc., which is not the case in architecture.

Furthermore, the realisation of works of architecture is usually dependent on patronage. The products of architecture – whether buildings, landscapes, cities – usually require substantial financial resources. The work that is achieved tends to be that wanted by those with access to or control over the resources needed to support its realisation. They decide what is built and often influence its form.

The conditions under which one can engage in architecture are therefore complex, perhaps more so than for any other art form. There are the physical conditions imposed by the natural world and its forces: space and solid, time, gravity, weather, light…. There are the conditions imposed by those who will use the products of architecture, and by those paying for them. There are also the more fickle political conditions provided by the interactions of human beings individually and in society. Architecture is inescapably a political field, in which there are no incontrovertible rights and many arguable wrongs. The world can be conceptually organised in infinitely diverse ways. And just as there are many religions and many political philosophies, there are many divergent ways architecture is used. The organisation and disposition of places is so important to the ways people live and interact with each other that it has in the course of history become less and less a matter of *laissez faire*, more and more subject to political control.

People make places (or have places made for them) in which to do the things they do in their lives – places to eat, to sleep, to shop, to worship, to argue, to learn, to store things and so on and on. The way people organise their places is related to their beliefs and their aspirations, their world view. As world views vary, so does architecture: at the personal level; at the social and cultural level; and between different sub-cultures within a society.

Which use of architecture prevails in any situation is usually a matter of power – political, financial or that of assertion, argument, persuasion. Launching design into conditions like these is an adventure only to be undertaken by the brave-hearted.

A definition of 'place'

In his 1982 address to the Architectural League in New York, the architect Vittorio Gregotti said: *'The marking of the ground, rather than the primitive hut, is the primordial tectonic act.'* But architecture begins before even that; it begins with a mind's motivation to make that mark, with its desire to identify a place.

'Place' is a word which, like many other words, has variable meanings. Often in architectural discussion it is used in the sense suggested by the sentence, 'New York (or wherever else) is a place; it has a particular visual character, which consists in the heights of buildings, the scale and layout of the streets, the materials used for building, the shapes and detail of doors and windows, etc.' (with the consequential implication that new architecture might in some way relate to that ingrained character – its *genius loci*). The word is used in a different, more rudimentary, way in this book. This use may be illustrated by the following steps:

Architecture, however complex and subtle it may be in its more sophisticated forms, can begin with something as simple as sitting on a sand-dune looking out to sea. By doing so you establish a place. Even after you have moved on, the impression of your body persists in identifying the place as a seat, the place where you sat.

- Imagine you are in an open landscape. With no more than a look you select a specific spot on the land. You have, in that look, established, if only in your mind, a place. **'Place' is where the mind touches the world**.

Maybe you see that place as a potential spot to settle, if only to rest for a moment.

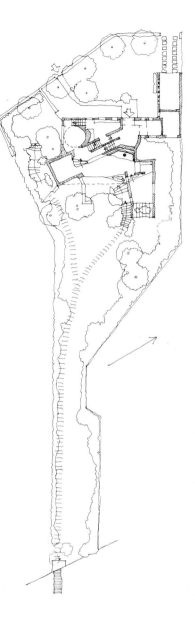

Maybe you associate that place with a particular experience – passing from the sunshine of an open field into the shade of a forest – or with a particular event – being startled by a snake – or perhaps with a particular set of emotions – a sensation of peace and safety.

- You decide to change that place, maybe just by occupying it, or by clearing bracken or stones to define an area of ground. Then you build a wall around that ground, or a circle of stones, or a small house or temple.

  A 'place' is established by a configuration of architectural elements that seems (to the mind informed by its senses) to accommodate, or offer the possibility of accommodation to, a person, an object, an activity, a mood, a spirit, a god.

- As you stand inside it, the boundary of your ground – the wall, the circle of stones, your house – defines you in your place; or, in the case of a small temple, defines the spirit or god in its place.

  'Places' mediate between life and the wider world – its surroundings.

- Even outside it, you know where you are by reference to your place.

  Through identifying 'places', and organising them, you make sense of the world you inhabit.

  Places set the spatial matrix of the life they accommodate; they orchestrate our experience of the world and manage our relationships with other people, our environment, our gods.

  By all this, you change the world (or small parts of it at least).

These steps illustrate a way of understanding 'place' that is about more than visual character. It is about 'place' as a consequence, an inescapable consequence, of being in the world. Architecture conceived and experienced as identification of place manages our being in the world. Places such as New York can be analysed and understood in this way too (as well as in terms of their apparent visual character) but it would involve deeper investigation of how life meshes with the space it occupies (in light and time), mediated by the architecture (spatial organisation) of its rooms and streets, squares and yards, entrances and windows, steps and pavements, hearths, altars, tables, benches etc.

The design of the house above – the Moll House (1936-37) by Hans Scharoun – began with a decision on where to place the sofa (marked with a dot) on the site.

'Vocabulary', 'syntax' and 'meaning'

The analogy between architecture and language can be helpful in understanding what it is to do architecture. In using language we take words (vocabulary), compose them according to particular arrangements (syntax) into 'sentences', and hopefully convey messages (meaning) to others. Something similar happens in doing architecture: the basic architectural elements (wall, roof, doorway etc.) listed in the next chapter constitute the equivalent of vocabulary; the ways in which they may be arranged, as illustrated in subsequent chapters, constitute the equivalent of syntax; and 'place' (as defined above) is the equivalent of meaning. Thus to return to the case of the two parallel walls on the beach: each wall is a 'word'; their arrangement in parallel constitutes the 'syntax' of the composition ('sentence'); and the result is the identification of a 'place' (the 'message' conveyed by the 'sentence').

As with all analogies, it is important not to overstretch this comparison between language and architecture. Walls are not words, nor *vice versa* (except perhaps when we write 'KEEP OUT' by a gateway). It is enough to suggest (tentatively) that just as we use language – composing words according to syntax into sentences to convey meaning – we seek to communicate and make sense of the world verbally, so we use architecture – composing walls (and other elements) in particular arrangements to identify places – we seek to situate ourselves in and make sense of the world spatially. It is not a step too far to suggest also that in both language and architecture we can be pragmatic, but we can also aspire to philosophy and poetry.

A place can be identified by a range of basic elements: defined area of ground, wall, platform, columns, roof, doorway, path.

BASIC ELEMENTS OF ARCHITECTURE

'Clearing-away brings forth the free, the openness for man's settling and dwelling. When thought in its own special character, clearing-away is the release of places toward which the fate of dwelling man turns in the preserve of the home or in the brokenness of homelessness or in complete indifference to the two... clearing-away brings forth locality preparing for dwelling.'

Martin Heidegger – 'Art and Space', in Leach, editor – *Rethinking Architecture*, 1997, p. 122.

BASIC ELEMENTS OF ARCHITECTURE

1

2

Now that we have a working definition of architecture and its fundamental purpose – *intellectual structuring* and *identification of place* – we can look at the elements available in design. These are not the physical materials of building – bricks and mortar, glass, timber etc. – but the compositional elements of architecture, and should be considered not as objects in themselves but in the ways they contribute to the identification of places.

The primary elements of architecture are the conditions within which it operates (1). These include: *the ground*, which is the datum to which most products of architecture relate; the *space* above, which is the medium that architecture moulds into places; *gravity*, which holds things down; *light*, by which we see things; and *time* (few if any examples of architecture can be experienced as a whole all at one time – discovery, approach, entry, exploration and memory are usually involved).

3

Within these conditions the architect has a range of elements with which to compose. It cannot be said that the following list is complete but at the most basic level the range of elements includes:

• *defined area of ground* (2)

The definition of an area of ground is fundamental to the identification of many if not most types of place. It may be no more than a clearing in the forest or it may be a pitch laid out for a football game. It may be small or stretch to the horizon. It need not be rectangular in shape nor need it be level. It need not have a precise boundary but may, at its edges, blend into the surroundings.

4

• *raised area, or platform* (3)

A raised platform creates a horizontal surface lifted above the natural ground. It may be high or low. It may be large – a stage or terrace; it may be medium-sized – a table or altar; it may be small – a step or shelf.

• *lowered area, or pit* (4)

A pit is formed by excavation of the ground's surface. It creates a place below the natural level of the ground. It may be a grave, or a trap, or even provide space for a subterranean house. It might be a sunken garden or perhaps a swimming pool.

• *marker* (5)

A marker identifies a particular place in the most basic way. It does so by occupying the spot and by standing out from the surroundings. It may be a pole planted in the sand, a standing stone or a statue, a tombstone or a flag on a golf course; it might be a church steeple or a multi-storey office block.

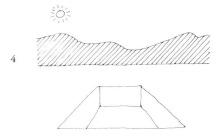

5

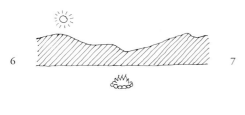

6

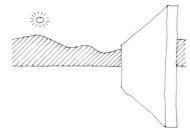

7

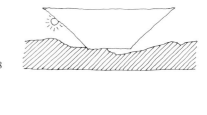

8

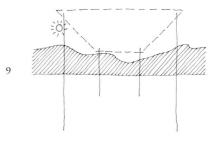

9

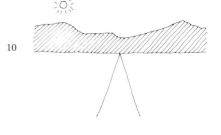

10

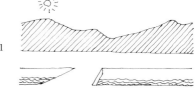

11

- *focus* (6)

The word *focus* is the Latin for 'hearth'. In architecture it can mean any element upon which concentration is brought to bear. This might be a fireplace, but it could also be an altar, a throne, a work of art, even a distant mountain.

- *barrier*

A barrier divides one place from another. It could be a wall (7); it may also be a fence, or a hedge. It could be a dyke or a moat, or just the psychological barrier of a line on the floor.

- *roof, or canopy* (8)

The roof divides a place from the forces of the sky, sheltering it from sun or rain. In so doing, a roof also implies a defined area of ground beneath it. A roof can be as small as a beam over a doorway or as large as a vault over a football stadium. Because of gravity a roof needs support. This could be provided by walls, but it could be by *supporting posts* or *columns* (9).

Other elements include:

- *path* (10)

… a place along which one moves. It may be straight but could trace an irregular route across the ground surface avoiding obstacles. A path may also be a *bridge* (11) across a gap or be inclined as a ramp. It may be formally laid out or merely defined by use – no more than a line of wear across the land.

- *openings*

… *doorways* (12) by which one may pass through a barrier from one place to another, but which are also places in their own right; and *windows* (13) through which one can look and which allow passage of light and air.

A more recent basic element is the *glass wall* (14), which is a barrier physically but not visually. Another is the *suspension rod* (15) or cable, which can support a platform, bridge or roof, but which also depends upon a structural support above.

12

13

Reference for wall:
Simon Unwin – *An Architecture Notebook: Wall*, Routledge, 2000.

Reference for doorway:
Simon Unwin – *Doorway*, Routledge, 2007.

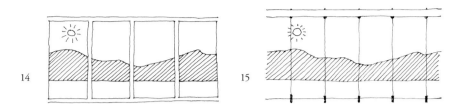

Combined elements

Basic elements such as these can be combined to create rudimentary architectural forms. Sometimes these combined elements have names of their own.

Barriers can be combined to form an *enclosure* (16), which defines an area by putting a wall around it. Floor, walls and a roof create a *cell* (17) or room, separating a space from everywhere else and making it a place. And giving a roof the supporting columns it needs creates an *aedicule* (18), one of the most fundamental of architectural forms. Arranging a series of small platforms at an angle makes a *stair* (19). And arranging them vertically makes a set of *shelves* (20). These basic elements and rudimentary forms recur again and again in the examples in this book. They are used in architecture of all times and regions of the world.

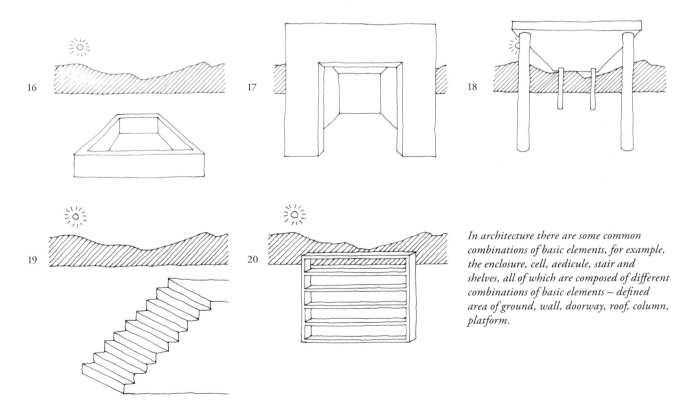

In architecture there are some common combinations of basic elements, for example, the enclosure, cell, aedicule, stair and shelves, all of which are composed of different combinations of basic elements – defined area of ground, wall, doorway, roof, column, platform.

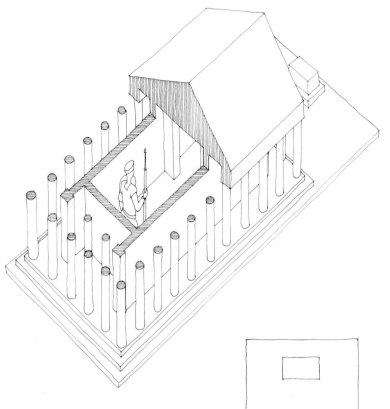

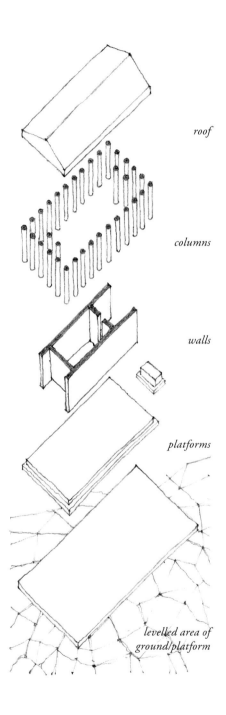

roof

columns

walls

platforms

levelled area of
ground/platform

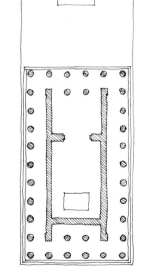

An ancient Greek temple (above) consists of
some of these basic elements, used in a clear
and direct way to identify the place of a god.
The building stands on a platform, *and
consists of* walls *that define a cell, which is
surrounded by* columns. *The columns
together with the walls of the cell support the
roof. The cell is entered through a* doorway,
outside of which is a small platform *in the
form of an altar. Together, this composition
of basic architectural elements organises the
space and orchestrates one's experience of the
temple. See how the* doorway *establishes a
relationship between the statue of the god
and the altar. See also how the* columns *veil
the* cella *or core cell of the temple. Imagine
too how it would feel to enter the temple, or
to walk between the* columns *and the* cella
wall. *Such a temple, often sited on a hill,
as a whole acts as a* marker *that can be seen
from far away.*

Together, the platform, walls, columns, roof
and altar identify the place of the god who
is represented by the carved statue within,
which is the focus of the whole complex and
the city around.

References for Greek temples:
A.W. Lawrence – *Greek Architecture,* 1957.
D.S. Robertson – *Greek and Roman
Architecture,* 1971.

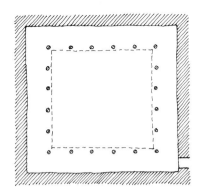

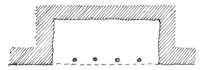

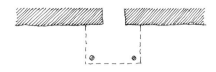

A cloister *is an area of ground (a garden open to the sky perhaps) enclosed by the* walls *of buildings with a row of* columns *set in from each side to create a* pathway *with a* roof. *This is the form of the garden of a typical Roman house; it is a standard element in the composition of a medieval monastery and of a Renaissance palace.*

A porch *shelters a* doorway *with a* roof, *perhaps supported on* columns.

A loggia *is a place defined by* walls *but open to one or more sides through* columns.

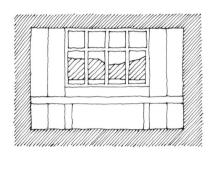

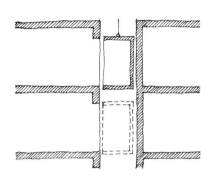

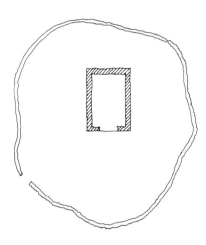

A temenos *is an* area of ground *enclosed by a* wall *to distinguish it as special, with a* cellular building *at its heart. This is the arrangement of many sacred places: the sanctuary of the ancient Greek temple; the medieval church in its graveyard; and of the cottage in its plot of garden.*

A street is a pathway *lined by the* walls *of buildings. With a glass* roof *it becomes a* mall *or arcade – an inside street (right).*

A window seat *is a place composed of a* window *and a* platform *(seat) set within a* wall.

A lift *or elevator is a place that moves. It is a* cell *that transports people from one* floor *to another.*

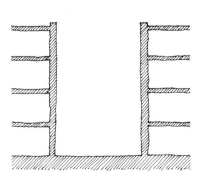

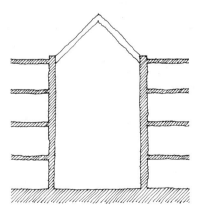

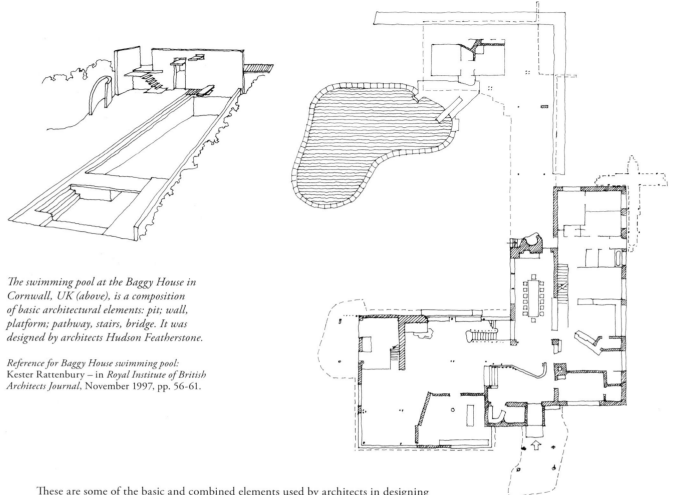

The swimming pool at the Baggy House in Cornwall, UK (above), is a composition of basic architectural elements: pit; wall, platform; pathway, stairs, bridge. It was designed by architects Hudson Featherstone.

Reference for Baggy House swimming pool:
Kester Rattenbury – in *Royal Institute of British Architects Journal*, November 1997, pp. 56-61.

These are some of the basic and combined elements used by architects in designing works of architecture. In some cases, such as the swimming pool of the Baggy House (above, designed by Hudson Featherstone in 1996), a work of architecture can be a clear compositions of basic architectural elements. But more complex and subtle works of architecture are composed of these basic and combined elements too. Above right is the ground-floor plan of the Villa Mairea, a house designed by the Finnish architects Alvar Aalto and his wife Aino, and built in 1939. Although it is not drawn in three dimensions, you can see that even if the underlying geometry of the building is not as simple as that of the Baggy House swimming pool, its composition is one of basic and combined architectural elements.

Doing architecture is not merely a matter of knowing the basic elements. The basic elements of architecture are constructs of the mind, which introduces them into the world as instruments by which space may be organised into places. A large portion of the subtlety of architecture lies in how its elements are put together. In literature, knowing all the words in the dictionary would not necessarily make you a great novelist. Having a good vocabulary does however give greater choice and accuracy when you want to say something. In architecture, getting to know the basic elements is only the very first step, but knowing them provides the beginnings of a repertoire of ways to give identity to places.

The places that constitute the Villa Mairea (above) are defined by the basic elements of wall, floor, roof, platform, column, door, window, pathway, defined area, pit (the swimming pool), and so on. Some places – the approach to the main entrance (indicated by an arrow) for example, and the covered area between the main house and the sauna – are identified by roofs (shown as dotted lines) supported by slender columns. Some places are identified by particular floor materials, timber, stone, grass, etc. Some places are divided by low walls, others by full-height walls (hatched) or glass walls.

References for Villa Mairea:
Richard Weston – *Villa Mairea*, in the *Buildings in Detail* series, 1992.
Richard Weston – *Alvar Aalto*, 1995.

It is impossible to convey fully in drawing, but the architecture of these steps consists in more than just their visible form. They are in the Generalife, near the Alhambra in Granada, Spain. The place shown in the drawing stimulates nearly all the senses: the deep greens of the leaves, the colours of the flowers and the patterns of light and shade stimulate the sight; there is the sound of moving water in nearby fountains; the smell of warm vegetation, and the perfume of oranges; the variations in temperature between the hot sunny places and the cooler shady places; the cold water for bathing hands and feet; the textures of the cobbled pathways; and, if one were to pick one of the oranges or a grape, the taste would contribute to the place too. And then there is the time that it would take you to climb to the doorway at the top.

MODIFYING ELEMENTS OF ARCHITECTURE

'From the outside, the house, shaded by the almonds in the Park of the Evangels, appeared to be in ruins, as did the others in the colonial district, but inside there was a harmony of beauty and an astonishing light that seemed to come from another age. The entrance opened directly into a square Sevillian patio that was white with a recent coat of lime and had flowering orange trees and the same tiles on the floor as on the walls. There was an invisible sound of running water, and pots with carnations on the cornices, and cages of strange birds in the arcades. The strangest of all were three crows in a very large cage, who filled the patio with an ambiguous perfume every time they flapped their wings. Several dogs, chained elsewhere in the house, began to bark, maddened by the scent of a stranger, but a woman's shout stopped them dead, and numerous cats leapt all around the patio and hid among the flowers, frightened by the authority in the voice. Then there was such a diaphanous silence that despite the disorder of the birds and the syllables of water on stone, one could hear the desolate breath of the sea.'*

Gabriel García Márquez, translated by Grossman – *Love in the Time of Cholera*, 1988, p. 116.

MODIFYING ELEMENTS OF ARCHITECTURE

The basic elements of architecture as described in the previous chapter are abstract ideas. When, by being built, they are given physical form, various additional factors come into play. In their realisation and our experience of them, basic elements and the places they identify are modified: by light; colour; sound; temperature; air movement; smell (and possibly taste); the qualities and textures of the materials used; use; scale; and the effects and experience of time.

Such modifying forces are conditions of architecture; they can also be used as elements in the identification of place. Possible configurations of basic and modifying elements are probably infinite. A room might be sombre, lit by one dim light-bulb, or bright with sunshine streaming through a window; sounds might be muffled by fabrics or reflect off hard surfaces. The temperature might be warm or cool; the air dank or fresh; there could be a smell of stale sweat or rotting fruit, fresh cooking or expensive perfume. The floor might be rough or polished as smooth as ice; the bed might be as hard as rock, or soft, padded with foam or feathers. Outside there may be a garden, continually changing with the weather, the time of day and the seasons.

A place may be no more than a patch of light, or a moment on a journey.

As abstract ideas, basic elements are subject to complete control by the designing mind; modifying elements may be less compliant. You might decide on the precise shape and proportions of a *column*, a *cell* or an *aedicule*, but the matter of how it sounds, or is lit, or smells, or changes with time is a more subtle issue. Control over modifying elements is a continuing and evolving battle. For example: in prehistoric times, light would have been that provided by the sky and not controllable; now there is electric light that may be controlled precisely. In the distant past, materials for building, whether stone or timber, were rough hewn; now their textures and qualities can be finely finished.

Though use of the basic elements may be the primary way a designing mind conceptually organises space into places, modifying elements contribute a great deal to the experience of those places.

Light

The first modifying element of architecture is light. Light is a *condition* of architecture, but it can also be an element. Light from the sky is the medium through which sighted people experience the products of architecture; but light, both natural and artificial, can be manipulated by design to identify places and to give places particular character.

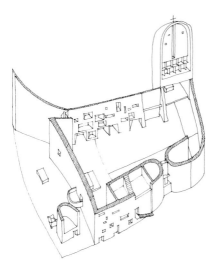

If one is thinking of architecture as sculpture it is by light that it is seen and its modelling appreciated. If one is thinking of architecture as identification of place, then one is aware that there can be light places and dark places; places with a soft even light and places with the strong brightness and sharp shadows of sunlight; places where the light is dappled or constantly but subtly changing; places, such as theatres, where there is a stark contrast between light (the stage – the place of the action) and dark (the auditorium – the place of the audience).

Light can be related to activity (below left). Different kinds of light are appropriate for different kinds of activity. A jeweller at his workbench needs strong light over a particular area. An artist painting in her studio needs constant and even light. Children in school need good general lighting for work and play.

Light changes and can be altered. Light from the sky varies through the cycles of night and day, and during different times of the year; sometimes it may be shaded or defused by clouds. Daylight can be exploited in making places. Its qualities can be changed by the ways it is allowed into a building. Some old houses have broad chimney stacks (below middle). Open to the sky they allow a dim 'religious' light to illuminate the hearth (when there is no fire). Le Corbusier used a similar effect in the side chapels of Notre-Dame du Haut at Ronchamp (above and below right). Using light 'scoops' he illuminated the side altars with daylight softened by its reflection off white roughcast walls. The same sort of effect is

The way light is admitted into the side chapels at Ronchamp (above and below) is similar in effect to that of light filtering down an old broad chimney stack.

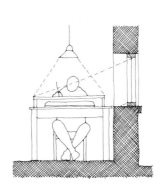

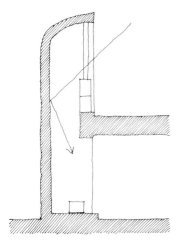

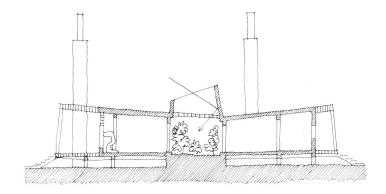

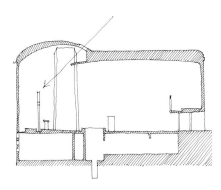

used in this crematorium at Boras, Sweden, by Harald Ericson (above right). It was built in 1957, three years after the Ronchamp chapel. The drawing shows its long section, with a concealed source of daylight over the sanctuary. In the same year, Ralph Erskine used a roof-light cum light scoop to identify the place of a small winter garden in the middle of a single-storey villa which he built at Storvik, also in Sweden (above left). Also in Sweden, though some twenty years earlier, Gunnar Asplund designed the Woodland Crematorium in the outskirts of Stockholm. The main chapel, set in extensive grounds, has a large detached portico. Near the middle of this portico is a large statue that appears to be reaching for the light through an opening in the roof (below).

The sources of daylight in religious buildings are often indirect or hidden, to increase their sense of mystery.

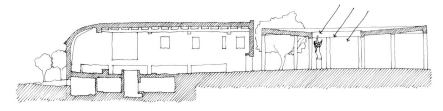

Light from an electric bulb is more constant and controllable than daylight: it can be switched on and off or precisely varied in intensity, colour and direction. One of the most intense uses of electric lighting is in the theatre but any place can be considered as a 'theatre' and lit accordingly. A spotlight can identify the place of an actor, a singer, a painting, an object, anything on which attention is to be focused (below). Beams of light can also work in the opposite way, drawing attention to their source (right).

In identifying places through architecture, light – both the varying light from the sky and the precisely controllable light from electric bulbs – can contribute in many ways. The way light contributes to the identification of place is part of architecture. Decisions about light play their part in the conceptual organisation of space and affect the ways basic elements of architecture are used. Light contributes to the character and ambience of a place.

A spotlight can identify the place of anything upon which one wishes to focus attention, or draw attention towards itself.

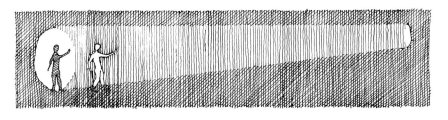

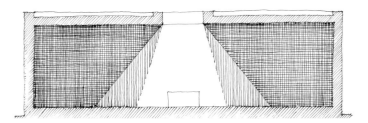

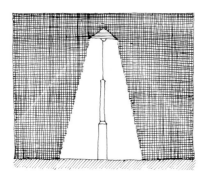

One is likely to make the quality of light in places of contemplation or worship different from that in places for playing basketball or for performing surgical operations.

Without changing the physical form of a place, its character can be radically altered by changing how it is lit. Think of the dramatic change in the appearance of a friend's face when you hold a flashlight under her chin. The same can occur in a room when it is lit in different ways, at different intensities and from different directions. A room's character changes radically when, in the evening, the electric lights are put on and the curtains are drawn; the fading dusk light is replaced with a constant brightness. We are perhaps so familiar with this event that we do not recognise its drama. The device of reversing the lighting conditions in a theatre when the house lights go out and the stage is lit is an important ingredient in the magic of theatre. Light can make the fabric of a building seem to dematerialise. A well-lit, completely smooth surface (of a wall or a dome for example), of which one cannot see the edges, can appear to lose its substance and become like air. The absence of light can have a similar effect. The surfaces in the distant recesses of the interior of a church can seem to disappear in the gloom. There are places where light is constant and others where it changes. In some buildings (hypermarkets or shopping malls for example) electric bulbs supply light that is the same all the time, at 9.30 on a winter night and at noon on a summer day.

Making a clearing in a forest is an architectural act. It removes the obstruction of tree trunks but it also changes general shade into a place with bright light from the sky. The removal of obstruction means that the place becomes a 'dancing floor'; the admission of light accentuates the place and allows it to be a garden rather than a forest. Erecting a roof under desert sun creates a patch of shade. The creation of a place of shade is essential to the architecture of a Bedouin tent (right). A roof, which might in some climates be considered primarily as protection against rain, is also a shade. Putting a roof-light in it can be like making a clearing in a forest, creating a pool of light surrounded by shade (above left). A lone lamp in a dark street identifies a place (above right); a red light maybe identifies somewhere more specific.

The doors of ancient Greek temples usually faced the morning sun. At dawn, the golden light from the east must have dramatically illuminated the figure of the god within. Like a cannon operating in reverse, the sun's horizontal light, striking deep into the interior of the temple, helped to identify the place of the image of the god at a particularly significant time of day. In the high ceiling of the large church of the abbey of La Tourette in southern France (built in the 1960s), the architect Le Corbusier designed a relatively small

A roof-light in a room, like a clearing in the forest, identifies a place of light, which might by used to draw attention to an altar. A street lamp makes a cone of light in the darkness of the night.

A tent in the desert identifies a place of shade.

A wall can be a screen on which shadows are projected. Inside the tower of Brockhampton Church, designed by William Richard Lethaby in 1902, the windows cast shadows of their tracery as a pattern of sunlight on the white walls.

Imagine the statue of the god illuminated by golden light from the rising sun striking in through the door of a temple (left).

rectangular roof-light. As the sun moves across the sky, through the dark interior a rectangle of its beams tracks like a slowly moving searchlight – the eye of God? In the side chapel of the same church Le Corbusier used deep circular roof-lights, like broad gun barrels with brightly coloured inner surfaces, to illuminate the places of the altars. These roof-lights are themselves like suns in the 'sky' of the chapel's ceiling. In the crypt chapel of the church intended for the Güell Colony in southern Spain, the architect Antonio Gaudi created a place of darkness in which columns and vaults melt into shadow, lit only by the stained-glass windows. This chapel, rather than making a clearing, recreates the forest, with stone tree trunks and coloured dappled light seeping under a canopy of shade.

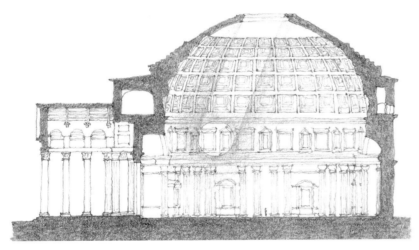

In the Aye Simon Reading Room (above, in the Guggenheim Museum of Art, New York, designed by Frank Lloyd Wright) Richard Meier, who was remodelling the room, used three existing roof-lights to identify three specific places (from top to bottom): the built-in seat; the reading table; the receptionist's desk.

In the Pantheon (left), built in Rome nearly two thousand years ago, the oculus in the dome allows a beam of sunlight to pan around the circular space.

Colour

Issues of colour are of course inseparable from those of light. Light itself can be any colour; coloured glass changes the colour of light that passes through it; the apparent colours of material objects are affected by the colour of the light that falls on them, adjacent colours and colours reflected from nearby surfaces. Colour, with light, can play a part in identifying place. A room painted a particular shade of green has a particular character (and is likely to be known as the 'Green Room'); a room lit only by a blue electric lamp has a particular character; a room lit by daylight passing through coloured glass windows has a different character. Various colours and qualities of light may seem

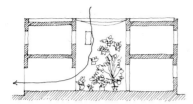

The patio courtyards of houses in southern Spain (left) are shaded by their high walls and, when the sun is at its highest, by awnings. They are packed with many plants and maybe a small fountain. Evaporation from these creates cool air that flows through the rooms and into the narrow streets.

An air-conditioning outlet can identify a warm place to stand on a cold day.

to suggest different moods. Colour is not only a matter of decoration or the creation of places with particular moods. Colour plays a part in place recognition. The importance of colour in place recognition is underlined by camouflage, which conceals by destroying or obscuring colour differences. Colour is also used in coding. In directing someone to your house, you might describe it as the house with the red (or blue, or green, or whatever colour) door (or walls, or windows, or roof). A coloured line can indicate a place where you should wait (to have your passport checked). A change in the colour of paving slabs or a carpet might indicate a particular pathway (giving it special importance, as when a red carpet is laid down for an important person) or help people find their way.

Temperature

Temperature plays a part in the identification of place too. The first huts were built either to contain the heat of a fire or to provide cool shade. The chief purpose in building an igloo is to organise a small place of relative warmth amid the snow fields of the arctic north. A reason for the shaded patios, full of plants, in the houses of Cordoba is that they create a relatively cool place as a respite from the strong sun and summer heat of southern Spain. Temperature may or may not be associated with light. In the temperate zones of the northern hemisphere a south-facing wall can make a place that is both bright and warm from the light and heat of the sun. An air-conditioning outlet, however, which emits no light, can identify an attractively warm place on an icy day. A bright room can of course be cold; a dark one, warm. The interiors of some buildings have constant, unvarying temperature in all parts, carefully controlled by air conditioning and computer systems. In other buildings, a rambling old house for example, there may be places with different temperatures: a warm place by a fire, a cool hallway, a warm attic, a cool cellar, a warm living room, a cool passageway, a warm courtyard, a cool pergola or verandah, a warm conservatory, a cool larder, a hot kitchen oven, a cold ice-house; moving from place to place, one passes through zones of different temperatures, related to different purposes and providing different experiences.

Ventilation

Temperature is involved with ventilation and humidity. Together they can identify places that may be warm, dry and still; cold, damp and draughty; warm, humid and still; cold, dry and draughty; and so on. A fresh breezy place can be refreshing after a warm, humid

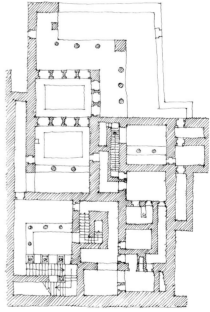

The residential quarters in the palaces of ancient Crete were well shaded. They were also provided with many openings and small light wells that, by providing ventilation, helped keep the rooms cool in the severe Cretan summer heat. (This is part of the royal apartments of the palace of Knossos.)

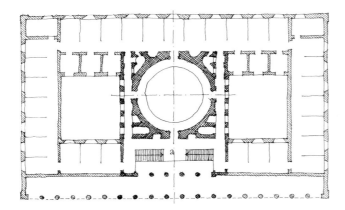

The loggia on the first floor of the Altes Museum in Berlin, marked 'a' on the plan (left) and section (below left), provides a moment of fresh air on a promenade through the galleries. Above is a drawing of the loggia from Schinkel's own Collection of Architectural Designs, *originally published in 1866 but republished in facsimile in 1989.*

one; a warm, still place is welcome after a cold, windy one. In the ancient palaces of the Mediterranean island of Crete, which has a hot, dry climate, royal apartments had open terraces and tiny courtyards shaded from sun and positioned to catch or produce air movement to cool the interior spaces.

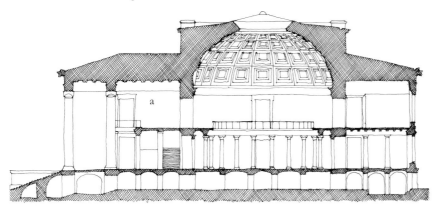

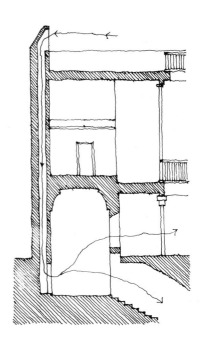

In the front elevation of the Altes Museum in Berlin (above), designed by Karl Friedrich Schinkel in the nineteenth century, there is a loggia (a), once open to the outdoor air, containing a pair of stairs from ground to first floor and looking over the square (the Lustgarten) in front of the museum. Before it was enclosed with a glass curtain wall (in the early 1990s) this loggia, which is encountered during one's progression through the museum as well as at the beginning and end of a visit, provided a reminder of the fresh air and the openness of the outside, as a contrast to the enclosed galleries.

Sound

Sound can be as powerful as light in identifying place. Places can be distinguished by the sounds they make or by the ways they affect sounds made in them. Religions use sound to identify their times and places of worship: by bells, gongs or the call to prayer from a minaret. In Greek Orthodox monasteries a plank of wood is beaten at significant times of the day to announce services. They also use bells that chime across the landscape. A place might be

*Traditional houses in Iraq had windscoops (*badgir*) to help bring air down into the lower rooms and courtyard.*

Reference for traditional houses in Iraq:
John Warren and Ihsan Fethi – *Traditional Houses in Baghdad*, 1982.

51

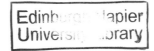

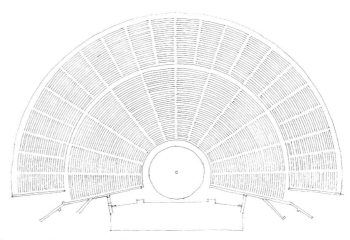

Standing at the centre of an ancient Greek theatre, any sound you make is reflected back from each tier in turn, extending it into a string of echoes that sound like a rapid machine-gun.

distinguishable by the sound of the wind in the leaves of its trees or by the sound of a stream or fountain of water. One's experience of a hotel room might be spoilt by the constant hum of its air-conditioning. A particular place in a city might be associated with the music of a particular busker. A place – an examination room or a library or a monastery refectory – might be distinguished by its silence; a restaurant by its taped background music.

Places can be identified by sound but they can also be identified by the ways they affect sounds made within them. A sound in a cathedral that is large and has hard surfaces will echo. A sound in a small room with a carpet, soft upholstered furniture and curtained windows will be muffled. A hall for the performance of music or for drama, or a courtroom in which witnesses, lawyers and judges must be heard, has to be made with careful consideration of the quality of sound it will allow. In the large church that is part of the monastery of La Tourette (the church with the rectangular roof-light) Le Corbusier has created a space that seems to hum of its own volition: its hard, parallel, concrete surfaces reflect and even seem to magnify every small noise: someone's shoe scraping on the floor, a door closing, someone clearing their throat or whispering. When the monks sang in this space….

Sometimes odd acoustic effects can be produced inadvertently. In the early 1960s the American architect Philip Johnson designed a small art gallery as an extension to a house. Its plan is based on nine circles arranged in a square; the central circle is a small open court; the other eight circles form the galleries and entrance lobby. Each of the galleries has a shallow domed roof (right). At the centre of each gallery one's voice seems amplified as the circular surfaces of the walls and the spherical surface of the domed ceiling reflect it directly back. A related effect occurs in an ancient Greek theatre. If one stamps one's foot at the central focus, the sound reflects back from each step in turn, producing a very rapid 'machine-gun' sound. This is a different phenomenon from the claim that such theatres (above) have good acoustics; but the rake of the tiers of seats did help the audience hear the actors and chorus performing in the *orkestra* – the circular 'dancing floor' at the centre of the theatre.

Some composers have written music specially to exploit the acoustic effects of particular buildings. The sixteenth-century composer Andrea Gabrieli wrote music especially for the cathedral of St Mark's in Venice. For his *Magnificat* he would position three choirs and an orchestra in different parts of the church, producing a quadrophonic effect.

There have also been occasions when the fabric of a building has been used as a musical instrument. Apparently, this happened at the opening of an arts building at Gothenberg University, Sweden, in the early 1990s, when the balcony rails were used as percussion instruments.

Sound can be a powerful component of the drama of a place:

'He would throw open the window in his room, even when the wintry stars were still in the sky, and warm up with progressive phrasings of great love arias until he was singing at full voice. The daily expectation was that when he sang his do at top volume, the Villa Borghese lion would answer him with an earth-shaking roar…. One morning it was not the lion who replied. The tenor began the love duet from Otello… and from the bottom of the courtyard we heard the answer, in a beautiful soprano voice. The tenor continued, and the two voices sang the complete selection to the delight of all the neighbours, who opened their windows to sanctify their houses with the torrent of that irresistible love.'

Gabriel García Márquez – 'The Saint', in *Strange Pilgrims*, 1994, pp. 41-2.

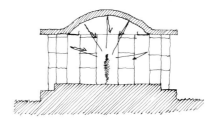

If you stand at the centre of one of the galleries in this building by Philip Johnson, your voice is reflected back to you by the curved surfaces of the walls and the ceiling, making it sound louder than elsewhere.

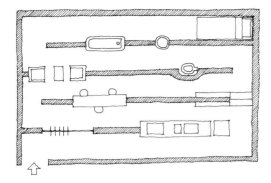

Usually we find our way around a building by sight. The 'Wall House' (left) was designed by Akira Imafugi to be navigated by touch. It is for a blind person. The walls are arranged in parallel lines an arm's width apart so they are never out of reach. All the principal places within the house – kitchen, dining table, clothes storage – are arranged within or in relation to these walls so they can be found easily.

Reference for the Wall House by Akira Imafugi: Japan Architect '92 Annual, pp. 24-5.

Smell

A place can be identified by its smell; a smell can make a place. Smell can be pleasant but it can also be repulsive. A schoolboy's stink bomb identifies a place to avoid. A public lavatory tends to smell one way, a ladies' hairdressers another, a perfume shop another, a fishmonger's another. The character of an old library is partly due to the smell of polished wood and musty leather book-bindings; that of an artist's studio to the smell of oil paint. Food halls in department stores cultivate odours of roasted coffee, delicate cheeses and fresh-baked bread. Some parts of cities with breweries smell of hops. Chinese temples are pervaded by the perfume of burning incense. When the spice warehouses of the Shad Thames area of London were in operation one could tell where one was with eyes closed, by the smell of cumin, cardamom, coriander…. The bedroom of an adolescent boy might be distinguished by the smell of dirty socks or deodorant. The lounge in a gentlemans club might smell of polish and old leather armchairs. Different parts of a garden might be distinguishable by the perfume of roses, honeysuckle, jasmine, lavender. Some of these odours are results of chance and occupation but an architect (whether of a garden or a building) may orchestrate the smells of spaces by using materials that have particular perfumes.

Texture and touch

Texture is a characteristic one can see – in this it relates to light and the sense of sight; but it is also a characteristic one can feel – in this it relates to the sense of touch. In both ways, texture may contribute to the identification of place. Texture can be achieved by surface application, of paint or of polish or of fabric; but texture is also intimately related to the innate qualities of materials and the ways they can be treated and used.

We identify places by changing their texture. We do this inadvertently when, for example, by repeatedly walking the same route across a field or a yard, we (or some sheep) wear away a smooth path. We do it consciously when we define a pathway with grit, or cobbles, or paviours, or tarmacadam. These changes are apparent to our eyes but they are also appreciated by our sense of touch, through our feet, and provide a harder wearing surface than the earth. On some roads the white lines that mark the verges are textured with rough ridges. If a car deviates from its lane it is communicated to the driver by the vibration and the noise of the tyres on the ridges; the place of the roadway is identified not only by sight, but by vibration (and sound) too.

'The moment was magical. There stood the bed, its curtains embroidered in gold thread, the bedspread and its prodigies of passementerie still stiff with the dried blood of his sacrificed lover…. What affected me most, however, was the unexplicable scent of fresh straw-berries that hung over the entire bedroom.'

Gabriel García Márquez, translated by Grossman – 'The Ghosts of August' (1980), in Strange Pilgrims, 1994, p. 94.

'The rooms adjoining the large parlour were protected by thick masonry walls that kept them in autumnal shadow. Jose Palacios had gone ahead to have everything ready. The bedroom, its rough walls covered by a fresh coat of whitewash, was dimly lit by a single green-shuttered window that looked out on the orchard. He had the position of the bed changed so that the window facing the orchard would be at the foot and not at the head of the bed, and in this way the General could see the yellow guavas on the trees and enjoy their perfume. The General arrived on Fernando's arm and in the company of the priest from the Church of La Concepcion, who was also the rector of the academy. As soon as he walked through the door he leaned his back against the wall, surprised by the scent of the guavas lying in the gourd on the windowsill, their luxuriant fragrance saturating the entire bedroom. He stood with his eyes closed, inhaling the heartbreaking aroma of days gone by until he lost his breath.'

Gabriel García Márquez, translated by Grossman – The General in His Labyrinth, 1990.

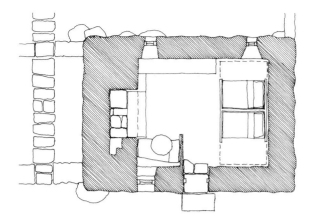

Traditionally, the surfaces of areas of floor that would be used most were given a texture that would be hard-wearing. In this cottage, flagstones protect the area just outside the doorway and have also been carefully placed to form a garden path. The area around the hearth is paved with stone to withstand the heat from the fire. Elsewhere the textures range from the large boulders of the wall to the smooth timber of the table and bench seat, to the soft feather mattresses of the beds.

Changes of texture are useful in the dark, and for people with partial sight. In some places road crossings are indicated by a change in the pavement texture. In old houses, when the making of hard pavements was a laborious activity, the places of hardest wear around the doorways were often identified and protected by large slabs of stone or aprons of cobbles.

Floors and pavements figure so prominently in discussion of the ways textures can identify place because it is through our feet that we make our main tactile contact with the products of architecture. Carpets change the texture of floors, making them warmer and more comfortable, particularly to bare feet. In some places consideration of bare feet is more problematic; around a swimming pool there is conflict between the need for comfort and the need for a non-slippery texture. Texture is important in other places where we come into contact with architecture. It can be a combination of aesthetics and practicality. If the top surface of a low wall is also intended as a casual seat, then one might change its texture from hard stone, brick or concrete to soft fabric or timber, thereby identifying it as a place to sit. The change is apparent to the eye but also to other parts of the body. Texture is also important where our hands or upper bodies touch buildings: door handles, counters, sleeping places, and so on. Beds are essentially matters of changes of texture – making a place upon which it is comfortable to lie and sleep.

Scale

The drawing on the right shows a man standing on a rather small stage. If however one is told that this man is only a piece of stage dressing, and that the real man on the stage is actually the dot between its legs, one's perception of the size of the stage is dramatically changed. Scale is about relative sizes. A scale on a map or drawing indicates the sizes of things shown on it relative to their sizes in reality. On a drawing which is at 1:100 a doorway that in reality might be one metre wide would be shown as one centimetre wide.

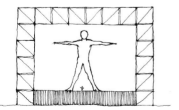

In architecture scale has another meaning, still to do with relative sizes. It refers to the size of something relative to oneself – 'human scale'. The experience of a place is radically affected by its scale. A football pitch and a small patch of grass in a back garden, though both defined areas of grass, present very different experiences because of their different scales.

(Scale is also discussed later, in *Geometries of Being,* under 'Measuring'.)

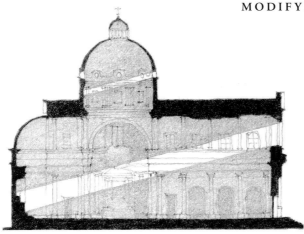

Time

If light is the first modifying element of the products of architecture then time is perhaps the last. Light provides instant stimulation; but time takes… time. Time plays a part in architecture in various ways. Although architecture produces lasting products, none of them is immune to the effects of time. The light in a space changes as the sun moves in the sky; materials change – develop a patina or deteriorate into ruin; original uses become more ingrained in a building or are displaced by others; people make places better or alter them for new uses; in war, and by terrorism, people destroy the places belonging to those others who they consider to be their enemies.

Sometimes the effects of time are positive, sometimes negative. They are usually considered to be 'natural' in that they are not subject to control by human decision; but that does not mean that they cannot be anticipated and used positively. It is possible to choose materials, or to design generally, with maturity rather than early use in mind.

Time is a modifying element of architecture in another sense, one that is more under the control of the designer, though not totally so. Although it takes time to achieve a profound understanding of a great painting, one is able to take in an initial impression literally in the blink of an eye. With a piece of music it takes the duration to be able to get even this initial impression; the achievement of a profound understanding probably takes many listenings. It takes time to assimilate architecture too. Though we see a great deal of the products of architecture illustrated, as pictures, by photographs in books and journals, this is not of course the way they are intended to be experienced.

When we experience a building in its physical existence there are many stages in the process. For example, there is the discovery, the view of outward appearance, approach, entrance and exploration of interior spaces (the last of which probably takes the greatest amount of the time). All processional architecture encapsulates time. In ancient Athens there were processions which led from the agora, up the acropolis to the Parthenon. The route took time. Great churches and cathedrals seem to encapsulate and manage the time it takes to pass from the entrance, along the nave, to the altar; as in a wedding. The production line in a car plant takes cars through a process of assembly, which takes time. The owners of great country estates made visitors approach their houses on long, and sometimes meandering, driveways so that they would have time to admire their property and wealth. It usually takes time to reach the managing director's office in an office building; and even when you reach it you have to wait.

Il Gesù (left) is a church in Rome, designed in the sixteenth century by Vignola. There is a clear window high in its west façade. Late in the afternoon the sunlight streams in like a searchlight down the nave to light the sanctuary and altar. Like the Pantheon and Le Corbusier's church at La Tourette, *the building is an instrument for managing time as manifest in the movement of the sun.*

Buildings are changed through time, as the demands of their uses change. This opening in a wall in Chania, Crete, has been changed many times.

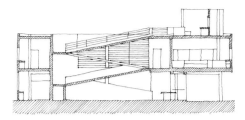

4 Section

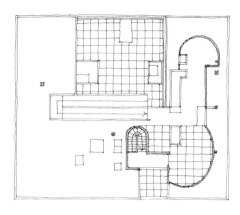

3 Roof, Solarium

Although architecture is sometimes discussed as if it were merely a sculptural or visual art – standing outside of the passage of time – some architects have realised the temporal dimension of their art. In the Villa Savoye at Poissy near Paris (1929), Le Corbusier used time as a modifying element of architecture. He knew it would take time for people to experience the house and so orchestrated routes through it. The three floor plans and a section are shown on the right. Approaching it, entering it and exploring within it, he created a route – an 'architectural promenade'. The approach works whether one is on foot or in a car. The 'front' entrance into the house is on the right of the ground floor plan (1); but one approaches from the rear. In a car one passes under the building following the sweep of the glass wall around the hallway. Entering the house, there is a ramp that takes one, slowly, up to the first floor which is the main living floor. You can see the ramp on the section (4). At that level (2) there is the salon, kitchen, bedrooms, bathroom and a roof terrace, which is itself like a large room. From the roof terrace the ramp continues to an upper roof terrace (3), where there is a solarium and a 'window' just above the entrance, completing the route; like a piece of classical music (another temporal art), the 'melodic' route through the Villa Savoye returns eventually to its home 'key'.

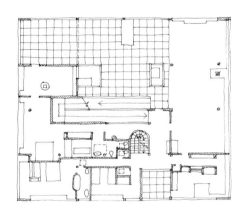

2 First floor

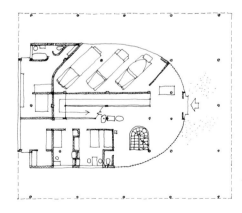

1 Ground floor

A window can 'do' many things architecturally at the same time. It lets light into a room, or out. It provides a view out, or in. It might set up an axial relationship, like the 'sight' of a rifle, lining up with something in the distance. The formation of an opening creates a sill, which can be a shelf for books or plants. The window can be a place for display. All this without even considering its role in the pattern of the overall layout of a wall.

ELEMENTS DOING MORE THAN ONE THING

'Follow out the destiny of the Column, from the Egyptian tomb-temple in which columns are ranked to mark out the path for the traveller, through the Doric peripteros in which they are held together by the body of the building, and the Early-Arabian basilica where they support the interior, to the façades of the Renaissance in which they provide the upward-striving element.'

Oswald Spengler, translated by Atkinson –
The Decline of the West (1918),
1926, p. 166.

ELEMENTS DOING
MORE THAN ONE THING

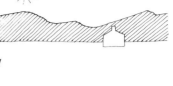

1

In architecture elements often do more than one thing at once. A gable wall of a house, for example, which plays its part in enclosing the interior of the dwelling, can also be a marker identifying a place where someone lives (1).

The top of a wall can be a pathway, for a child or a cat, as can the promenade of a pier or the battlements of a castle (2).

And the side surface of a wall can be a place for display, as in a cinema or an art gallery; or in the way that any building presents a 'face' to the world (3).

This ability of an element to identify different places in a variety of ways is an essential feature and one of the most intriguing aspects of architectural design. It involves the mental processes of both recognition and creation in an interactive way – creation of one place leads to recognition of others – and comes into operation at all scales.

2

Occurrences are innumerable. This will be seen to be a theme that recurs over and over again in the examples used in this book.

Part of the reason for the importance of this theme in architectural design is that architecture does not (or should not) operate in its own hermetic world. Its work is (almost) always relating to other things that already exist in the conditions around.

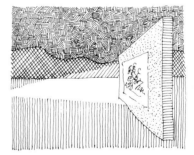

For example, any wall built in a windswept landscape creates at least two places – one exposed, one sheltered. If the sun is shining it will also divide a shady from a sunny place (4). All this as well as maybe dividing a public place from one that is private, or a place where there are sheep from one where there is a garden.

3

If the wall forms an enclosure or a cell then it divides an 'inside' from the 'outside'; giving something to and taking something from both. Even in such a simple arrangement the walls can be seen to do many things. As well as separating a sheltered inside from everywhere else they also probably support the roof. They provide surfaces on which things can be displayed or against which furniture can be positioned. And their geometry, together with the position of the doorway, seems to give them a hierarchy of importance. The theme also reaches into the work itself. A single 'party' or dividing wall makes two rooms, with the dividing wall serving both equally.

4

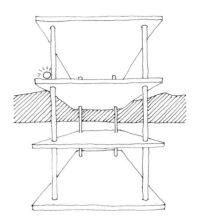

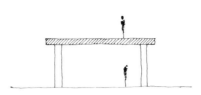

A flat roof is also a platform. The ceiling of one place is the floor of another (above). A vertical series of roofs, which are also floors, makes a multi-storey building (right).

Walls are often (though not always) structural – they hold up a roof; but their primary architectural role is to define the boundaries of place. Other structural elements can have this role too. A line of columns can also define a pathway.

A roof may also be a platform (above left). A stack of roofs/floors makes a multi-storey building (above).

A line of columns also defines a pathway (left).

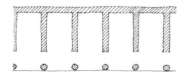

In this apparently simple plan (variations on which can be found in the stoa of an ancient Greek agora, the cloister of a medieval monastery, the shop-houses of Malaysia and streets and urban squares across the world) a few basic architectural elements are composed to identify a number of different places: the cells themselves; the street or square outside; and the covered pathway (defined by the columns and the ends of the party walls of the cells), which also makes a transition space between the street and the insides of the cells.

One of the indispensable skills of an architect is to appreciate the consequences of composing elements and be aware that they are likely to do more than one thing. These consequences can be positive: cut a window into a wall and one has a view as well as light and a sill for books or a vase of flowers; build two parallel rows of houses and one also makes a street between them. But the consequences can also be negative: build two houses too close together but not joined and you create an unpleasant unusable space between; build a wall for display, and you may also create a 'non-place' behind.

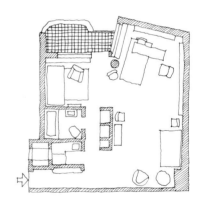

In this small apartment by the Swedish architect Sven Markelius, a number of elements do more than one thing at once. For example: the one structural column (near the balcony door) helps to suggest different places within the generally open plan; the bathroom and kitchen are grouped together and form a division between the entrance lobby and the rest of the apartment.

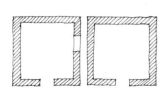 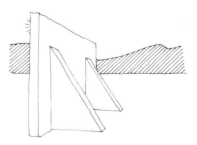

Ill-considered arrangements of walls can result in the creation of 'non-places' (left)

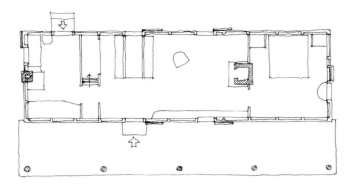

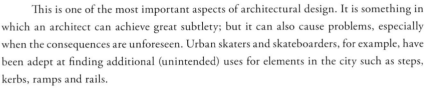

In this small summerhouse (shown above in plan and section), the five columns not only hold up the roof, but also help to define the boundary of the veranda – a place for sitting and looking over the nearby lake which is at Muuratsalo in Finland. It is called the Villa Flora, and was designed by Alvar and Aino Aalto in 1926.

This is one of the most important aspects of architectural design. It is something in which an architect can achieve great subtlety; but it can also cause problems, especially when the consequences are unforeseen. Urban skaters and skateboarders, for example, have been adept at finding additional (unintended) uses for elements in the city such as steps, kerbs, ramps and rails.

Some problems associated with elements doing more than one thing are evident in the work itself, rather than in how others interpret it. In such examples it seems the architect has not cared, or been able, to design the problems out.

On the right is the plan of an English house from the early part of the twentieth century. The forecourt is a square with cusps taken out of three sides. The cusp that bites into the house may help to identify the place of the entrance but it also causes problems with its internal planning. In the awkward spaces alongside the doorway the architect has placed the butler's pantry (to the left) and the cloakroom and lavatory (to the right). A similar problem occurs in the drawing room where the same device is used to identify the place of the fire; but here it also makes an odd shaped garden room (in the bottom right corner of the house). These are examples of an element (a wall with a particular geometry) having a positive effect on one side but a negative effect on the other.

Elements can readily be found to be doing two things at once (it is actually difficult to find elements in architecture that are only doing one thing!) but sometimes one finds elements that are doing many things. (Maybe this is one of the measures of quality, or at least sophistication, in architecture.)

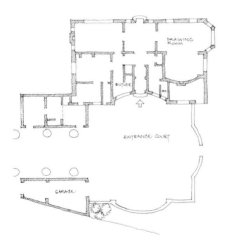

In the Royal Festival Hall, London, the stepped floor of the auditorium also provides a distinctive raked ceiling for the foyer spaces. The building was designed by Robert Matthew, Leslie Martin and others, and was completed in 1951.

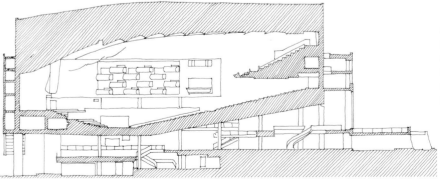

61

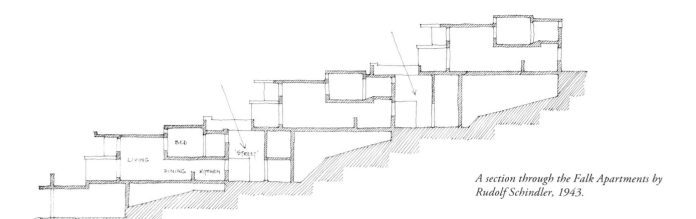

A section through the Falk Apartments by Rudolf Schindler, 1943.

In this section through a hillside house – The Wolfe House (right) designed by Rudolf Schindler in 1928 – you can see that the simple thin horizontal concrete slabs, some of which are tied back into the hillside, act not only as floors and ceilings but also as outdoor terraces and sunshades. Their precipitous edges are protected by balustrades which are also planting boxes.

In the Falk Apartments of 1943 (above and below), also by Schindler, it is not only the elements but the ways they are positioned that do more than one thing at once. The party walls between the apartments have been angled so that the living rooms face a lake. But this device has other effects too. It allows the terraces outside each apartment to be larger; it also gives these terraces more privacy. Deeper into the plan the angled walls open up a place for each staircase, which would otherwise be more cramped. The non-orthogonal geometry also enables the end apartments to be larger and different in plan from the intermediate ones. Schindler has been careful not to let the deviation from right-angles create awkward shaped rooms; it is as if almost all the problems that might have been caused by the shift from rectangular geometry have been reduced down to one tiny triangular cupboard in the right-hand end apartment. These apartments, like the Wolfe House, were also designed for a hillside, though one that is less steep. Their section (above) is stepped so that a roof can also be a terrace. In the section of an individual apartment you can see that the bedroom is almost like an enclosed gallery in the living room. This device too does more than one

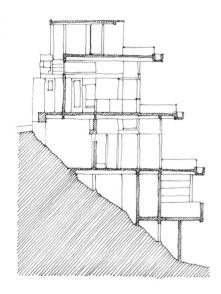

A section through the Wolfe House by Rudolf Schindler, 1928.

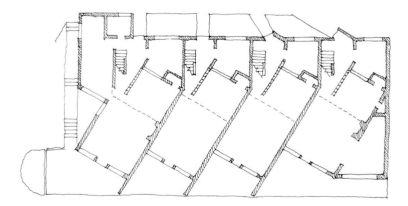

In the plan of the Falk Apartments (left), the angle of the party walls does more than one thing. In the section (top of page) the streets between the blocks allow access, as well as light and air, to the rear of the apartments. The siting on a hillside allows one apartment to look over the top of those in front.

Reference for the architecture of Rudolf Schindler: Lionel March and Judith Scheine – *R.M. Schindler*, 1993.

This is the plan of a village in the Ticino region of Switzerland. It shows cellular houses (hatched), low walls and some platforms adjacent to houses. In such places it is difficult to find an element that is not doing more than one thing at once. Most house walls also define outside pathways, private gardens or small public spaces. The result is an integrated web of places, some private, some public and some in between. There are no vague, open, non-specific spaces.

thing. One can see from the bedroom down into the living room; thus the bedroom is less enclosed than is traditionally the case. But the position of the bedroom in the section also creates two different ceiling heights, which relate to the places they cover: a high ceiling over the living room making it more spacious; a low ceiling over the entrance and kitchen. The line where the low ceiling changes to the high also suggests the division between the living room and the dining area. The dining place is identified by the lower ceiling.

One of the drawbacks with stepped sections is that inside spaces close to the hill can be dark. Schindler counters this problem in the Falk Apartments by making 'streets' between the blocks. These pathways do at least three things at once: they give access into the apartments; they provide light into the back spaces – the kitchens, hallways and bathrooms; and they allow cross-ventilation through the apartments.

Many small villages across the world that have been inhabited and gently modified over many centuries show the subtle ways in which simple elements can be used for more than one thing. House walls, for example, usually not only enclose the private interiors of the dwellings or their gardens but also define the pathways, small public squares and roads between them. In this way the villages have an intimate interrelationship between spaces, creating a tightly woven web of places that also seems to be a metaphor for the tightly knit communities that live in them.

Reference for Swiss villages:
Werner Blaser – *The Rock is My Home*, WEMA, Zurich, 1976.

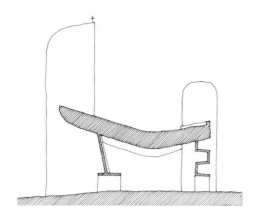

Allegory and metaphor

Elements often do more than one thing in the ways they organise space or contribute to the structural stability and environmental performance of a building. But they can be expressive too. Architecture can express meanings, draw allusions, evoke metaphors, tell stories. The capacity of a work of architecture to be symbolic can lift it out of the pragmatic and experiential to the level of allegory, in which some message is communicated through association.

Some works of architecture seem metaphorical in ways that emerge from deep in the human psyche. Three millennia ago, Minoan people, living on the island of Crete, carved deep slits into the living rock (right), with chambers at their ends for the interment of the remains of the dead. It is hard not to interpret these tombs as metaphorical 'wombs' to which those who had died could be 'returned'.

When prehistoric chieftains erected large stones to identify their territory such standing stones tend to be interpreted not only as markers but also as symbols of the chieftains themselves and of their manhood.

Such symbolism in the identification of places may have been subconscious, but all through history, at the behest and with the collusion of their patrons, architects have used allusion, allegory, association and metaphor deliberately. They have used architecture to convey, openly or subliminally, messages, meaning, propaganda, status.

When wealthy Renaissance gentlemen wanted their villas fitted with porticoes in the form of Roman temples, they were not just asking for practical porches that would help keep out the weather, nor were they merely wanting to extend the experience of moving

The chapel at Ronchamp, designed by Le Corbusier in the 1950s, seems to draw on the images of standing stones and ancient burial chambers as symbols of places of pilgrimage, worship, and sacrifice.

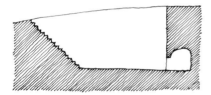

Early Minoan graves are like wombs carved into the solid rock.

When Renaissance architects built villas with 'temple' fronts they were not only building a practical house, they were using architecture to draw allegorical allusion to a particular period of history that they admired, and with which they wished to be associated.

When eighteenth-century architects built rustic cottages, they were alluding to a particular imagined way of life – the romantic rural idyll.

from outside to inside their houses. They were seeking to associate themselves, through the style of their houses, with a historical age they considered to be heroic.

When nineteenth-century English gentry built houses for their estate workers in the style of rustic cottages, they wanted to evoke the idea of simple rural life, as well as perhaps to reaffirm through architecture the lower social status of their employees.

When architects in the first half of the twentieth century wanted to turn their backs on history and explore architecture at the level of basic and modifying elements, they stripped their work of stylistic ornamentation. Even so, such buildings can be interpreted as symbolic expressions of 'modernism'. To use the analogy of fashion: if the Renaissance villa was dressed as a Roman temple, and the estate worker's house as a country cottage, then even the 'naturism' of the modernist house could be interpreted as a fashion statement.

When Modern architects stripped their buildings of overt historical allusions, maybe they sought to avoid symbolism. But nevertheless their work symbolised their rejection of history, their forward-looking attitude and their attempts to re-invent architecture from first principles.

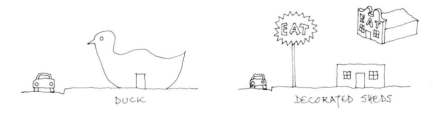

DUCK   DECORATED SHEDS

One might want to try to escape the symbolic dimension of architecture because it seems fickle, rhetorical, prone to variable interpretation. It may be interesting to interpret the symbolic meaning of dreams but often divergent interpretations of the same dream are possible and one has no way of determining which (if any) interpretation is (in whatever sense) 'right'. Just as in other media, the symbolic meaning of works of architecture can be open to variable interpretation. A single work might be interpreted in different ways by different people, even if its architect intended no symbolism at all. And even when symbolism is intended, the message sent may be interpreted differently in the minds of its recipients.

Fickleness of interpretation has less scope when, as in the case of the Minoan tomb or prehistoric standing stone, the symbolism is deeply rooted in the human psyche, or when, as in the case of the house that looks like a temple or another that looks like a cottage, the 'language' of symbolism is so well established that it is shared and understood by all (within their particular culture). To use the analogy of language: words are symbols; it is through familiarity that we come to share an understanding of their meanings, though new or unfamiliar words can still cause problems. In architecture it can be problematic

'We shall emphasize image – image over process or form – in asserting that architecture depends in its perception and creation on past experience and emotional association and that these symbolic and representational elements may often be contradictory to the form, structure, and program with which they combine in the same building. We shall survey this contradiction in its two main manifestations: 1. Where the architectural systems of space, structure, and program are submerged and distorted by an overall symbolic form. This kind of building-becoming-sculpture we call the duck in honor of the duck-shaped drive-in, "The Long Island Duckling", illustrated in God's Own Junkyard by Peter Blake. 2. Where systems of space and structure are directly at the service of program, and ornament is applied independently of them. This we call the decorated shed.'

Robert Venturi, Denise Scott Brown, Steven Izenour – *Learning from Las Vegas*, 1977 (2nd edition), p. 87.

to use symbolism that is not widely shared. People who have the resources to produce works of architecture may operate with a symbolic 'language' which is different from that accepted and understood by those who will encounter their buildings, though the dialectic interplay may be dynamic – unfamiliar symbolism may come to be widely accepted and understood with time.

Symbolism plays its part in the identification of place. Within a shared cultural language of symbolism, the appearance of a house will match people's expectations of what a 'house' should look like, a church will look how people think a 'church' should look, a bank will look like a 'bank'. Each is read as a symbol of itself; a symbol which, like Venturi's 'duck', identifies its place and purpose. Challenging expectations about how different building types should look is no doubt healthy and vital, but if it causes confusion it will usually provoke complaint.

The symbolic dimension of architecture is a powerful one. Individuals, multinational corporations, local and national governments, all take interest in what their buildings say about them, and may use them as advertisements for the image they want to project. Built in the 1880s, the Eiffel Tower has become a symbol of Paris and French culture, just as the Parthenon has been a symbol of Athens and ancient Greek culture for over two thousand years and St Peter's has been a symbol of Rome and Roman Catholicism for five centuries. In the 1970s the Sydney Opera House (by Jørn Utzon) became a cultural symbol for Australia. In the 1980s Richard Rogers revitalised his client's image with the Lloyds Building in the city of London. And in the 1990s the fortunes of the northern Spanish city of Bilbao were revived when Frank Gehry's Guggenheim Museum attracted huge attention. In some cases (the Parthenon and St Peter's, for example) the architects of these iconic buildings raised a shared symbolic language of architecture to a new level; in the others, symbolic power derived in part from shocking 'newness'.

The many dimensions of architectural elements doing more than one thing cannot be covered adequately here. They are too rich and complex. This is a characteristic of architecture at all scales and types, and from all periods of history. When an ancient Mycenaean king hung his shield on a structural wall of his megaron, he was using an architectural element to do two things at once. If that wall was also the side of his bed-place, then it was doing three. Whether he made his megaron look like his ancestors', or if he made it look radically different (maybe not in the shape of a duck), it was also a symbol of the identity he wished to present to the rest of the world.

A cave that is used as a dwelling is architecture, just as much as is a built house, by reason of having been chosen as a place.

USING THINGS THAT ARE THERE

'… the temples and the subsidiary buildings of their sanctuaries were so formed in themselves and so placed in relation to the landscape and to each other as to enhance, develop, complement, and sometimes even to contradict, the basic meaning that was felt in the land. From this it follows that the temples and other buildings are only one part of what may be called the "architecture" of any given site, and the temple itself developed its strict general form as the one best suited to acting in that kind of relationship.'

Vincent Scully – *The Earth, the Temple, and the Gods*, 1962, p. 3.

USING THINGS THAT ARE THERE

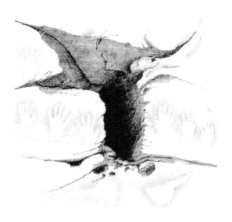

Even a crevice in a rock face may become a subtle and moving work of architecture.

In this small crevice in a huge rock face (right, in the Carnarvon Gorge in Queensland, Australia), an aborigine family laid the dead body of a small child, wrapped in bark. They marked the place with silhouettes of their hands, made with pigment. This grave is as much a piece of architecture as is the Great Pyramid of Giza (and more poignant). It is architecture *by choice*. Although architecture is always an activity of the mind, it does not follow that architecture always entails building something physically. As identification of place, architecture may be no more than a matter of recognising that a particular location is distinguishable as 'a place' – the shade of a tree, the shelter of a cave, the summit of a hill, the mystery of a dark forest. In daily life, one is constantly recognising places, thousands at any one moment. This is how one knows where one is, where one has been and where one is going. With many of these thousands of places one does not interact; they are left unchanged except for the recognition itself, which may be fleeting and hardly acknowledged. Some places stay in the mind. They are acknowledged because of some particular distinction: a fine view, shelter from the wind, the warmth of the sun; or through association with a particular event: falling off a bicycle, fighting with a friend, making love, witnessing a miracle, winning a battle.

The next significant step in a relationship with place is that one might choose to use it for something – the shade of that tree for a brief rest on a long and arduous walk, the cave as a hiding place, the hill top to survey the surrounding countryside, the darkest part of the mysterious forest for some spiritual ritual. The recognition of a place may be shared with other people; the memory and use associated with it then becomes communal. In these ways places acquire significance of many kinds – practical, social, historical, mythical, religious. The world has many, many such places: the cave in Mount Dikti on the island of Crete, believed to have been the birthplace of the Greek god Zeus; the route of the Muslim pilgrimage – the *hajj* – in and around Mecca; the mount from which Christ delivered his sermon; the stretch of boulevard in Dallas, Texas, where President Kennedy was shot; places in the Australian outback that are identified and remembered in the 'songlines' of aborigine culture and so on.

Recognition, memory, choice, sharing with others, the acquisition of significance: all these contribute to the processes of architecture. Of course architecture also involves building – the physical alteration of a part of the world to enhance or reinforce its establishment as a place. Recognition, memory, choice, sharing operate at the rudimentary levels of identification of place. Architecture makes more difference when it proposes and puts into effect physical changes to the fabric of the world.

Castle builders throughout history have built their fortifications on sites which, though often powerfully dramatic, were chosen primarily for their defensibility. Even if identically rebuilt somewhere else, such buildings could never be architecturally the same on another site.

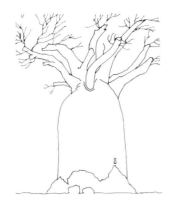

African baobab trees have thick trunks and soft wood. With space carved out inside, they can be made into dwellings.

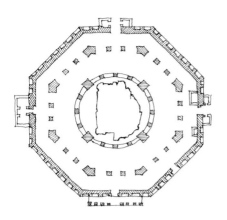

The Dome of the Rock in Jerusalem is built over a rock that is sacred to Jews, Christians and Muslims.

Architecture always depends on things that are already there. It involves recognising their potential or the problems they present; it involves, maybe, remembering their associations and significances; it involves choice of site and sharing with others. Fundamentally all terrestrial architecture depends upon the ground for its base, something that we perhaps tend to take for granted. In a flat and completely featureless landscape the establishment of a place would have to be an arbitrary decision; though once established the place would provide a catalyst for other places. The irregular shape of most ground, together with the water-courses that flow through it, the wind that blows across it and the things that grow on it, all under the sun, often suggest places that are seeds of architecture. Dealing with them, taking advantage of them, mitigating their effects, exploiting their character can be important challenges. In the untouched landscape, architecture can involve using hills, trees, rivers, caves, cliffs, breezes from the sea: things said to be 'provided by nature'.

Examples of the ways natural features or elements contribute to architecture are innumerable. They can be aesthetically and intellectually engaging in the way they symbolise a symbiotic relationship between people and their conditions. People have lived in caves since time immemorial. They have altered them, flattened their floors, extended them by excavation, enclosed their entrances, built outwards from them to make them more commodious. It is said that proto-people descended to the ground from the trees; people still make houses in trees. Since ancient times too people have used the walls of caves and of cliff-faces as places for the display of images – wall paintings and carvings. Through history people have found ways to cool and dry their dwellings with natural breezes and warm them with the sun. Domineering or frightened people have chosen hills and craggy rocks as places for fortresses or defensible villages. The constant need for water and food has led people to build near rivers and adjacent to fertile land. The examples are innumerable.

Simeon the Stylite lived in a cave dwelling within one of the volcanic cones of the valley of Göreme in Anatolia. The caves were extended and refined by carving into the rock. (The plans of such a house are shown below.)

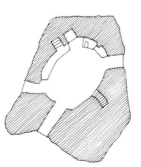

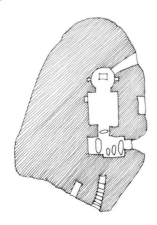

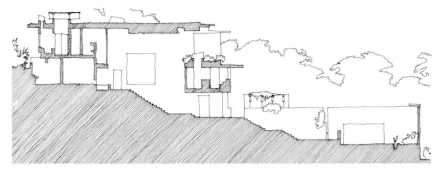

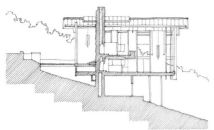

Since ancient times, many architects have either had to contend with the problems caused by having to build on sloping ground, or take advantage of them. Two approaches are illustrated in the sections above, both from twentieth century buildings. In the Lutz Residence (Shell Knob, Missouri, 1978, above right), the architect Fay Jones has created a platform on which the house stands. You enter across a bridge, and by the time you reach the other side you find yourself raised above the ground. Donovan Hill, by contrast, uses the ground slope in a different way in his 'C' House (above, Brisbane, Australia, 1998). Here the levels inside the house follow the slope downwards in a series of terraces.

Each of the major buildings on the acropolis in Athens (below) identifies (takes advantage of) a place that was already there in the landscape. The Parthenon identifies the highest point of the rocky outcrop, dominating the city around; the Erectheion stands on a sacred site associated with an ancient olive tree; the Propylaea mark the easiest access onto the summit from the plane below; and each of the theatres occupies an accommodating bowl of land where spectators probably watched performances even before they were fitted out with formal performance areas and stepped seating. Archaeologists have found remnants of much earlier temples on the acropolis, suggesting that this rocky hill had been used as a place of refuge, safe-keeping and worship for hundreds of years before the present temples were built some two and a half thousand years ago.

In the case of the monasteries at Meteora in Greece, the choice of site was an important ingredient in the architecture. They would not be the same on a flat plain. The choice of site affects the experience of them – the way monks entered in a basket hauled up by a rope, for example – as well as their dramatic appearance.

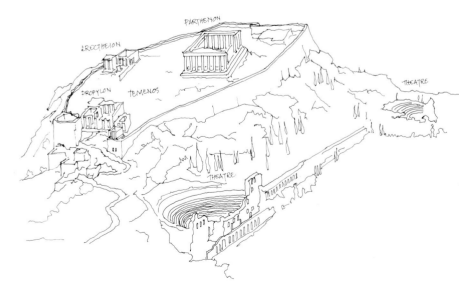

References for architecture using natural forms:
Bernard Rudofsky – *Architecture Without Architects*, 1964.
Bernard Rudofsky – *The Prodigious Builders*, 1977.

Reference for the 'C' House:
Clare Melhuish – *Modern House 2*, 2000, p. 150.

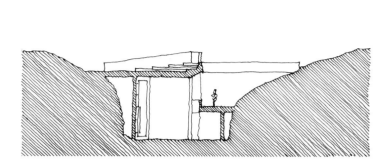

At the base of Ayer's Rock in central Australia (above right) there are some natural alcoves, apparently carved out by wind erosion. Each provides a place of shade, stones to sit on, and also a surface on which to draw. Some of them appear to have been used as schoolrooms.

This cottage in Leicestershire (UK, below) was designed in the 1890s by Ernest Gimson. It was built hard against a natural rocky outcrop, which contributes part of the enclosure of the house and also affects the levels of its floors. The land, as found and chosen, is an integral part of the work of architecture.

In 1988 Sverre Fehn designed a small art gallery to be inserted into a large cleft in natural rock (above left).

Reference for Sverre Fehn art gallery:
Christian Norberg-Schulz and Gennara Postiglione – *Sverre Fehn: Works, Projects, Writings, 1949–1996*, 1997, pp. 198-200.

Reference for Stoneywell Cottage:
W.R. Lethaby and others – *Ernest Gimson, His Life and Work*, 1924.

In designing the Students' Union building at Stockholm University in Sweden (right), built in the late 1970s, Ralph Erskine used a particularly fine tree, already on the site, to determine the position of an outside space taken like a bite out of the plan of the building. The tree, with the contours of the ground, contributes to the place and to the views from inside the building.

The drawing at the top of the next page is a section through part of a small dwelling in Mexico, designed by Ada Dewes and Sergio Puente. It was built in the mid-1980s. The designers used basic elements of architecture to make a number of places. In concert with modifying elements and things already on the site, these are used to achieve the complete experience of the house. The house is built amongst trees on the steep side of the valley of a fast-flowing river. The first element of the house is a horizontal platform built out from the slope. This is approached from above by steps; and there is a stepped pathway down from it to the river below. This platform is further defined by a single screen wall on the upslope side, through the middle of which it is entered. It also has a roof over it supported by the screen wall and by two columns. The other

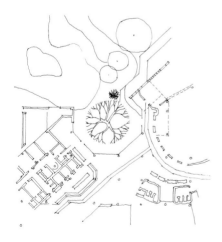

Reference for the Student Centre by Ralph Erskine:
Peter Collymore – *The Architecture of Ralph Erskine*, 1985.

The built form of this small house in Mexico is elemental and minimal. It depends on the surrounding trees for its completion. The living space, above the bedroom, has only one built wall. The forest provides the others and its roof.

three sides of the platform, which is a bedroom, are enclosed only by mosquito netting, keeping out biting insects but allowing in the calls of the birds in the trees. Steps in the platform lead to a shower room below. The roof of the bedroom is also the floor of the living room above. This 'room' has only one wall, a vertical extension of the screen wall below, through which it too is entered; the other 'walls' and its 'roof' are provided by the canopy of trees around.

The house below was built on a wooded site in France. Its main floor is lifted on columns, a full storey above the ground. Its architects – Lacaton Vassal – did not cut the trees down but built the house amongst them and around six of them in particular, which gives the interior a special character.

Using natural things that are already there is part of what has been termed, by Christopher Alexander, the 'timeless way of building'. This is as relevant today as ever, though in regions of the world that have been inhabited for many centuries one is less likely to have the opportunity to use natural features and elements, and more likely to have to relate to existing products of architecture.

A section through the house at Cap Ferret near Bordeaux, designed by Lacaton Vassal, shows how existing trees are retained and incorporated into the design.

Reference for Mexican house:
(Dewes and Puente) – 'Maison à Santiago Tepetlapa', in *L'Architecture d'Aujourd'hui*, June 1991, p. 86.

Reference for the house at Cap Ferret, near Bordeaux, by Lacaton Vassal:
Clare Melhuish – *Modern House 2*, 2000, p. 190.

Reference for the 'timeless way of building':
Christopher Alexander – *The Timeless Way of Building*, 1979.

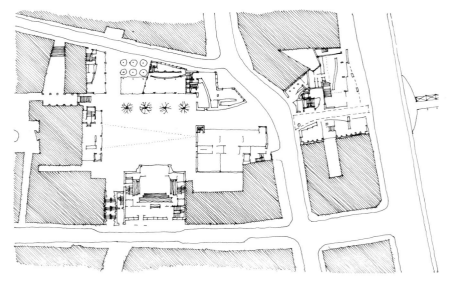

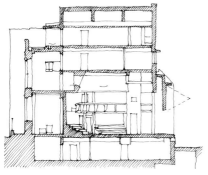

On a crowded beach, if there is a small space left amongst other people's towels, wind breaks, barbecues, deck-chairs, sunshades, etc., you make your own settlement, accommodating yourself to the space available, the direction of the sun and wind, the route to the sea, as best you can. Designing amongst existing buildings – in a village, a town, a city – involves interacting with what is already there. In cities the task is to make places in spaces between existing buildings and relate them to the places around. When Foster Associates designed a new Radio Centre for the BBC (below, not built) they took care to fit the building into its site at Langham Place in London – the junction between Regent Street and Portland Place and on the urban route between Regent's Park and Piccadilly Circus designed by John Nash in the early nineteenth century. Not only is the building's plan shaped to fit the site like a jigsaw piece, thus providing walls to define the adjacent roads, but it also provides a pathway, passing through the building from Cavendish Square into Langham Place. The design has a six-storey atrium at its heart; this is oriented towards Nash's All Souls Church across the road, which its large glass wall frames like a picture, using it to add character and identity to the atrium within the building.

When Group '91 architects won the competition to redevelop the Temple Bar area of Dublin in the early 1990s, they designed a series of interventions that used and fit in with existing buildings, streets and squares. The result, which fuses new buildings with old, was richer in character and more sympathetic to the history of that part of the city than would have been achieved by comprehensive redevelopment. The drawing (above left) shows Meeting House Square with the plans of Group '91's interventions. (Notice how it can be used as a outdoor cinema.)

The Ark, by Shane O'Toole and Michael Kelly (two of the Group '91 architects) at the bottom of the plan (section above) has a performance place that may be opened to the square outside.

Reference for Group '91 in Temple Bar:
Patricia Quinn (ed.) – *Temple Bar: the Power of an Idea*, Gandon Editions, Dublin, 1996.

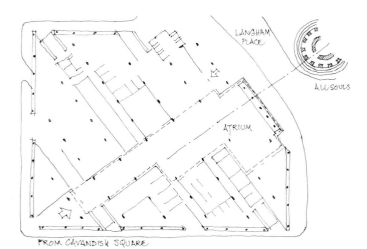

The atrium of the proposed BBC Radio Centre at Langham Place in London (left) was to have been oriented towards All Souls Church, using it as a focus for the space.

Reference for BBC Radio Centre:
(Norman Foster) – 'Foster Associates, BBC Radio Centre', in *Architectural Design 8*, 1986, pp. 20-27.

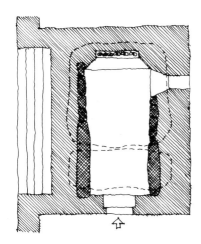

Maybe buildings that are already there count as part of nature. This is more so when the buildings are very old. In Brittany, north-western France, there is a small chapel attached to a church (above and right). It is called the *Chapelle des Sept-Saints* – the Chapel of Seven Saints – and is near Plouaret. It is a Christian chapel but it has been built around an ancient dolmen – a stone age burial chamber or temple built of huge megaliths or very large stones (above left). The chapel uses the space (place) established by the earlier builders thousands of years earlier. It is curious that a pagan building should be used in this way. Maybe it was economical to use a space that had already been enclosed; but maybe this chapel identifies a place that has been used for worship continuously for many centuries, from pre-Christian through to Christian times.

Sometimes architecture involves using an existing building or its ruins. When the Victorian architect William Burges was given the commission to design a hunting lodge a few miles north of Cardiff for the Marquis of Bute, he was presented with the ruins of a Norman castle as the starting point (below left). His reinterpretation of the castle (below right) grew from little more than a ground plan, already there in stone. Using these remains as a base, physically and creatively, Burges designed his own version of a medieval castle. The result is a collusion of the past with Burges's present. *Castell Coch* (The Red Castle) is not an accurate reconstruction of the original castle. In the 1870s when it was built, it was a new building (except, that is, for the foundations), but one in which Burges took prompts from what was already there. His imagination benefited from working on a base and on a

The Chapelle des Sept-Saints (above) is built around an ancient burial chamber.

Reference for Chapelle des Sept-Saints:
Glyn Daniels – *Megaliths in History*, 1972, p. 30.

References for Castell Coch:
John Mordaunt Crook – *William Burges and the High Victorian Dream*, 1981;
David McLees – *Castell Coch*, Cadw: Welsh Historic Monuments, 2001.

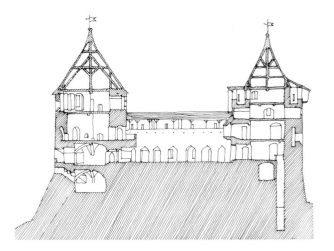

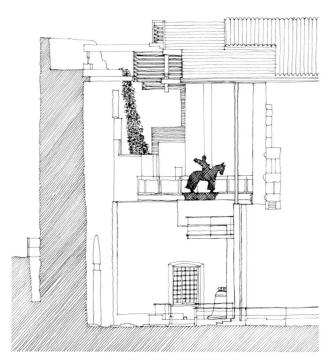
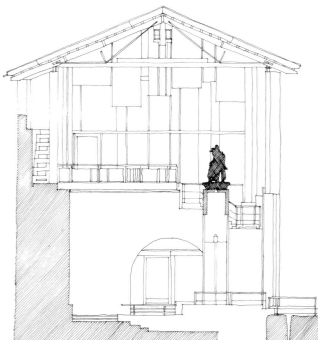

Cangrande space, sections

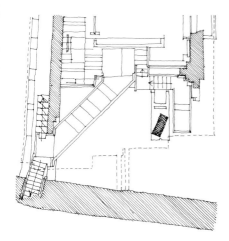

Upper level plan (at a different scale)

Reference for Castelvecchio:
Richard Murphy – *Carlo Scarpa and the Castelvecchio*, 1990.

site (the castle overlooks the Taff Valley running north from Cardiff) inherited from seven centuries earlier. His intention was to make a romantic recreation of a medieval place as an entertainment for his client and an ornament in the landscape.

In the late 1950s and early 1960s the Italian architect Carlo Scarpa was given a commission that involved refurbishing an old building and making it into a new work of architecture. His base (there was more remaining of it than Burges had at *Castell Coch*), was a fourteenth-century castle – the *Castelvecchio* (Old Castle) – in the northern Italian city of Verona. Scarpa's attitude to the past and how its built remains might be used architecturally was different from that of Burges. It was not his intention to realise a romantic image of the past, but rather to use the remains of the past as a stimulus to present aesthetic interest and poetic interpretation. In dealing with and remodelling the Castelvecchio, Scarpa created an architectural experience that is of the present but also exploits accidents and collisions, juxtapositions and relationships, that were in the building before he came to it. To these he has added interventions from his own responsive imagination, as one more historical layer – belonging to the mid-twentieth century – on a building that already had many from various earlier periods. The result is more complex and poetic than a restoration. Perhaps the most impressive place in Scarpa's *Castelvecchio* is the 'Cangrande space', named after the equestrian statue it frames (above and right). This is a place that had not existed in the castle before, but it is deeply conditioned both by the existing fabric of the old stone walls and by an appreciation by Scarpa of the historical changes that had occurred in that particular part of the building.

The way something that is there is incorporated in a work of architecture can be an expression of a conflict in ideologies between those people with influence over what gets built. When Peter Aldington designed and built three houses in the English village of

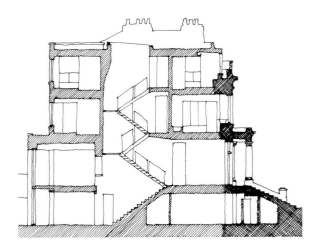

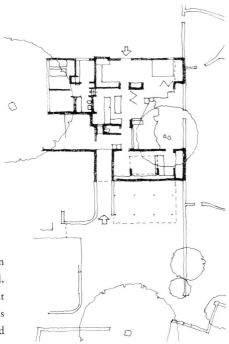

Haddenham in the 1960s (right) he was keen to exploit the existing stone walls and trees in his own composition. But when Rick Mather designed this modern house in Hampstead, London (above), with its high white atrium and glass stairs, one gets the impression that he would rather not have had to incorporate the existing Victorian front elevation. This condition had been imposed on him by the planning authorities so that the design would not disrupt the existing street and upset the neighbours.

Frank Gehry adopted a different attitude when he adapted his own house (below) in Santa Monica at the end of the 1970s. He started with a conventional suburban house and set about subverting its ordinariness. He screened and shrouded the house with materials unusual in such situations, distorted its geometry with non-orthogonal additions, and ignored the traditional uses of the rooms. The new kitchen is positioned just outside one of the bay windows of the original house, and retains for its flooring material the tarmac of the driveway that was there previously. Some parts look like a stage set, others like a defensive base for the military. The result may be interpreted as a witty critique of suburban American culture.

In some works of architecture there is a profound harmony between what was there and what has been added. When the Danish industrialist Knud Jensen commissioned Jørgen Bo and Vilhelm Wohlert to design the Louisiana Art Museum north of Copenhagen,

This is the plan of Peter Aldington's own house, Turn End, in Haddenham, England.

Reference for Turn End:
Jane Brown – *A Garden and Three Houses*, Garden Art Press, 1999.

Reference for the house in Hampstead, above left, by Rick Mather:
Deyan Sudjic – *Home: the twentieth century house*, 1999, p. 186.

Reference for the Gehry House in Santa Monica, below:
ibid., p. 88.

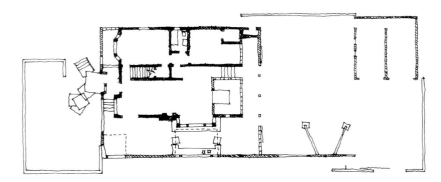

Gehry House, ground floor plan

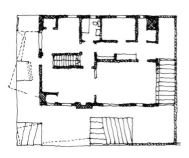

Gehry House, upper floor plan

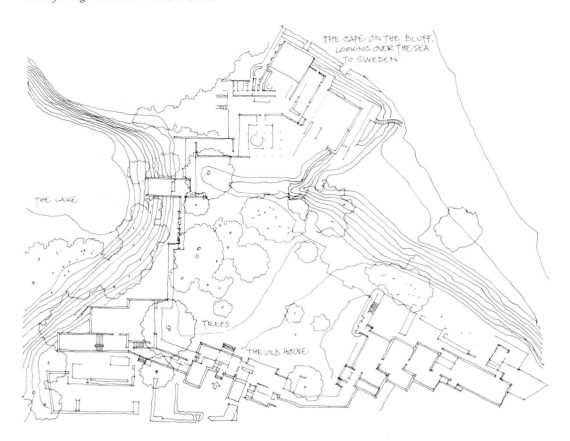

there were various existing feature of the site that he wanted the architects to use in their design. He wrote:

> 'First, the old house had to be preserved as the entrance. No matter how elaborate the museum might become in later years…. Second, I wanted one room … to open out into that view, about two hundred metres to the north of the manor, overlooking our lush inland lake. Third, about another hundred metres farther on, in the rose garden – on the bluff overlooking the strait and, in the distance, Sweden – I wanted to have the cafeteria and its terrace.'

The first phase of the art museum that was built in response to Jensen's brief occupies the left two-thirds of the plan (above). It uses all the innate features of the site that he identified. The old house, at the middle-bottom of the plan, is the main entrance. The route through the museum passes through some galleries and then north along a stepped series of walkways to one particular gallery that has a large glass wall looking out over the lake. The route continues through more galleries to the bluff, where there is a cafeteria looking out across the sea to Sweden. The architects also used other features already on the site, especially some of the mature trees and the contours of the ground, as well as the lake and the views. This building, the architecture of which takes its visitors on a tour of its site and of places that were already there, could not be the same anywhere else. The underlying ideas – the laying out of a route, the use of pairs of walls to frame views etc. – could well be applied elsewhere, but they would produce a different building because of the differences in location. The site, with its trees, lake, views and topography, is essential to the specific architecture produced.

The ground plan of the Louisiana Art Museum in Denmark, designed by Jørgen Bo and Vilhelm Wohlert. An old house is used as the entrance; the galleries and the cafeteria respond to other places on the site. One of the galleries is positioned to enjoy a view across the lake.

Reference for Louisiana Art Museum:
Michael Brawne – *Jørgen Bo, Vilhelm Wohlert, Louisiana Museum, Humlebaek*, 1993.

The ancient dolmen seems to have been an architectural metaphor for a cave, constructed as a place for the deposition of the remains of the dead.

PRIMITIVE PLACE TYPES

'The place had a stone circle – a Gilgal – which marked it as a sanctuary, and here young Eliphaz, the highway-robber, durst not have troubled him. In the centre of the Gilgal a peculiar stone was set upright, coal black and cone-shaped – obviously fallen from heaven, and possessing heavenly powers. Its form suggested the organ of generation, therefore Jacob piously saluted it with lifted eyes and hands and felt greatly strengthened thereby.'

Thomas Mann, translated by Lowe-Porter
– *Joseph and his Brothers* (1933),
1970, p. 90.

PRIMITIVE PLACE TYPES

As time has passed the places people establish and use have become more diverse, more sophisticated and more complex in their interrelationships. Some types of place are ancient: the hearth as the place of the fire; the altar as a place of sacrifice or a focus for worship; the tomb as a place for the dead. Other place types are more recent: the airport; the motorway service station; the cash-dispenser.

The most ancient types of place are those concerned with the fundamental aspects of life: keeping warm and dry; moving from location to location; acquiring and keeping food and water, fuel and wealth; cooking; sitting and eating; socialising; defecating; sleeping and procreating; defending against enemies; worshipping and performing rituals; buying or exchanging goods and services; story-telling and acting; teaching and learning; asserting military, political and commercial power; discussing and debating; fighting and competing; giving birth; suffering rites of passage; dying.

Place links architecture with life. The places people use are in intimate relation to their lives. Living necessarily involves the conceptual organisation and physical arrangement of the world into places: places to work, places to rest; places to be seen, places to spectate; places that are 'mine', places that are 'yours'; places that are pleasant, places that are nasty; places that are warm, places that are cold; places that are awe-inspiring, places that are boring; places that protect, places for exhibition; and so on.

Like language, architecture is not stagnant. Both language and architecture (as identification of place) exist through use and are subject to historical changes and cultural variation. Social institutions evolve; beliefs differ about the relative importance of particular facets of life and hence so do the places to accommodate them. Aspirations become more or less ambitious; some places become redundant; needs for new types of place become apparent; fashions come and go; linkages (physical and electronic) between places become more sophisticated. In language a particular meaning can be conveyed in different ways using different words in different constructions. The words and their patterns have to be in accord with the intended meaning, otherwise it is lost in nonsense or a different, unintended meaning emerges. The various ways of saying something may just be different, but variations in vocabulary and construction can also add subtlety, emphasis, stylistic nuance or aesthetic quality. It is the same in architecture; places with similar purposes can be identified architecturally in different ways.

Places are identified by the basic and modifying elements of architecture. A place for performance might be identified in any of a number of ways: by a platform, by a spotlight, by a circle of stones, by a number of marker poles setting out an area of ground. A place of imprisonment might be a small dark cell, an island, a deep pit or the corner of a classroom. The identity of a place also depends on the ability of someone to recognise it as such. A person has to be able to recognise a place as a place; otherwise, for that person, that place does not exist. A place may have many interpretations. A person might see a wall as a barrier, another see it as a seat, another see it as a path along which to walk; a third might see it as all three at the same time.

Places can overlap with others. A bedroom has a place to sleep (the bed) but it also has places for getting out of bed, for sitting and reading, for dressing and undressing, for looking in a mirror, for standing looking out of the window, maybe for doing press-ups. These places are not distinct but overlap within the room and perhaps change their identities from time to time. At a larger scale, a town square can be a market place, a car park, a place for eating, talking, performing, for wandering... all at once.

Primitive place types

Amid this complexity, some place types have acquired their own names – *hearth, theatre, tomb, altar, fort, throne* – that reach far back into history. Their ancient names are testament to their age-old roles in the lives and architecture of people through history. Although such place types are ancient and have a consistent conceptual identity related to purpose, their architecture (their conceptual organisation by the use of basic and modifying elements) can vary greatly. A purpose does not necessarily determine the architecture of its place; many purposes, even the most ancient, have been accommodated architecturally in very different ways.

The relationship between architecture and the names of place types with ancient purposes can be confusing. The word *tomb* might evoke a particular example in one's mind but the architecture of tombs through history has been very diverse. The names of place types in architecture can seem clear, yet be vague. If one says that a place is 'like a theatre' one might be exact in so far as it may incorporate a place for performance with a place for spectating, but architecturally it might be an amphitheatre, a courtyard, a street, or have a stage, with or without a proscenium arch.

There is often a rough and ready relationship between architecture and the words through which it is discussed. Words that are specific in one context may be imprecise and analogical in another. Words such as *hearth, theatre, tomb, altar, fort, throne* are not necessarily specific in the architectural forms to which they refer.

Primitive place types are evident in one of the oldest stories, Homer's Odyssey, *which was written nearly three thousand years ago, but had probably been told orally, around the hearth, for many years previously. The primitive places Homer used are fundamentally those we use today:*

Seat: *'He then conducted her to a carved chair, over which he spread a rug, and seated her there with a stool for her feet. For himself he drew up an inlaid easy chair.'*
'The elders made way for him as he took his father's seat.'

Tomb: *'No barrow would have honoured his remains.'*

Cooking place: *'When the thighs were burnt up and they had tasted the inner parts, they carved the rest into small pieces, pierced them with skewers and held the sharp ends of the spits to the fire till all was roasted.'*

Hearth: *'He found the lady of the lovely rocks at home. A big fire was blazing on the hearth and the scent from the burning logs of split juniper and cedar was wafted far across the island.'*

Hearth – the place of the fire

The hearth has had a traditional significance in many cultures, as the heart of the home or the focus of a community – a source of warmth, for cooking, a point of reference around which life revolves. Its essential component is the fire itself, but the ways the place of the fire is identified can vary greatly. Even a simple outdoor fireplace can be formed of different configurations of basic architectural elements (some of which are found in larger structures too). The circle of scorched earth may be contained with a circle of stones; the fire might be set against a large stone which protects it from excessive draught and stores some of its heat; or it may be flanked by two parallel walls of stone that channel draughts and provide a platform for cooking pans.

Gottfried Semper identified hearth *as one of the four fundamental elements of architecture, along with the* earthwork, *the* roof, *and the* screen wall. *With regard to these 'Four Elements', in the present book the* hearth *is categorised as a 'primitive place type', the* earthwork *and the* screen wall *both as the 'basic element' of* wall *or* barrier, *and the* roof *as the 'basic element' of* roof.

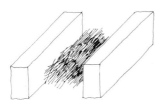

The place of a fire might be identified in more elaborate ways too: maybe provided with a tripod from which a cooking pot is hung, but which also forms an aedicule emphasizing the hearth; or perhaps set in a more sophisticated construction, like a seat or table that lifts it off the ground for convenience; or perhaps provided with its own small building.

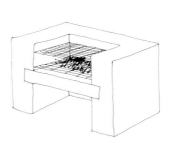

A fire not only has its own place but also creates a place where people can occupy its sphere of light and warmth. The extent of this sphere can vary. It might be defined by a tight circle of people around a campfire on a cold night; or it might be the extensive circle of visibility of a hill-top beacon seen across miles of countryside.

Through history the architectural role of the hearth as an identifier of place of human occupation has been to do with how its sphere of light and warmth has been defined, contained or controlled. In the countryside – the landscape of the primitive family or the present-day camper – a fire makes its own place by its light and warmth. But when one wants to make a fire, a place for it has to be chosen. In doing this various factors may be taken into account, factors related to the purpose of the fire. If there is a dell, protected from the wind and provided with rocks for seats, and if the purpose of the fire is to provide a cooking place and a focus for a summer evening of eating and talking, then it is likely to be chosen as a place for the hearth. In doing this the dell becomes a container of the sphere of light and warmth from the fire. It also becomes a room within which friends may talk while cooking and eating.

This fire is in the middle of natural room; its light and warmth seem bounded by the rocks around and the canopies of the trees above.

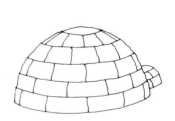

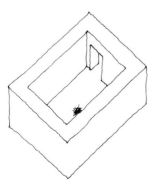

In many cultures, particularly in cool and cold regions of the world, domestic architecture has been primarily concerned with enclosing the place of the fire and containing its sphere of light and warmth. An igloo contains the sphere (or hemisphere when the fire is on the flat surface of the earth) literally – with a dome. Materials more difficult to shape than ice are not so easy to form into a dome, so a teepee limits the hemisphere with a cone. The primitive round house is similar. And an orthogonal room converts the hemisphere of warmth into a rectangular volume of space (right).

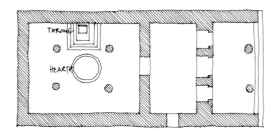

In an ancient Mycenaean megaron (left, shown in plan) the place of the fire was identified by a circle on the ground, by the four columns that held up the roof, and also by the rectangular form of the room itself, which was the place of the king on his throne.

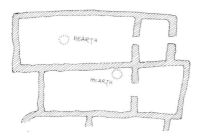

In some ancient houses the position of the hearth can seem arbitrary (above).

The architecture of the fireplace within a dwelling cell affects the organisation of the space around it into subsidiary places. As a source of warmth and light the fire is a focus for life; but it can also be an obstacle. In the remains of some early dwellings archaeologists have found hearths located arbitrarily on the floor, with little clear organisational relationship between their position and the space around them (right). Other ancient remains suggest tidier, more formal arrangements. In the megaron of the palace of Mycenae (c.1500 BC, above) there is a clear relationship between the hearth and the throne, the entrance and the structure of the room. Sitting here, the king of ancient Mycenae, Agamemnon, was enthroned within his own 'fireplace'.

The consequences of changing the location of the fireplace from a central position to a peripheral one is shown in two Norwegian traditional timber houses. Their plans (right) are similar, except for the position of the hearth. In the upper plan the space of the living room is dominated by the central hearth. Subsidiary places – for sitting and eating, for storage – are arranged around this central focus. Moving around the room is a matter of moving around the fire. In the lower plan the fireplace is situated in the corner of the room and built as a small cell of stone, non-combustible, to protect the timber of the outer walls. The consequence of this change is that, although the fire no longer occupies its central symbolically important position, movement within the room is less constrained. The floor becomes more open for human occupation – a 'dancing-floor'.

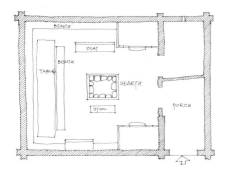

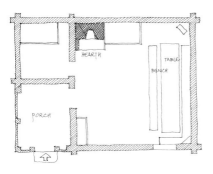

The decentralised fireplace need not be positioned in the corner of its room. In this small Welsh cottage (below left) the hearth takes up almost all of one wall. A consequence of putting a fireplace on the periphery of a room is that the fabric of the hearth (and of the chimney stack it acquires) contributes to the enclosure and structure of the room; it assumes another architectural role, as wall. In another Welsh example (below right) it is the fireplace that divides the cell of the house into two rooms. In fact the fireplace stack in this example does more than that. Each of its four sides contributes a wall to four places: the two rooms already mentioned plus an entrance lobby; and a stair to the upper floor, which the stack similarly divides into two.

The way a space can be used may be radically altered by changing the position of the hearth (above).

Chimney stacks are significant space-defining elements (left).

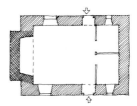

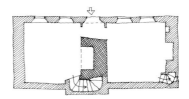

In another Welsh example (below left) the space defining role of the hearth and its massive chimney stack is taken further, with each of its four sides playing a part in the composition of each of four sections of the house – three wings of accommodation plus an entrance porch. Here the fireplace is once more central to the house, but in a way architecturally different from that of the open hearth in the centre of a room. The central stack generates four spaces like spokes radiating from a hub. The same idea is taken a step further

In this summer cottage, designed and built in 1940, Walter Gropius and Marcel Breuer used the chimney stack to separate the living area from the dining.

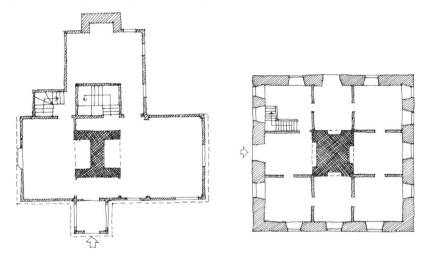

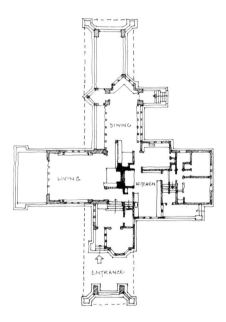

in the example alongside by being formalised into a square plan and enclosing the four corner spaces as rooms. These rooms do not have fireplaces and the route from room to room re-introduces the sort of circulation problems of the hearth in the centre of the floor, though of a different order.

In the house at the top of the next page, another building by Rudolf Schindler, designed (but never built) when he was an apprentice fellow of Frank Lloyd Wright, the fireplace plays a number of the roles already mentioned. It provides the focus of the house and is its main structural anchorage. It divides the living room from the work room. It also contributes a wall to the entrance lobby. Its fourth side is however more curious. The fire itself is not set beneath the chimney stack, but on a low platform between the stack and the outer wall. It seems the idea was that in this way one fire could warm both rooms.

In large rooms a fire can only warm a fraction of the space; its sphere of warmth does not extend to the walls. In these circumstances the fire, like an outdoor fire, identifies its own

In the Ward Willits House (above), designed by Frank Lloyd Wright in 1901, the central chimney stack plays a pivotal role in the organisation of the accommodation into four wings. (Compare the organisation of this plan with that of the small Welsh cottage on the far left)

Reference for Welsh rural houses:
Peter Smith – *Houses of the Welsh Countryside*, 1975.

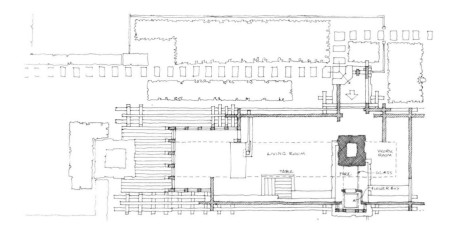

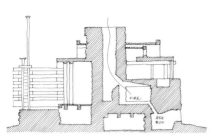

In this cabin by Rudolf Schindler, one fireplace heats two rooms. It is also provided with an ash pit that can be emptied from outside.

small place within a larger one. Sometimes this is recognised architecturally too. Below is the plan of two of a number of 'co-operative dwellings' that Barry Parker and Raymond Unwin designed (in about 1902) for 'a Yorkshire town'. If they had ever been built they would have formed part of a quadrangle of similar houses, also provided with common rooms for social activities. In the right-hand plan one can see that the place around the fire is identified architecturally as an 'inglenook'. Notice too how Parker and Unwin identified other 'sub-places' within the living room: a place to sit by the window; a place at the table to eat; a place for the piano; a place to study.

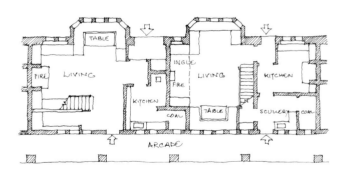

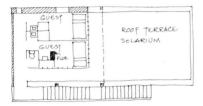

second floor

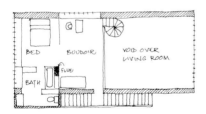

first floor

In houses with central heating the hearth is less important as a source of warmth, but it can retain its role as the focus of a particular place for sitting and reading, talking, knitting or perhaps dozing. Rather than the hemisphere of warmth having to fill the interior of the cell, it can be used merely to heat and more importantly provide a vital focus for a small portion of the space within the cell, leaving the rest of the space to be heated by the background central heating system. In Le Corbusier's 1920 design for a Citrohan House (right) the fireplace is the focus of a small part of the living room, under the 'boudoir' balcony and rather like a simplified inglenook. The rest of the house was to be heated by radiators fed from a boiler positioned under the outside steps to the roof, which therefore did not contribute to the conceptual organisation of the living spaces of the house.

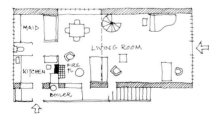

ground floor

The hearth in this house by Hugo Häring is a stable centre amongst the irregular geometry of the other spaces.

The Schindler Chase House (below), designed by Rudolf Schindler, has outdoor fireplaces that make the point that the outside rooms in the garden are just as much for living in as the rooms inside the house.

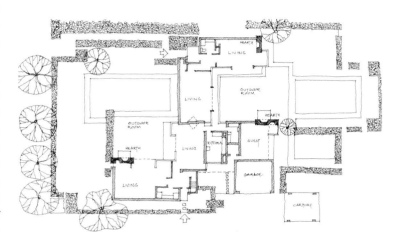

With central heating the hearth in a dwelling is practically redundant, or at least not required to heat the whole space. In these circumstances its role in spatial organisation can change. It can become more like a fireplace set in an internal landscape.

In this house by Hugo Häring (top, 1946) the fireplace is almost completely detached from the rest of the fabric of the house. From its central position, other places, defined by the activities they accommodate, radiate with an irregularity more associated with the outside landscape. The next plan (middle) is of two houses designed by Rudolf Schindler, in 1922, for himself and his wife, and another couple. Set in the reasonably comfortable climate of southern California, the gardens are treated as external rooms. The outdoor rooms, as well as those inside, were provided with fireplaces. The three chimney stacks are positioned between the rooms with roofs over them and those without. Below this is a plan of *Fallingwater*, by Frank Lloyd Wright (1935). This house is well known as built over a waterfall. Its floor platforms and flat roofs echo the horizontal strata of the geology. The symbolic power of the hearth was important in many of Wright's houses. Though it does not provide all the heating, here it is the social focus and heart of the house. Set on the natural rock, it is as if the hearth has escaped from the containment of the cell and returned to its place in the landscape.

In Fallingwater it is as if the hearth has returned to the landscape.

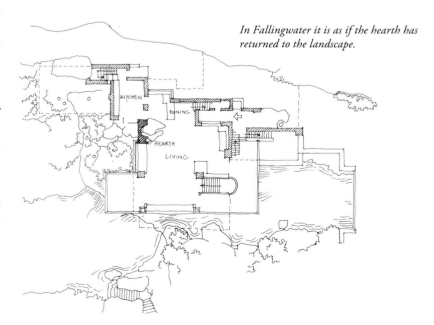

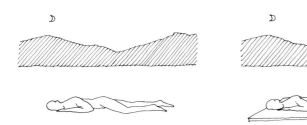

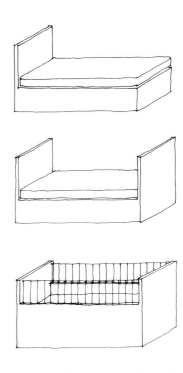

Bed – a place for sleep, sex, sickness

A bed is not just a piece of furniture; conceptually it is a place. It might be argued that the most fundamental purpose of a house is as a secure place for sleep. The bedroom is the innermost, most private, most protected part of a house. It is a place where one must feel safe enough to sleep or be ill, and private enough for sex. The earliest houses were, and the most primitive houses are, little more than bedrooms, with most other activities associated with dwelling taking place outside. The development of the house through history involves the invention of the separate bed chamber and its progressive segregation from other internal living places in the interests of increasing privacy and security. The bedroom has become a room on the conceptual, and often also the physical, periphery of a house – upstairs or set aside from the living rooms, private to its owner and often considered less important than the reception rooms.

A bed can be a separate piece of furniture, with its own self-contained form, or it can be fixed into the architecture of its house. Like a hearth, a bed may be no more than the patch of ground a sleeping creature occupies. Or it might be identified as a defined area by a material that makes it more comfortable – leaves, soft grass, a ground sheet, a foam mattress, a towel, a rug. A bed may be a platform, lifting the sleeping surface off the ground and fitted with one, two, three or four walls.

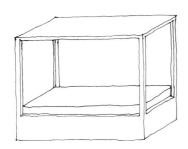

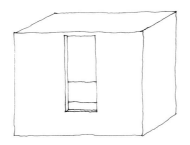

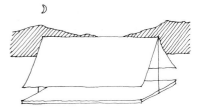

A bed might be fitted with a roof supported on its own columns, making it into a bed-aedicule. It might even be a complete room in itself – a bed-cell.

Not only do beds have their own architecture, they also contribute to the composition of more complex places. A hiking tent, like a primitive bivouac made of branches and leaves, is a bed-roof – a small building.

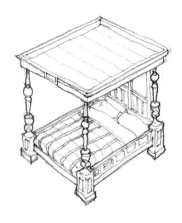

A bed may be an aedicule, provided with its own roof supported on columns, or walls.

In more complex buildings the bed does not occupy the whole internal space but it does play its part in the organisation of spaces into places.

According to accounts in the writings of Homer some three thousand years ago, ancient Greek kings slept in beds in their megarons (below left), while their visitors slept in the porches, as someone nowadays might sleep on a veranda.

Some small old houses had sleeping floors built between the side walls at the end of an open hall, lifting the bed up into the warmer air that collects in the upper levels of any heated space and freeing more space on the ground floor. On the right below is a long section through a tiny Welsh cottage.

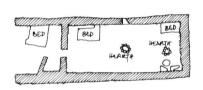

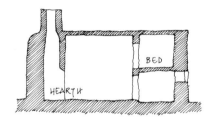

In Powis Castle in Wales there is a state bedroom that is spatially organised like a proscenium arch theatre: the bed is the stage and is set in an alcove framed by a proscenium arch, outside of which is an area for those seeking an audience.

Some had box-beds – sleeping-cells like cupboards built alongside the hearth. Below is the plan of a house the inside of which was illustrated earlier in this book (in the chapter *Architecture as Identification of Place*). The bed upstairs does more than one thing: it also forms a box space in the ceiling below, which collects warmth and makes a place for storing and smoking meats.

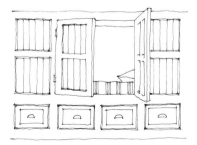

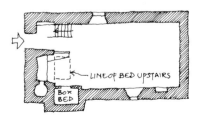

Bed: *'Nestor arranged for Telemachus to sleep at the palace itself, on a wooden bedstead in the echoing portico…. The king himself retired to rest in his room at the back of the high building.'*

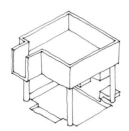

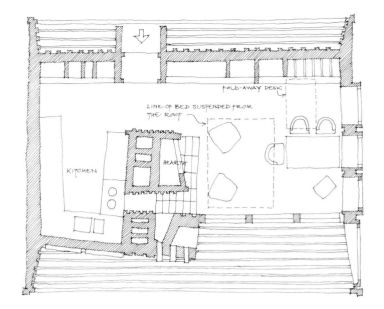

In this house (left), which Ralph Erskine built for himself when he went to live in Sweden, space is saved by having furniture that can be stowed away; the bed, for example, lifts into the ceiling space.

In some of his houses, Charles Moore made 'bed aedicules' with sitting places beneath (above).

In the small woodland house (above) that Ralph Erskine built for himself when he went to live in Sweden during the Second World War, the bed could be lifted into the ceiling during the day, to save space.

In some of the houses that Charles Moore has designed, the bed is a platform on top of an aedicule, with the space defined beneath used as a sitting place with its own hearth (above right).

Even an 'ordinary' bed – a movable piece of furniture – contributes to the architecture of its room. The Victorian architect Robert Kerr, in his book *The English Gentleman's House* (1865), devoted four and a half pages to discussing the relative positions of windows, doors, hearth and bed in a sleeping-room, and comparing typical English arrangements, where the bed stood as a free-standing piece of furniture positioned to avoid draughts (below left), with French bedrooms where the bed was sheltered in its own alcove (below right).

Reference for Ralph Erskine:
Peter Collymore – *The Architecture of Ralph Erskine*, 1985.

Reference for Charles Moore:
Charles Moore and others – *The Place of Houses*, 1974.

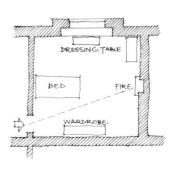
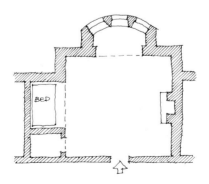

According to Robert Kerr, the English Victorian architect, the English gentleman's bedroom should be arranged so that the bed avoided draughts; one should be able to draw a straight line from the door to the hearth without it cutting across the bed (far left). In French examples (near left), he said, beds were protected from draughts by being provided with their own alcoves planned into the bedrooms.

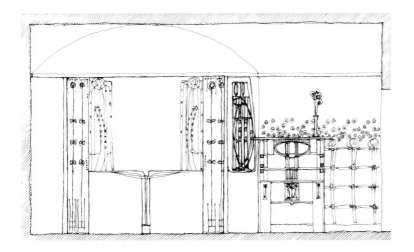

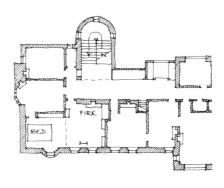

Hill House was built at Helensburgh, Scotland, in 1903, designed by the architect Charles Rennie Mackintosh. The main bedroom is at the bottom left of this plan (above right), which shows part of the first floor of the house. Though apparently very simple, Mackintosh subtly divided the room into various places for particular purposes. There is a hearth with a seat. The washstand is just inside the door. There is a dressing place by the pair of windows, between which stands a tall mirror. The bed lies in its own generous alcove with a vaulted ceiling. Originally Mackintosh intended to define the bed-alcove even more with two decorated side-screens making an entrance, but these were not built. The drawing above shows these screens, the bed, the washstand and the decorative scheme for the bedroom walls.

In the Farnsworth House (below) by Mies van der Rohe, the places of the two beds are not as definitely identified by the architecture. Though their positions are hinted at by the organisation of space in the house, they take their own places rather than have them given to them by the architecture. In this house, in contrast to traditional houses, the only places defined as rooms with walls around them are those that require privacy, the bathrooms.

In the main bedroom in Hill House (above, in section and plan), the architect Charles Rennie Mackintosh placed the bed in its own alcove, with an arched ceiling.

Bed: *'Meanwhile in the shadowy hall the Suitors burst into uproar, and each man voiced the hope that he might share her bed.'*

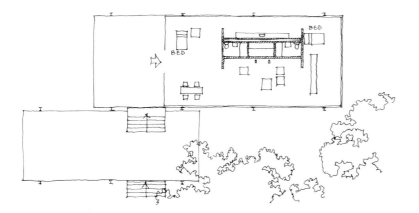

In the Farnsworth House, by Mies van der Rohe (left), the bed places are not identified by rooms but in more subtle ways.

Reference for Mackintosh:
Robert Macleod – *Charles Rennie Mackintosh, Architect and Artist*, 1968.

Reference for Mies van der Rohe:
Philip Johnson – *Mies van der Rohe*, 1978.

92

At Stonehenge the place of the altar is identified by a circle and a horseshoe of standing stones. The altar is positioned not quite at the geometric centre of the circle, offset in response to the approach to the circle and the open end of the horseshoe.

Altar – a table for sacrifice or worship

The architecture of an altar may be more consistent than that of a hearth or of a bed. It is almost always a table (a platform) for ritual or symbolic sacrifice, or which plays the role of focus for worship.

In ancient Egypt altars were tables on which nourishment for the dead pharaoh was placed. Altars were hidden away in the deepest recesses of mortuary temples attached to the bases of the pyramids. Though they were concealed from public view and attended only by the priests, they were usually positioned on the east–west axis of the pyramid and the long axis of the temple. Above right is a small early example from the pyramid of Meidum.

The same principles of arrangement apply in the much larger and more complex example at the pyramid of Chephren (one of the well-known group at Giza, right). The mortuary temple lies at the base of the pyramid (at the top of the drawing); the altar is in a small chamber close to the pyramid; the spirit of the pharaoh would reach the food through the *image* of a doorway apparently leading from inside the pyramid.

In ancient Greece altars were positioned outside the temples. The image of the god was housed within. The altar and the god inside the temple are linked by the long axis they share. As in Egyptian pyramids, this was often the east–west axis.

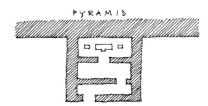

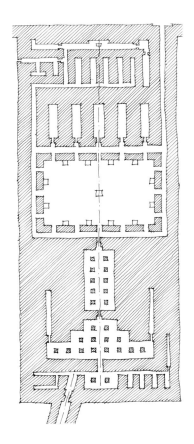

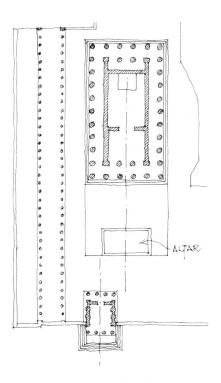

In the pyramid temple of Chephren (below left) the altar is hidden away at the end of labyrinthine corridors. The spirit of the god king would come to collect the food through an false doorway that 'connected' the chamber with the inside of the pyramid (at the top of the drawing).

The altar in an ancient Greek sanctuary (above) was placed outside the temple. This is the temple of Athena Polias at Priene.

93

The spire of a traditional church acts as a marker identifying the place of the altar in a way that can be seen for miles around.

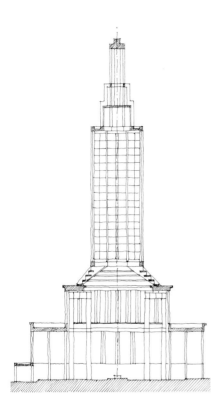

In medieval churches and cathedrals the altar is inside. The altar of S. Maria del Mar in Barcelona (below left) relates to an east–west axis that provides the backbone for the whole building. The principal purpose of all Christian churches is to identify the place of the altar. Here the way that the structure of the building focuses on the altar is clear.

During the Renaissance, some architects and theologians wondered whether the altar should be positioned at the centre of the church rather than at one end. In the church of St Peter in Rome (below right) the high altar is placed at the centre of the main part of the building. An extension to the nave stops the building being a fully centralised church. Some twentieth-century churches have centralised plans too. On the right are the section and plan of one in Le Havre, France, designed by Auguste Perret and built in 1959. The church is essentially a large spire which, like spires on traditional medieval churches, also identifies the place of the altar. In Perret's church the altar is placed on three axes: the two horizontal axes and the vertical.

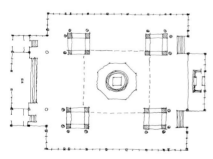

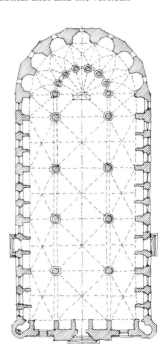

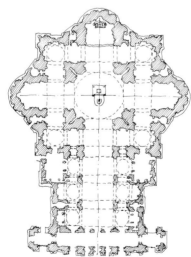

In the church of S. Maria del Mar in Barcelona (left), the geometry of the structure focuses on the altar at its heart. In St Peter's, Rome, the altar stands near the focus of two axes (above).

This church (above, in plan and section), designed by Auguste Perret, is one big spire. The altar is positioned centrally, directly under the spire.

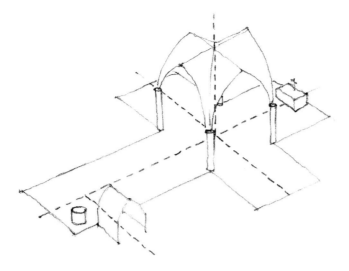

The place of the altar in a traditional church is identified by the axis of the building. Often the entrance is placed so that people coming into the church do not confront this axis directly.

Another way the place of the altar can be identified is by the effect of the perspective of a long space. This effect works because the altar is on the long axis of the building. Such axes are so powerful, symbolically as well as architecturally, that entrances into churches are often positioned to avoid confronting it directly. This arrangement, which we tend to associate with Christian churches and cathedrals, seems to stretch all the way back through history to the mortuary temples at the bases of the Egyptian pyramids. But by the twentieth century the symmetrical arrangement had become so orthodox that architects were keen to explore other ways of positioning an altar in a church.

The axis of a church is part of a perspective that focuses on the altar.

Altar: *'A whistling wind blew up, and our ships made splendid running down the highways of the fish, reaching Geraestus in the night. And many a bull's thigh we laid on Poseidon's altar after spanning that weary stretch of water.'*

95

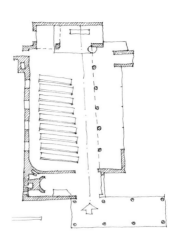

Altar: 'She then drew a polished table to their side, and the staid housekeeper brought some bread and set it by them with a choice of dainties, helping them liberally to all she could offer. Meanwhile a carver dished up for them on platters slices of various meats he had picked from his board, and put gold cups beside them, which a steward filled up with wine as he passed them on his frequent rounds.'

In the Cemetery Chapel at Turku, Erik Bryggman experimented with a non-symmetrical arrangement about the axis of the altar.

The Cemetery Chapel at Turku in Finland (above), designed by Erik Bryggman and built in 1941, has an asymmetrical plan but the altar remains the focus of the building. Attention is drawn to it by the axis of the entrance and the pathway leading to it (as in more traditional church plans), but in making an asymmetrical layout the architect recognised the relationship between the inside of the church and the outside. The context of the church is not symmetrical; the layout allows the sun in to illuminate the altar alcove and the congregation to look out through the glass south wall.

Some things in architecture, without actually being altars, can be like them. This is a part of the old plan for the Abbey of St Gall in Switzerland (right). It dates from the ninth century AD, and shows the intended infirmary. The operating table has the same sort of architectural relationship with its room as the altars in their chapels.

Many ordinary everyday things can be like altars. When someone devotes a table to

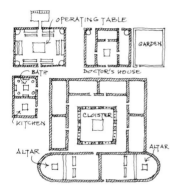

In the abbey of St Gall (part of the plan is above) the operating theatre had a layout similar to a chapel, making the operating table like an altar. The old plan, from which this portion is taken, is displayed on its own 'altar' in the Stiftsbibliotek in St Gallen, Switzerland.

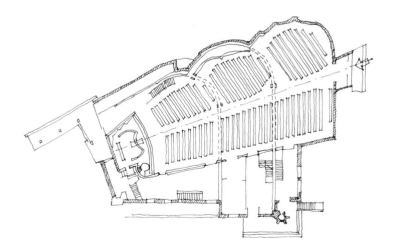

Alvar Aalto's design for the Vuoksenniska Church at Imatra in Finland is asymmetrical in its plan. But still, by various means, the building focuses on the altar.

1

2

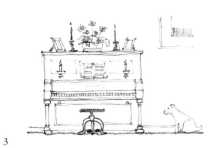

3

4

5

6

memorabilia of a favourite football club, it can be like an altar (1). A museum curator may place precious objects on their own altars (2). A grandmother might put photographs on her piano, making it into an altar to her family (3). A bar might be considered by some to be an altar to drinking (4), a table to eating (5). A kitchen stove might be like an altar to cooking (6). A mantelpiece can be an altar to the fire in its hearth and a support for ornaments (7). A dressing table is an altar to one's self (8). Many games are played on 'altars': a gaming machine is an altar to the acquisition of money by luck, a pool or snooker table is an altar to a mystical game of skill and chance (9). An operating table might be seen as an altar on which patients are treated by 'high priest' surgeons (10); a mortuary table is an altar to their failures (11).

As a platform, an altar lifts whatever it carries onto a plane above the ordinary and by so doing makes its burden special and worthy of attention. The drawing boards and computer screens on which architects work are altars to the mysterious processes of architectural design.

9

10

7

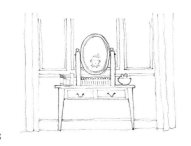

8

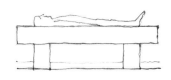

11

When a clown performs on a patch of ground it becomes a stage.

Performance place: '*They now swept the dancing-floor and cleared a ring wide enough for the performance…. The minstrel then moved forward to the centre; a band of expert dancers, all in the first bloom of youth, took up their positions round him; and their feet came down on the sacred floor with a scintillating movement that filled Odysseus with admiration as he watched.*'

Theatre – a place for performance

A performance requires space: for religious ritual, dance, music, drama, football. It is not as focused a place as a hearth or an altar. A performance place also requires protection from encroachment by those not involved in it, who may be spectators.

When a clown performs in a field it becomes a stage. He defines its area by his movement and by positioning his props. He protects it from encroachment by the force of his presence and pretend personality. The ring of spectators that he attracts also contribute to the identification of place, to the architecture of this impromptu theatre.

In primitive times a place for the performance of ritual may have been no more than a clearing in a forest or a trampled piece of grassland. But by the powers of architecture performance places can be made more formal and more permanent.

In Minoan and Mycenaean times, about 3500 years ago, the 'dancing floor' – *orkestra* – was a specific place. On the right is an example from the Palace of Knossos on the Mediterranean island of Crete. It is thought to have been built by Daedalos, architect to King Minos, as a place for his daughter Ariadne to dance. But it might also have been a place for displaying bulls before they went into the courtyard of the palace to be fought by young Minoans. This small dancing floor is a flat, almost rectangular, paved area, with low sitting steps on two sides. The rake of the steps takes advantage of the natural slope of the ground.

By a thousand or so years later, architects had formalised the outdoor theatre into the ancient Greek theatre, which was much larger and more geometrically organised but which also made use of the lie of the land.

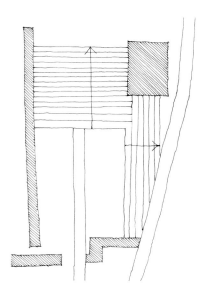

Just outside the Palace of Knossos there is a small performance place defined by tiers of sitting steps around a flat pavement (above).

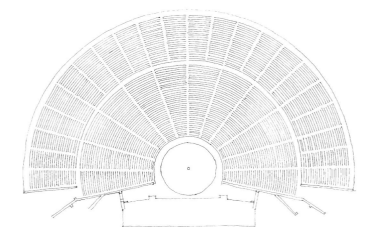

The ancient Greek amphitheatre is a formalisation of performance places in the landscape.

Behind the *orkestra* in a Greek theatre there was a building – the *skene* – which in Greek drama was a background to the action. Through Roman and into modern times this building came to be used as a performance place in its own right – a stage. It was also, like the altar, brought inside. The stage became framed by a proscenium arch. In the Greek theatre the magic of the place of performance had been defined by the circle of the *orkestra*. In this type of theatre the separation of the special world of the actors and the ordinary world of the audience was defined by the platform of the stage and by its rectangular opening – a window into a make-believe world. With the development of cinema and television the window into other worlds became more far-reaching, and encroachment impossible.

Some architects have tried to design performance places in which the separation between performers and spectators is reduced. In designing the Philharmonie in Berlin (1956, below right), Hans Scharoun was determined to be non-orthogonal. In this plan, he has placed the performers on their stage, not in opposition to the audience but surrounded by them. Listeners sit in tiers as if on the slopes of a small valley. The sanctity of the performance place is preserved by the platform, but the separation between audience and players is reduced.

Many places can be thought of as performance places. Street theatre, like the clown in the field, makes its own stage where it can in the public spaces of a city. Religious ceremonies and services are performed in the setting of churches, mosques, temples…. Sports pitches, bull rings, boxing rings are the stages for competitive confrontations. Sitting in the window of a cafe, the passing life on the pavement outside is like a subtle play with many unsuspecting actors. The rooms of a house are the sets of daily rituals and domestic dramas.

The proscenium arch in a theatre is a metaphorical window between the ordinary world and an imaginary world. The effect of separation is enhanced by the contrast in light between the auditorium and the stage. Similar effects can be achieved in more everyday situations: a window looking onto a street; a park seat in dark shade watching people pass on a lit path; a veranda overlooking the everchanging sea.

* * *

There are many other primitive place types, too many to cover here: places to cook; places to store things (garages, boat sheds, coal and wood sheds, libraries, larders, cupboards, closets, museums, archives); places arranged for people to discuss things (council chambers, parliaments, meeting rooms, chapter houses); shrines; thrones; places for selling and exchanging things (shops, banks); places to work (studies, workshops, offices); places to stand and

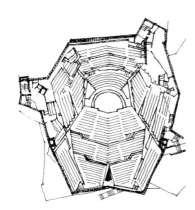

In the Philharmonie, a concert hall in Berlin designed by Hans Scharoun, the performers are surrounded by their audience. The effect is like an internal landscape of terraced slopes around a clearing where the orchestra perform.

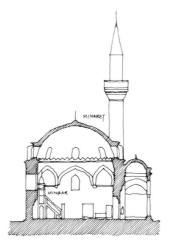

Bath: *'In the meantime, the beautiful Polycaste, King Nestor's youngest daughter, had given Telemachus his bath. When she had bathed him and rubbed him with olive oil, she gave him a tunic and arranged a fine cloak round his shoulders, so that he stepped out of the bath looking like an immortal god.'*

The traditional hamam *(below, upper drawing) and Zumthor's thermal baths at Vals in Switzerland (below, lower drawing) are compositions of places where you can enjoy a variety of sensual experiences.*

speak; places to bathe. A place to stand and speak may be no more than a prominent rock above a place for an audience, like the rock on which the oracle Sybil stood in the sanctuary at Delphi (above). It might be a lectern at a business conference or the desk in a lecture theatre or classroom; the pulpit in a church or the minbar of a mosque.

A place to bathe may be the sea, a river, or a pool of clear cool water beneath a crashing waterfall. It might be the usual bathtub found in a domestic bathroom or it might be the complex of rooms in a Roman baths or Turkish *hamam* (right) where you can be steamed and massaged. In the thermal baths at Vals in Switzerland (below right), designed by Peter Zumthor and built in 1996, there are rooms to provide for every human sense. There are pools in which to bathe: one outdoor (into which you can swim from inside) and another inside. There are also smaller pools hidden in what appear to be massive structural columns: a cold pool; a warm pool; a pool with the fragrance of flower petals strewn on the water; a pool in a murmur-resonating chamber of rock, into which you must swim through a tunnel. There are also steam baths, showers, massage rooms and a shrine where you can drink the thermal waters. Half into the hillside, and half facing across a Swiss valley to the mountains opposite, the baths at Vals achieve a sophistication that appeals to the primitive sensuality of the human being.

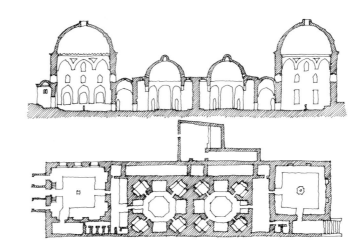

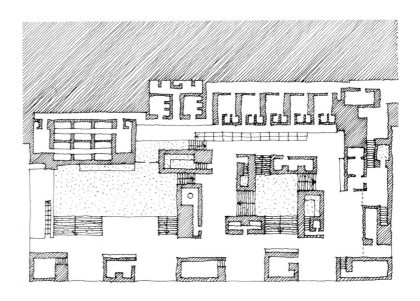

In this carving the image of a person (called Rhodia) is framed by the representation of a building. It is a pictorial composition and a memorial but it also illustrates a recognition that buildings are 'frames' within which people live and that buildings can be identified by the people that inhabit them. (The carving is a grave stele from Egypt, and is about 1200 years old.)

ARCHITECTURE AS MAKING FRAMES

'When a child was born in a coral house, the female members of the household performed a ritual that marked that child's social position. The baby was taken around the house and in each area the child was told who slept or worked there, what those persons owned, and what their relationship was to the child. The child of course understood none of this, but the women in the group learned or reinforced their rank and everyone else's…. The areas of the house and associated objects became cues for behavior toward the individuals who occupied the spaces. This ritual was needed to make the power relationship clear to everyone in the house….. As a child grew up in the house he or she learned his or her place in the house and society.'

Linda W. Donley-Reid – 'A structuring structure: the Swahili house', in Susan Kent, editor – *Domestic Architecture and the Use of Space*, 1990.

ARCHITECTURE AS MAKING FRAMES

Architecture is more to do with making frames than painting pictures; more a matter of providing an accompaniment to life than the dance of life itself.

Certainly it is within the capacity of architecture to frame 'pictures' – as the rectangle of a window frames a view of distant hills, or a doorway the figure of a person, or an archway the altar of a church.

It is also possible to compose works of architecture, in townscape or landscape, as if they themselves were objects in a picture, maybe to be seen from a particular point of view or ready to be painted by an artist.

But architecture is not primarily about contriving 'picturesque' compositions (though sometimes it is presented as such); nor is the power to frame limited to distant hills or someone standing in a doorway. The dimensions of architecture include more than the two of a picture-frame. It is obvious that they include the third spatial dimension, but there is also the dimension of time – which accommodates movement and change – and those more abstract and subtle dimensions: patterns of life, work and ritual. The products of architecture can frame gods; they can frame the dead; they can even frame the family pet. But perhaps their noblest purpose is to frame life.

A window frames a view into a room. But the room itself frames the life it accommodates. The doorway frames people coming in and going out. The chair is a frame waiting for a sitter. The cupboard frames possessions. The table frames meals. Even the small vase frames its single flower. And the television frames views of the remote world outside.

We are used to looking at the world through frames: the frames of windows, of pictures, the frames of television screens, the frames and sub-frames of computer screens. It might be argued that since these frame remote places they constitute an abstract, supra-real architecture. The World Wide Web, for example, is a form of architecture that reinterprets or overlays the physical world.

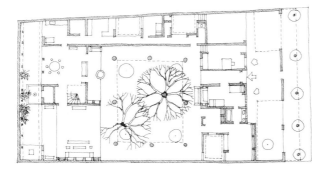

Thinking about architecture as frame-making is part of conceiving it as identification of place. Frames define boundaries. Frames mediate between that which is framed and the 'outside world'. Products of architecture are multi-dimensional and multi-layered frames: the rooms within which we work, the pitches on which games are played, the streets along which we drive, the table where a family eats, the gardens in which we sit, the floors on which we dance are all 'frames'; and together they constitute a complex and extensive *framework* within which we live, which, though vast, can be like the musical accompaniment that sets the metre of a song, both a support and a discipline.

The plan above illustrates how a work of architecture frames life. It is a house in Colombo, Sri Lanka, designed by the architect Geoffrey Bawa and built in 1962. The house as a whole is framed by the outer boundary wall, but it contains many other frames too. The living and bedrooms frame social activities and sleeping; the dining table frames dinner parties; the courtyards frame the trees, plants, fountains and large stones they contain; even the bath is a frame, and the garage frames the car.

The word 'frame' comes from the old English word *framian,* which means 'to be helpful'. A frame is 'helpful' in that it provides support. The physical frame of something – a loom, a body, a building – is its structure, without which it would be formless. A frame also 'helps' by defining space: creating demarcations and an ordered relationship between 'insides' and 'outsides'. A frame is a principle of organisation. Whether it is a picture frame, or a sheep pen, or a room, it is rarely (if ever) sufficient by itself (except perhaps in the poetic device of the 'vacant frame'). It has a relationship with what it frames (actually or potentially) and with what is 'outside', setting something in its place. That 'something' may be a picture or an object, but it might also be a person (the hermit in his cave, 'Mrs Clark' in her house, St Jerome in his study, one's self in a room), an activity (tennis on a court, car manufacture in a factory), an animal (a pig in its sty, a bird in its cage), a god (Athena in the Parthenon, Vishnu in his temple).

This painting (right) is of *St Jerome in His Study*. It is by the fifteenth-century Italian painter Antonello da Messina. As a picture it has a frame, but within the picture St Jerome is framed, physically and symbolically, by the architecture of the building in which he sits.

A frame can be a structure and a boundary but its helpfulness also comes from being a frame *of reference*, according to which one develops an understanding of where one is. The squares on a chessboard, or the floors of an apartment block, or the streets of a city make frames that condition how pieces, people or vehicles move, and by reference to which their locations can be described.

A photographic image portrays the building as an object and is unable to let us experience it as a frame. Our experiences of a building in reality – when the building is framing us rather than being contained within the frame of a picture – is very different from when we see it in a photograph.

Photographs often portray buildings not as frames but as objects. This is a consequence of the process of photography, which involves placing a two-dimensional frame around something. This process deprives us of our experience of buildings as frames, turning them into objects that are themselves framed. The same problem afflicts computer representations of buildings.

Photographs also tell lies. Photographs in architectural periodicals are often composed or cropped to show buildings at their best, and maybe cut out unattractive aspects of their surroundings.

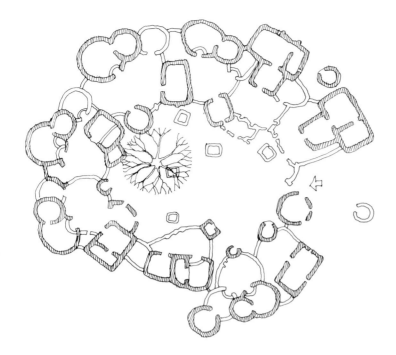

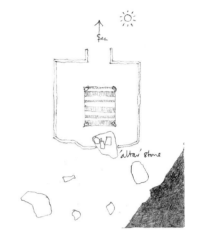

Not only is the plan of this African village a diagram of the communal life it accommodates: the village itself is a conceptual frame that responds to the order in the lives of its inhabitants.

We frame our selves on the beach when we spend time by the sea; maybe just with a towel, or maybe by drawing a line around our area of ground.

In an abstract sense, a frame can be a theory. (The intention of this book, for example, is to be 'helpful' by offering a framework of concepts for analysing architecture.) Architecture involves considering how things should be framed, theoretically (philosophically) as well as physically. Designing a museum involves thinking about how objects should be exhibited and the routes people might take through its galleries. But it also involves taking a theoretical stance on the notion of a museum and its role in culture. Designing an opera house involves thinking about how the spectacle of an opera, and the dressed-up people who come to see it, might be displayed, which depends on a theory of the culture of opera. Even the design of a kennel poses the theoretical problem of how a dog should be framed.

In more complex cases, the design of a house involves theorising about how the lives it will accommodate might be lived and producing an appropriate frame. The design of a church involves understanding the liturgy – the theory of how it is to be used for worship and ritual. Architecture, in all these cases, involves the responsibility of proposing a physical and a theoretical framework within which art can be viewed, opera watched, dances danced, gods worshipped, meals eaten, produce sold, or whatever.

A picture frame, or a museum exhibition case, or an ancient Greek temple, holds something static, something for which time has been halted. Through architecture, however, people also make frames for movement and for change. A football field is a frame on which an artificial battle is fought; a street frames the movement of traffic; the track of a fairground ride describes the passage of its carriages; a church frames a ceremonial route, from lychgate to altar. Frames (physical and theoretical) are used to give the world, or part of it, some sort of order. These pages, which are themselves frames, have been organised into two-dimensional rectangles – the graphic 'architecture' of the page. Some computer programmes are based on the use of frames for different tasks. The range of types of frames in architecture is greater; and they are not always simple or rectangular.

The sixty-four squares of a chessboard set the frame for the game of chess. The board is simple and fixed, as is the framework of rules, but the games that can be played are almost infinitely variable.

105

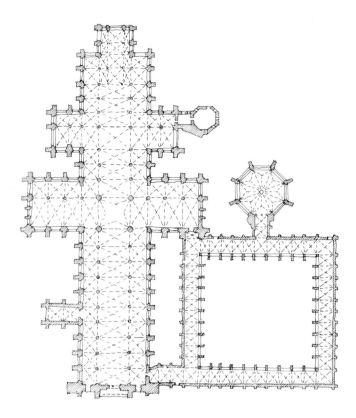

Salisbury Cathedral is composed of a number of frames for different purposes: the porch frames the entrance; the cathedral frames the altar; the altar frames the ceremony of preparation for communion; the square cloister frames a place of contemplation; the octagonal chapter house frames a place for communal discussion.

A conceptual requirement of a frame is that it must have something to frame, whether or not that something is temporarily or even permanently absent. A chair is not always occupied. A cenotaph is literally an empty tomb; though permanently empty it is a frame for the 'idea' of the dead. It is not necessary that a frame always contains something, but its relationship with content, and the extrinsic, is essential.

One usually assumes that a picture frame is of lesser importance than the work of art which it contains. One similarly assumes that the glass case that protects, for example, the bust of Nefertiti in the Egyptian Museum in Berlin is less important than the bust itself. But the question whether the products of architecture are of lesser, or greater, importance than the things they frame is more difficult.

The answer of moderation is that the two are in a symbiotic relationship. It may be that a frame is secondary to its contents, but the contents also benefit from their frame – in the protection it gives, in the accommodation it provides, in the amplification it gives to their existence. A room provides a service as a frame; as does a chair, a bookcase, a pulpit, an aircraft hangar, even a bus shelter. Each protects, accommodates and reinforces the existence of its contents (or its inhabitants). The relationship between contents and frame is pivotal.

Architecture is most often a matter of framing the ordinary and the everyday, but famous instances make the point and are memorable. The simple blue garage in Laugharne on the South Wales coast is the frame within which Dylan Thomas wrote his poetry; the new palace in Bucharest, Romania, was intended to frame and amplify the political power

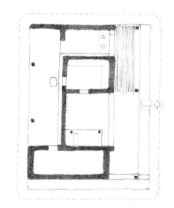

plan

section

This simple but subtle house in Kerala, India, frames the life of the old lady who lives in it.

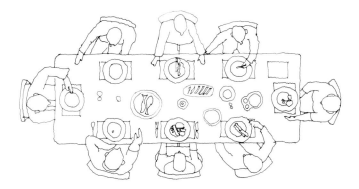

A table, in its space, frames the life of a meal. It even frames the people sitting around it, though they are outside of its rectangle.

of the dictator Nicolae Ceausescu; the Dome of the Rock in Jerusalem frames a sacred place; the concentration camp at Auschwitz framed the deaths of a million people.

Thinking in this way, one realises that human beings surround themselves with frames, by which they organise the world architecturally. Sitting writing this I am surrounded by many frames: the frame of streets of the planned village in which I live; the frame of our piece of ground, our house, my study. In the study there are: shelves that frame books (which themselves frame ideas and facts, stories and other worlds); a table that frames a surface for work; a drawing board; windows; a door; a fireplace; lights; pictures; cupboards; and computers, which frame many images and pieces of information from all over the world.

Architectural frames, and the ways in which they can be used, are innumerable. There are simple frames (an aedicular porch), and complex (the network of routes in a modern air terminal). There are small frames (a keyhole) and large (a city square). There are basically two-dimensional frames (for example, a snooker or pool table), three-dimensional (a multi-storey structure), four-dimensional (a labyrinth, which includes the dimension of time), and many dimensional (the Internet).

Frames need not be constructed of tangible material – a spotlight can frame an actor on a stage – and can apply to senses other than the visual. A beautiful woman might be framed by an aura of scent. Warm air from an air vent might frame a group of people trying to keep warm on a cold day. A mosque, or even the whole of the Muslim religion, is in a way framed by the sound of the *muezzin* calling the faithful to prayer.

Russian dolls

Frames in architecture often overlap one another or fit one within another. Frames can be like Russian dolls, each of which has an inside into which fits a slightly smaller doll, to the

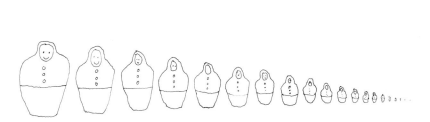

The aedicule of the Albert Memorial in London frames a statue of Prince Albert, but in death it also frames his memory.

107

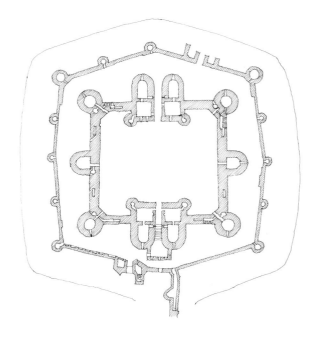

Beaumaris Castle on the island of Anglesey, off the coast of North Wales, consists of a concentric series of defensive barriers.

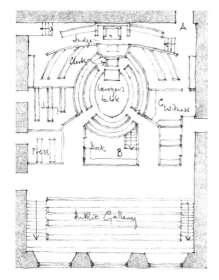

limits of practicability. Some works of architecture can be like this. The plan of Beaumaris Castle (above) on the island of Anglesey shows five concentric layers: the moat; the outer defensive wall; the outer ward; the inner defensive wall; and the inner ward.

In architecture frames are rarely simply concentric like Russian dolls; frames overlap, combine in complex and sometimes contradictory ways, intrude one on another, and operate at vastly variable scales, from the keyhole to the city.

Imagine a walled town. The 'first' frame is the wall itself; next there are the gateways through the walls; then there is the network of streets, geometric or organic; each of the houses or church or civic buildings is a frame itself, but together they might define a market place or town square; in the square there might be a fountain set in its own frame of water; inside each of the houses there are a number of rooms, each of which contain frames of different kinds – tables, chairs, fireplaces, cupboards, chests, beds, a bath, a sink, even a carpet can frame a place; a table might be set for a meal, each person having their own place framed by a chair and some cutlery; the table may be framed in a pool of light; a desk might frame work in progress; a television frames views of the outside world; and so on.

A traditional court room is a carefully arranged composition of boxes, seats and tables. The judge is framed on the bench, with the Clerk to the Court just below; the lawyers are framed at their table; the witness in the witness box; the journalists in the press box; and the jury in the jury box. In the dock the accused is framed, whilst the public watch from the gallery.

A characteristic of the civilisation of the Romans was that their cities and their houses had a very clear structure of frames for different purposes. This is the House of Pansa in Pompeii. It has hardly any elevation to the surrounding streets; its rooms and atriums are embedded in the block, surrounded by shops and other houses.

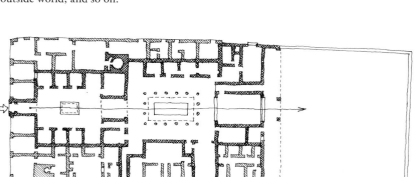

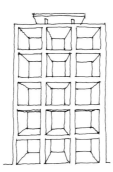
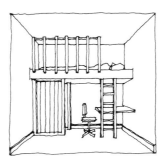
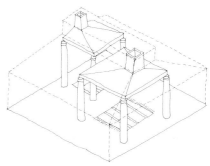

Buildings can be frames structurally, but architecture makes frames conceptually too. On the right is a diagram of a small house the American architect Charles Moore designed for himself and built in California in 1961. It is not a large house, but it contains two aedicules, like small temples. Each of these frames its own place: the larger, a living area; the smaller, the bath and shower. Both aedicules are lit by rooflights, so both places are also framed by light. The house as a whole is framed by the envelope shown dotted on the diagram. Other places within the house are framed by a combination of the aedicules and the outer envelope, together with pieces of furniture. Taken altogether the house is a complex matrix of overlapping frames.

A courtyard café (below) is also a complex overlapping composition of frames. The courtyard itself is the main frame, but the rooms off it are also frames. The umbrellas frame the tables – themselves frames around which people, framed by their chairs, eat their ice creams (framed in their bowls or cones) – in shade. The kitchens frame the cooks and the washers-up. The pool frames the fountain (after which this café in Malta is named). Amidst these many frames the waiters weave their intricate dance.

A condominium frames a number of apartments that frame rooms, each of which contains a number of smaller frames.

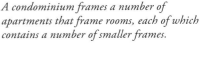

One of the houses that American architect Charles Moore designed for himself (above) contains two aedicules: one identifying the place of a sitting area; the other the place of the bath. Both are lit by their own small rooflights.

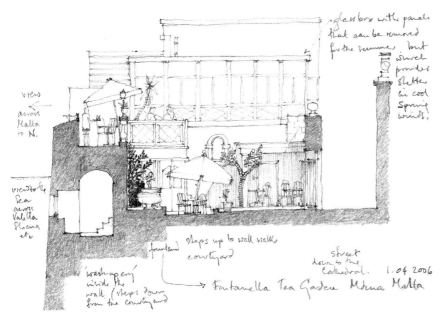

This courtyard café in Malta (left) is a complex composition of many architectural frames.

Reference for Moore House:
Charles Moore and others – *The Place of Houses*, 1974.

109

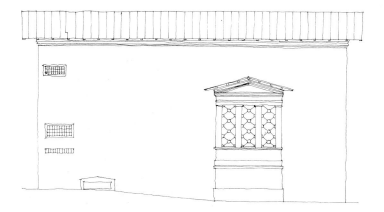

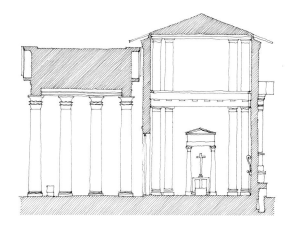

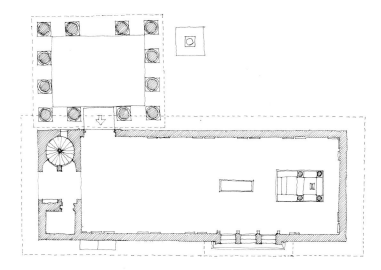

The Chapel of the Resurrection, designed by Sigurd Lewerentz, is composed of a number of architectural frames. The slightly askew portico frames the entrance; the aedicule frames the altar; the catafalque frames the coffin which frames the deceased, and which is framed by the light from the south-facing window. The blank mass of the chapel seems to frame death itself.

The Chapel of the Resurrection (above) was designed by Sigurd Lewerentz in 1925. It stands in the grounds of the Woodland Crematorium near Stockholm. This is another building in which 'nested' aedicules of different scales are used to frame places. Here the places are to do with death and bereavement. The entrance from the north is framed by a large porch of twelve columns supporting a pediment; this porch is not attached to the main part of the building. The body of the chapel itself is very plain, like an austere tomb. On the inside walls there are shallow relief columns, so that this cell is also a temple-like aedicule. Within the chapel, and very carefully positioned, is a smaller, more elaborate aedicule, which identifies the place of the altar and frames the cross. And in front of this aedicule there is the catafalque, which provides a frame for the coffin during funeral ceremonies. The coffin, of course, frames the corpse. All together, the coffin and the mourners, with the altar and cross in their own aedicule, are framed by the chapel itself. The Chapel of the Resurrection is composed of many architectural frames. The window in the south-facing wall (above) is also in the form of an aedicule. Its primary role is not to frame a view of the outside but, as the sole source of daylight in the chapel, to allow the sun into the cell to frame the coffin on the catafalque in a patch of light.

Reference for Chapel of the Resurrection:
Janne Ahlin – *Sigurd Lewerentz, architect 1885-1975*, 1987.

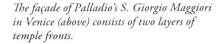

Layering

Sometimes frames are overlaid on top of each other, producing a complex layering. This can happen in the two-dimensional frames that architecture makes, but it can also happen in three or four dimensions. The façade of S. Giorgio Maggiore in Venice, designed by Andrea Palladio in the mid-sixteenth century, frames the entrance to the church (right). Its design is derived from Roman temples, but Palladio had to provide a front for an interior consisting of a nave with two side aisles with lower roofs. The simple temple form would not do this satisfactorily, so Palladio used the device of composing the façade as a combination of two overlaid temples.

Layering applies also to spatial frames. The Minoan Palace of Knossos on the island of Crete was built some three and a half thousand years ago, but its architects had a complex and subtle appreciation of spatial design. In the royal apartments (below left) they created layers of space using open colonnades to help ventilation in the hot climate. Some of the layers are roofed and some are open to the sky, allowing light into the heart of the building. In experiencing these spaces one is aware of a hierarchy of privacy and of a subtle pattern of layers of light and shade.

The façade of Palladio's S. Giorgio Maggiori in Venice (above) consists of two layers of temple fronts.

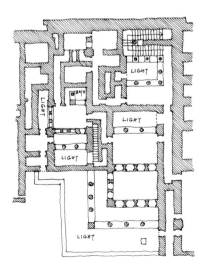

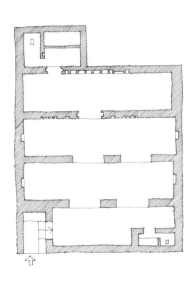

In this Swahili house (near left) there are layers of space, stretching back through the stepped section, from the most public to the most private. Different levels of the family occupy each of the different layers.

Reference for the Swahili house:
Susan Kent (editor) – *Domestic Architecture and the Use of Space*, 1990, p. 121.

111

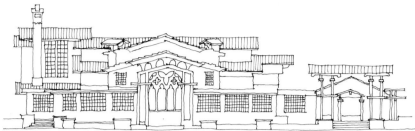

The First Church of Christ, Scientist, in Berkeley, California, is an aggregation of many aedicules layered one over another. It was designed by Bernard Maybeck and built in 1910.

Reference for First Church of Christ, Scientist:
Edward Bosley – *First Church of Christ, Scientist, Berkeley*, 1994.

Something similar would have happened in the Roman house earlier in this chapter, with layers of space – some light, some dark – being visible along the axis from the entrance to the garden, producing a hierarchical progression to the most important reception room in the house.

Layering has become part of the repertoire of compositional devices used by architects in the twentieth century. The interplay of layers produces a complexity and aesthetic intricacy. In his design for the First Church of Christ Scientist in Berkeley, California, built in 1910, Bernard Maybeck layered his building in various ways. The elevation (above) is layered in a similar way to the façade of Palladio's S. Giorgio Maggiore, except that here the composition is more three-dimensional, and composed of more 'temple' fronts. Maybeck's church is less about elevational design and more about the interweaving of three-dimensional aedicules, starting with the entrance canopies and culminating in the grand cruciform structure spanning over the congregation in the main hall. Furthermore, the layers of the external walls are supplemented by pergolas supporting climbing plants. The effect is to dematerialise the walls, making the church less of a building, more of a forest.

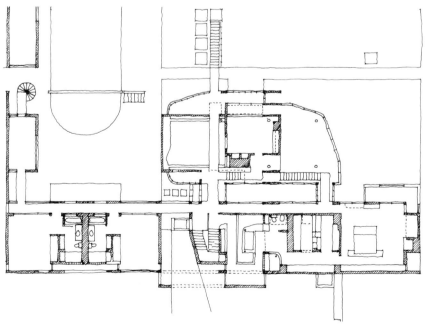

Richard Meier has a distinctive repertoire of ideas in his work. His buildings are white and have complex geometric forms. He also tends to layer the walls of his buildings, making them three-, rather than two-, dimensional. Sometimes he uses the spaces between the layers for specific purposes, but mostly it is done to increase the aesthetic intricacy of the appearance of the buildings. Below is the upper floor plan of the Palm Beach House he designed in the mid 1970s. There is hardly a wall that is not in some way layered.

Reference for the Palm Beach House:
Paul Goldberger and others – *Richard Meier Houses*, 1996, p. 110.

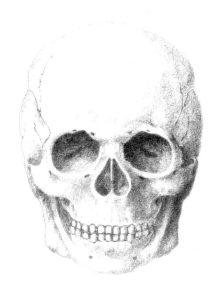

The form and character of our architecture is conditioned by our attitudes to the world around us and its various components.

TEMPLES AND COTTAGES

'To be, or not to be: that is the question:
Whether 'tis nobler in the mind to suffer
The slings and arrows of outrageous fortune,
Or to take arms against a sea of troubles,
And by opposing end them?'

William Shakespeare – *Hamlet*, Act III.i.

TEMPLES AND COTTAGES

In dealing with the world, people sometimes accept what the world provides or does, and at others, they try to change it to achieve a view of how it should be – how the world might be more comfortable, more beautiful or in better order than it is.

Our interaction with the world can be thought of as a mixture of these two responses: to accept or to change. Hamlet was not the only one to be afflicted with this quandary; it is particularly alive in architecture, where the designing mind has to engage directly with the world.

It is not possible to change everything by the powers of architecture. But neither is it feasible to leave everything as it is. Merely by lighting their campfire our prehistoric family changed the world. Architecture therefore involves both acceptance and change. The designing mind is faced with the double question, 'What should one try to change; and what should one accept as it is?'

In this question, architecture is philosophy (in a conventional sense). It is to do with trying to understand how the world works and what the response should be. There is no single correct answer but a mixture of wondering and assertion, considering which factors impinge on a situation and how they should be dealt with.

The following two quotations, both by writers concerned with architecture, illustrate different philosophical positions on how the designing mind should relate to the world. The first is taken from *The Ten Books on Architecture*, written for the Emperor Augustus by the Roman architect Vitruvius in the first century BC (he is paraphrasing Theophrastus, an earlier, Greek writer):

'The man of learning... can fearlessly look down upon the troublesome accidents of fortune. But he who thinks himself entrenched in defences not of learning but of luck, moves in slippery paths, struggling through life unsteadily and insecurely.'

The second is from *The Poetry of Architecture*, the first published work by the nineteenth-century British critic, John Ruskin. He is imagining the quintessential mountain cottage:

'Everything about it should be natural, and should appear as if the influences and forces which were in operation around it had been too strong to be resisted, and had rendered all efforts of art to check their power, or conceal the evidence of their action, entirely unavailing... it can never lie too humbly in the pastures of the valley, nor shrink too submissively into the hollows of the hills; it should seem to be asking the storm for mercy, and the mountain for protection: and should appear to owe to its weakness, rather than to its strength, that it is neither overwhelmed by the one, nor crushed by the other.'

The attitudes these two writers express are poles apart. Vitruvius puts forward the idea that architecture is about changing the world for the benefit of people, and that such change is to be achieved by the application of human intellect and the assertion of human will. Ruskin, on the other hand, unsteadies this simple idea by suggesting that it is not the role of human beings to contend against providence but to recognise that they are part of (not separate from) nature, and to accept its authority in the faith that nature 'knows best' and will provide and protect. (Ruskin first published the above passage in 1837, under the *nom de plume* '*KATA PHUSIN*', which is Greek for 'according to nature'.)

It would not be fair to suggest that these two quotations represent the full bodies of thought offered by Ruskin and Vitruvius. Nor do the attitudes presented belong only to these two writers; they have been echoed by many others through history. These two passages do however identify the horns of an abiding dilemma for architects.

In a previous section of this book it was suggested that to understand the powers of architecture one should be aware of the conditions within which they may be employed. The conditions the world presents can be categorised in various ways. Here is one way that seems appropriate for discussing architecture. Generally speaking, in architecture one has to deal with all or some of the following, which are extrinsic to the conscious designing mind:

- the *ground*, with its earth, rock, trees – its stability or instability, its changes in level, its dampness, its flatness or unevenness;
- *gravity* – its constant verticality;
- the *weather* – sun, breeze, rain, wind, snow, lightning;
- the *materials* available for building – stone, clay, wood, steel, glass, plastic, concrete, aluminium…, and their characteristics;
- the *size* of people and other creatures – their reach, their eyes, how they sit, move;
- the *bodily needs and functions* of people and other creatures – for warmth, security, air, food, disposal of waste…;
- the *behaviour* of people, individually or in groups – social patterns, religious beliefs, political structures, ceremonies, rituals…;
- *other products of architecture* (other buildings, places…) that exist, or are proposed;
- *pragmatic requirements* – the spatial organisation needed for various activities;
- the *past* – history, tradition, memories, narratives…;
- the *future* – visions of 'Utopia', or of 'Apocalypse';
- the *processes of time* – change, wear, patination, deterioration, erosion, ruin.

To each or all of these the designing mind (consciously or unthinkingly) may adopt different attitudes, maybe in differing circumstances. For example: to make shelter against a cold wind, or to enjoy the benefits of a cooling breeze; to try to control patterns of behaviour, or to allow (or accept, cultivate or concede to) their contribution to the identity of places; to subject materials to carving and polishing, or to accept their innate character or the texture they are given by the processes of their acquisition (such as that of stone broken by quarrying); to fight (or disregard) the effects of time, or to anticipate (or exploit) the patination of materials by sun, wind and wear; to provide for bodily needs and functions, or to dismiss them as beneath architectural consideration; to accept human size as a basis of architectural scale, or to create a hermetic rule for proportion, one which does not refer to anything outside itself; to follow the precedents of history (even to submit to the 'authority' of tradition), or to seek the new – making the future different from the past.

Any product of architecture (for example a building, a garden, a city, a playground, a sacred grove…) is informed by, and hence expresses, such attitudes. If an architect wishes to fight against the force of gravity then it will show in the form of the building produced (for example: a Gothic cathedral vault, or one of the cantilevers of Frank Lloyd Wright's design for the house called 'Fallingwater'). If an architect seeks to control the behaviour of people then it will show in the form of the building (for example in a 'panopticon' Victorian prison, in which all cells could be watched from a single central viewpoint). If an architect wants to cool the interior of a house with breezes then this too will affect the form of the building.

Products of architecture combine acceptance of some aspects with change of others. There is, however, no general rule to dictate which aspects are accepted and which should be changed or controlled. This fundamental indeterminacy lies at the heart of many of the great debates about architecture through history and in the present: should architects follow tradition or should they strive for novelty and originality; should materials be used in the state in which they are found or be subject to processes of manufacture that change their innate character; should architects dictate the layout of the places where people live or should cities grow organically, without a master plan? People find different answers to these and many other similarly difficult questions.

Designing minds combine *change* and *acceptance* in varying degrees. In some products of architecture the attitude of change and control seems to dominate; in others it is the attitude of acceptance and responsiveness that appears to prevail. The archetypal 'temple' and the archetypal 'cottage' illustrate these differences.

The archetypal 'temple'

The archetypal 'temple' is not a real temple but an idea. The illustration on this page shows a building that looks like an ancient Greek temple, but as we shall see later there are other buildings that might be classified as 'temples' in the philosophical sense.

This temple can be characterised in terms of the ways its architect dealt with various aspects of the world. It is not necessary to look at the temple in terms of all the aspects listed earlier; noting the treatment of some of them will illustrate the point.

This temple stands on a platform that replaces the uneven *ground* with a controlled surface as a foundation for building. This flat platform (or, in some historical examples, subtly curved platform – as that of the Parthenon on the acropolis in Athens) is a starting level (a datum) for the geometric discipline of the temple itself and detaches it from the found world. Even if the platform had no temple it would define a special place, distinct because of its flatness and its separation by its height and its edge (boundary, threshold) from the landscape around.

The temple provides shelter against the *weather* to protect its content (the image of a god) but its form concedes little to the forces of climate. It stands aloof, prominent in an exposed location.

Its *materials* are carved into abstract or geometric shapes and carefully finished – smoothed, painted and with precise mouldings. The stone is probably not that which is readily available at the site but has been brought some distance, with the consequent expenditure of substantial effort and money, because of its quality.

The scale of the temple relates not to the usual *size* of human beings but to the in-determinately larger stature of the god to whom it is dedicated. The module on which the size of the temple is based exists only in the dimensions of the building. The temple has its own ideal system of proportions within its own fabric. This contributes to its detachment from the found world.

As a house of a god the temple does not provide for the *bodily needs or functions* of mortals.

The temple is complete in itself and does not respond to *other architecture*. It is more likely that other architecture will relate to it as a focus and point of reference. The temple represents a stable centre. Though not responding to other buildings around it, the temple probably does relate, maybe by an axis, to something distant and above the ordinary: a sacred place on the peak of a distant mountain, a star, or perhaps the rising sun.

A temple stands aloof from the world, a manifestation of control, privilege, maybe arrogance.

A cottage is embedded in the world, submissive, a manifestation of responsiveness, humility, perhaps deprivation.

As a shrine the temple has a simple function that is not complicated by messy *pragmatic requirements*. Its form is ideal, dictated by geometry and axial symmetry rather than by the spaces needed for a mixture of activities.

The form of the classic Greek temples was the product of refinements made over a number of centuries, but as an idea the 'temple' is timeless – belonging equally to *the past* and *the future*.

Though ancient temples are now in ruins, they were not built with this fate in mind. They were intended to stand against the *processes of time* rather than submit to them. (For the later Romantic mind the reduction to ruin of these icons of human self-confidence – hubris – is filled with poetic significance, that of retribution.)

The archetypal 'cottage'

Like the 'temple', the archetypal 'cottage' is not a real building but an idea. Whereas the 'temple' manifests humanist detachment from the found world, the 'cottage' fits in with its context, in more ways than one. The drawing on this page shows what appears to be a British cottage (of somewhat obscure origin), but there are many other buildings (and gardens) that illustrate the 'cottage' idea.

Unlike the Greek temple, which stands aloof, this cottage sits on the *ground*. The unevenness of site is incorporated into its form. Not detached from the landscape, its walls may extend into the surroundings as field walls.

The cottage provides a refuge from the *weather* for people and animals. Its architect has responded to climate. Built for cold winters, it has a large hearth. It has a pitched roof to shed the rain, and is located to find what protection there is from trees and from the lie of the land. Its relationship with the sun does not involve setting up a significant axis but may be a matter of taking advantage of its warmth.

The cottage is built of *materials* ready to hand. Though subject to rough shaping and finishing, they are used in the state they were found or obtained from the quarry.

The scale of the cottage relates directly to the actual *size* of people and perhaps also of livestock. This is particularly evident at doorways, where height corresponds to human stature.

The cottage provides for *bodily needs and functions*. Its main purpose is to house people who spend their time working to keep themselves alive. There is the fire for warmth, around which there are places to sit, prepare food, eat and sleep.

'As a house, Barton Cottage, though small, was comfortable and compact; but as a cottage it was defective, for the building was regular, the roof was tiled, the window shutters were not painted green, nor were the walls covered with honeysuckles.'

Jane Austen – *Sense and Sensibility* (1811), 1995, pp. 24-5.

When building on rugged ground it is sensible to build a platform to make a level floor.

The cottage and the places around it accommodate many different *pragmatic requirements.* In response to these the layout is not formal but complex and irregular.

The cottage is mutable and accepts the *processes of time* – wear and age. It can never be said to be complete; additions may be added as more space is needed, or removed when redundant. Its fabric acquires a patina that deepens with age. Lichens grow on its stones and plants grow in their own way, establishing themselves in the crevices of the walls.

If the 'temple' stands apart from the world, the 'cottage' is grows from it.

Attitude

Though the above descriptions are analyses of the images of apparently real and plausible buildings – a 'temple' and a 'cottage' – the issue for the designing mind is the underlying one of attitude. The mind that is engaged in architecture must have an attitude, or an array of attitudes, to the conditions that impinge. Attitudes may be held unthinkingly or asserted consciously but they always affect the character of the work produced. There is not one attitude that informs all architecture; variety in works of architecture is the result of variety in the philosophical approaches of architects.

Broadly, the attitudes designing minds adopt exist on a dimension that stretches from submission, through symbiosis, to domination. One may submit to the conditions that prevail, seek to work in harmony with them, or seek to dominate them. But there are also many more subtle nuances of attitude: ignorance, disregard, recklessness, acceptance, resignation, acquiescence, responsiveness, mitigation, amelioration, exaggeration, exploitation, aggression, contention, subversion, subjugation, control… all of which may combine in a variety of ways and permutations in dealing with the many different aspects of the world perceived as conditioning the production of works of architecture.

With regard to climate for example: on a particular site you, as an architect, might be ignorant of a wind that blows with potential destructive force in the same month each year; you might know about the wind and yet disregard it; you might seek to mitigate or even exploit its effects for the environmental benefit of the users (with a wind turbine perhaps); or you might perhaps suggest a windbreak to deflect or control it. Some of the options may be negligent, foolhardy or downright stupid; others may be subtle, poetic and intelligent; some might exist in a grey zone between the two. But the options in attitude are always there, to be adopted with regard to different aspects of the conditions, according to your judgement.

'The Hamilton house grew as the family grew. It was designed to be unfinished, so that lean-tos could jut out as they were needed. The original room and kitchen soon disappeared in a welter of these lean-tos.'

John Steinbeck – *East of Eden*, 1952, p. 43.

Attitudes, consciously or unthinkingly adopted, are manifest in the character of the work of architecture that is produced. If an attitude of domination is adopted, it will be there in the work; if submission, it too will be there. Attitudes may be personally asserted by architects or be inherited by them from their culture; in which case their works manifest not just their personal attitudes but those of their culture or sub-culture.

The representation of attitude in works of architecture is also open to manipulation: by those who wish to use architecture as a means of poetic expression; by those who wish to use it as a medium of propaganda or symbol of national, personal or commercial status. When architects of Hitler's Third Reich in Germany during the 1930s wanted to use architecture to symbolise the power the Reich asserted, they used a style of architecture (based on Classical architecture and its 'temples') that evoked an attitude of control. When the Nazis wanted to suggest that their politics were of those 'of the people', they insisted on a folk style (based on 'cottages') that seemed to suggest acceptance and celebration of national traditions with roots deep in history. Neither the Classical style nor the traditional was, in these instances, born of an attitude of acceptance; both were employed with the intention of manipulating people's feelings and aspirations for political ends.

Manipulation of the appearance of works of architecture to suggest that they are born of particular attitudes is not always associated with dark or cynical political propaganda. It is also a facet of the poetic potential of architecture. The other face of propaganda in this regard is romance; whether it is the romance of the heroism of ancient Rome, of an idyllic rural life, of high technology, of ecological harmony, works of architecture can be made to appear to have been born of the appropriate attitudes.

It may seem cynical to say so, but sometimes the attitude superficially suggested by the appearance of a work of architecture may not be the same as the one that actually underlay its conception and realisation.

One attitude that is not compatible with being an architect is abdication. As an architect you may accept, respond to or change (the lie of the land for example), but if you abdicate from decision or try to suggest that the driving force lies elsewhere (in nature, nation, history, climate, function... as many architectural polemicists have done), then, in the fine grain of things, you are no longer an architect. Nature, society, history, climate, gravity, purpose, human scale... do not *determine* the way a work of architecture turns out. That depends on the architect's attitude to them and the decisions made. This is the case even though architects' attitudes and decisions may themselves be limited and conditioned by the cultures in which they work.

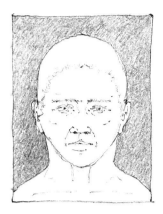

'Cottage' and 'temple' as ideas

'Cottage' and 'temple' are architectural ideas that are not restricted to cottages and temples. The difference is visually most evident in terms of formality and irregularity.

Is a human head a 'temple' or a 'cottage'?

Confusingly, it is quite easy to find cottages (i.e. small dwellings) that are to some degree 'temples' (architecturally, that is to say), and temples (i.e. shrines and churches, loosely speaking) that architecturally are 'cottages'. These architectural ideas are not restricted to their nominal roles as 'grand shrine for a god' and 'humble home of man'. Architectural ideas are not necessarily specific to purpose.

In its irregular composition of forms this church on a tiny island off Corfu (below), though functionally a temple, is architecturally a 'cottage'.

While the cottage and hut on the right, with their geometric order and axial symmetry, standing on their small plinths, are architecturally 'temples'.

The 'cottage' and 'temple' ideas can equally well be applied to garden design. In the traditional English cottage (and 'cottage') garden, plants in irregular groups are apparently allowed to grow in their innate ways, with no formal organisation. Whereas in the ornamental garden of a French chateau, for example, the plants are arranged in geometric patterns and clipped into unnatural shapes. One can interpret these differences as differences in attitude. The English cottage garden implies acceptance of the providence of nature, appreciation of the innate characters of the different species of

Even this house or hut might be considered to be 'temples'.

plant, and enjoyment of an aesthetic effect that appears independent of human decision and control. By contrast, the geometric garden of the French chateau celebrates a more overt human control over nature; the plants do not grow into their natural shapes but are clipped into regular forms.

Many products of architecture are neither pure 'cottage' nor pure 'temple' but a mixture of both. Parts of a rambling house may be little 'temples', such as the porch, the fireplace, the four-poster bed, the door-case, the bay window and the dormer window in this cutaway drawing (below).

In an 'English' garden (above left) it appears that plants are allowed to grow where they want and to their own shape. In a 'French' garden (above middle) plants are clipped into geometric forms and controlled in symmetrical beds. In a 'Japanese' garden (above right) there is a fine balance between nature and the mind.

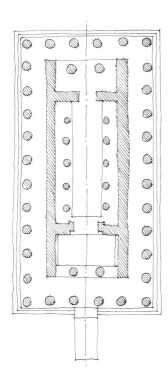

The architectural ideas of 'temple' and 'cottage' are evident in the plans of works of architecture, as well as in their outward appearances. On the right is the plan of the ancient Greek temple of Aphaia at Aegina. It illustrates the abstract characteristics of axial symmetry and regular geometry associated with the architectural idea of 'temple'. While the

The architectural idea of a temple is clear in its plan. It is based on order, geometry and the discipline of the axis (above).

123

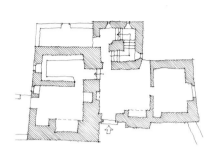

irregularity and absence of strictly orthogonal geometry in the plan of this Welsh farmhouse (Llanddewi Castle Farm, Glamorgan, above left) is typical of the 'cottage' idea: its plan is not complete within itself; some of its walls enclose patches of outside space while others stretch out into the landscape; the rooms are not laid out formally but more as an accretion of places for different purposes.

The Erectheion, a temple on the acropolis in Athens (below), has an irregular asymmetrical plan and relates to the lie of the land by responding to varying ground levels. It is composed of parts of three 'temples' combined but in its relation to the ground it also has some 'cottage' characteristics.

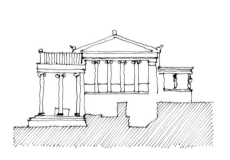

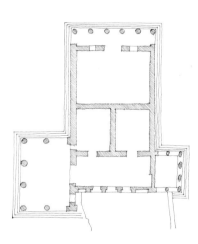

In some of its characteristics, this Welsh cottage (above) is, architecturally, a 'temple'. It is symmetrical in plan and section, and stands on a platform, separated from the natural lie of the ground. This temple (left), however, has some characteristics, architecturally, of a 'cottage'.

By contrast, the Welsh farmhouse above right exhibits some of the architectural characteristics of a 'temple'. It has a regular plan, is symmetrical in section and stands clear of the uneven ground on a level platform. However, in its use of rough timber, especially in the curve of the principal structural members ('crucks' – pairs of which are obtained by halving tree trunks with a natural curve) and in the imprecision of its geometry, it also has architectural characteristics of a 'cottage'.

So far in this discussion of the 'temple' and the 'cottage' as architectural ideas we have looked only at examples from the distant past. These ideas are ancient in the production of architecture but they have been apparent in the twentieth century too.

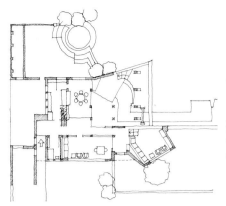

This house (left) by Hans Scharoun is architecturally a 'cottage'.

Reference for the Nationalgalerie (centre of page): Fritz Neumeyer – 'Space for Reflection: Block versus Pavilion', in Franz Schulze – *Mies van der Rohe: Critical Essays*, 1989, pp. 148-171.

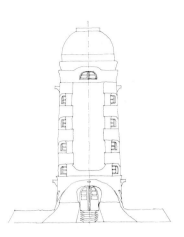

The Nationalgalerie in Berlin was built to the designs of Mies van der Rohe in the 1960s. Below is the entrance level of the building; the majority of the galleries are within the plinth on which it stands (not shown). The structure of this large pavilion is steel and its walls are almost completely of glass. By its plan and overall form it is clearly a 'temple' (to art): it stands on a platform clear of the natural ground level; its plan is a perfect square; and it is axially symmetrical. It is a reinterpretation in steel of the architecture of ancient Greek stone temples.

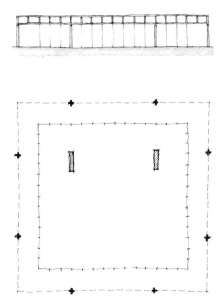

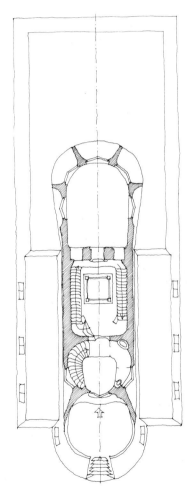

In contrast, the house at the top of the page, by Hans Scharoun and built in Germany in 1939, with its irregular plan that directly responds to the accommodation of different purposes, appears architecturally to be a 'cottage'.

The Einstein Tower (1919, right) by Erich Mendelsohn is, even with its curved forms, a 'temple' (to science). It stands on its platform and its smooth rendered surfaces, and colour, detach it from the surrounding landscape. (It cannot, however, resist the patinating effects of the weather without repeated cleaning, repair and resurfacing.)

Both the Nationalgalerie (centre) and the Einstein Tower (above) are 'temples'.

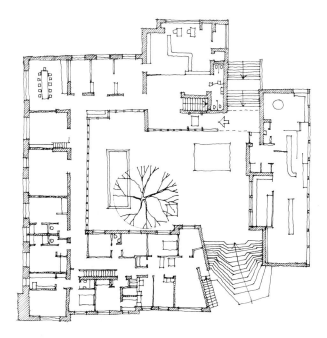

Aalto's Säynätsalo Town Hall (left) is architecturally a 'cottage'.

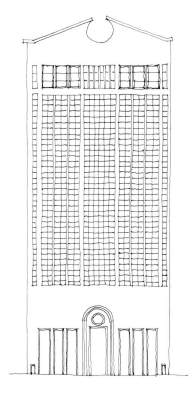

The civic centre at Säynätsalo, Finland (above), designed by Alvar Aalto (1952), with its careful but irregular planning, response to changing ground levels and incorporation of external places, tends more towards the architectural 'cottage' (with correspondingly appropriate political connotations).

Philip Johnson and John Burgee's AT&T Building in New York, built in 1982 (right), is a tall 'temple' (to money).

And from the same year, the Inmos Research Centre near Newport, Gwent (below), designed by Richard Rogers, is a wide 'temple' (to computer technology).

Difficulties

There is perhaps a temptation to interpret the 'temple'–'cottage' dimension as a dichotomy between human will and natural providence. Ruskin's description of the mountain cottage given at the beginning of this chapter almost suggests that the cottage is a natural creation, a product of its conditions, rather than of the mind of a human being.

Johnson's AT&T Building (above) is architecturally a 'temple', as is Rogers's Inmos Factory (below).

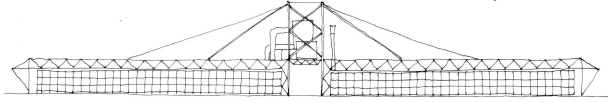

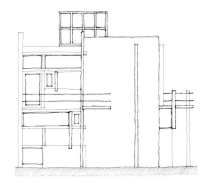

The Schroeder House in Utrecht, by Gerrit Rietveld (1923) may be irregular in its composition but it is clearly a 'temple'. Its abstract composition, geometrically complex but precise like a Mondrian painting made into a sculpture, seems to detach it from its mundane surroundings.

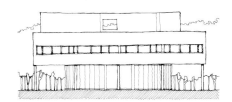

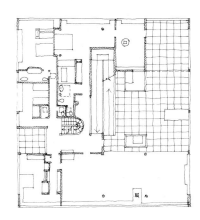

The implication is that the people who live in it are, like Adam and Eve before the Fall, 'at one with nature' rather than divorced from it.

If asked to identify examples at the very extremes of this dimension, one might suggest that the extreme 'temple' is a lunar module, and the extreme 'cottage' a cave. The lunar module is wholly a product of the human mind. It is its own self-sufficient world, independent of all conditions, with its own air supply and environmental control, and free even of the constraints of gravity. Not only does it sit on a platform, but it is able to break free of the ground completely, in dramatic fashion. The cave, on the other hand, is completely as provided by nature, unaffected by human will. Its form is that scoured from the rock by the forces of natural erosion, the wind and flowing water, rather than by human effort. It does not just sit directly on the earth, it is embedded in it like a womb inside a woman.

On this dimension one might position one's own situation as occupying an area somewhere in the middle. One might feel inclined (or persuaded by the media or a lifestyle guru) that one should move 'down' the dimension, towards a more 'natural' life in a cave, maybe to a teepee in the Welsh countryside or perhaps only as far as a smallholding in Virginia; or 'up' the dimension, to a technologically more sophisticated life, perhaps to a hi-tech 'living-pod' in a city tower or maybe (in the future) to the Arcosanti self-sufficient cities imagined by Paolo Soleri in the 1970s (like 'arcologies' in the SimCity computer game) or those drawn by the architectural firm Archigram in the 1960s.

Media commentaries alternately characterise both ends of this dimension as morally 'good' and morally 'bad'. It is a dimension that covers many aspects of culture, from the genetic modification of food crops, to cloning embryos, to euthanasia, to wars against terrorism and tyranny as well as many more mundane political issues such as the need for new roads and the curriculum in schools. The 'temple' extreme (humanist, scientist, wilful, controlling) is described both as 'heroic' (good) and 'hubristic' (bad); the 'cottage' end (responsive, submissive, accepting, faith-led) both as 'sustainable' (good) and 'naive' (bad). In popular culture one sees 'utopian' and 'dystopian' representations of both, from *Darling Buds of May* to *Bladerunner*. Advertising constantly pulls us in both directions, depending on whether it is trying to sell bread or fast cars. It is a dichotomy that often revolves around the question 'should we or shouldn't we?', which stems from the Garden of Eden when the implicit suggestion was that we should not.

In architecture, the dimension suggested by the ideas 'temple' and 'cottage' concerns a great deal more than regular symmetrical formality or irregular informality in the

There are twentieth-century buildings that appear to combine 'temple' with 'cottage' characteristics. From the outside, Le Corbusier's Villa Savoye (1929) is a 'temple' (though it is a house). Its main living spaces are lifted clear of the natural ground, not on a solid platform but on a series of columns, called by Le Corbusier 'pilotis'. Its outer form is generally symmetrical but with small deviations and it is ordered according to geometric proportions. But its plans, though based on a regular structural grid, are an irregular composition of spaces arranged without reference to axial symmetry but apparently with consideration of pragmatic needs and relationships.

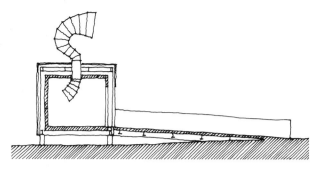
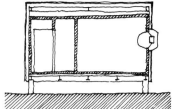

appearance of buildings, though this is often the level to which it is reduced. The irregularity of many works of architecture is just as artificial as the symmetry of a Greek temple, and it can be a disingenuous attempt to take the moral high ground to suggest otherwise.

There are many aspects of the professional role of architects that militate against adoption of an attitude anywhere close to the 'cottage' end of the dimension. Control and the predictability of results are central to the services architects offer their clients. Architecture, since ancient Egypt, has been an accoutrement of power, whether political or personal, plutocratic or aristocratic.

One might reasonably draw the conclusion that the 'cottage', in the terms described above, is a myth. It is part of the dream of a return to Eden before The Fall, before humanity was forcibly divorced from its 'natural' state. As soon as prehistoric people lit that fire in the landscape to establish a place, they had asserted their own will; they had begun to impose their own intellectual structure on the world, to change it in pursuit of their own desires. That first fire was itself a 'temple'.

But there is still something more to consider. Surely architecture cannot be condemned as irredeemably arrogant. It might reasonably be argued that architecture is concerned, through the identification and establishment of places, with making the world sensible, comfortable, beautiful, organised... for the benefit of human beings in pursuit of their aspirations, their activities, the care and protection of their possessions, the celebration and worship of their gods etc. This aim is not solely concerned with the appearance of works of architecture. It involves careful and intelligent consideration of which aspects of the world as it is encountered might be taken advantage of, beneficially used, exploited, cultivated.

Architecture is not a matter, as considered by Hamlet, of 'taking arms against a sea of troubles, and by opposing ending them', nor is it a matter merely, as the Bible suggests, of 'making straight in the desert a highway...'. It also involves celebrating the beautiful tree that has taken decades to grow, benefiting from the warming sun and cooling breeze, and enjoying the innate textures and perfumes of stone and wood that change over time. In doing this human beings neither submit themselves to the power of the storm, nor assert dominion hubristically; they seek some sort of harmony. The dichotomy in attitudes and related architectural ideas associated with 'temple' and 'cottage' run through all dimensions of architecture. An architect can impose an abstract order onto the world or respond to what the world provides. Usually architecture involves both at the same time.

At the Historical Park in Kalkriese, Germany, the Swiss architects Gigon and Guyer have built small temples to listening and to seeing.

Reference for the Historical Park in Kalkriese: (Gigon and Guyer) – *Architectural Review*, July 2002, pp. 34-41.

Geometry is innate in many aspects of architecture. It informs how we make things and how we occupy space.

GEOMETRIES OF BEING

*'Man's taking measure in the dimension
dealt out to him brings dwelling into
its ground plan. Taking the measure
of the dimension is the element within
which human dwelling has its security,
by which it securely endures. The taking
of measure is what is poetic in dwelling.
Poetry is measuring. But what is it
to measure?'*

Martin Heidegger, translated by
Hofstadter – '...poetically man dwells...' (1951),
in *Poetry, Language, Thought*, 1975, p. 221.

GEOMETRIES OF BEING

The previous chapter, *Temples and Cottages*, discussed some of the different attitudes that a designing mind can adopt towards the conditions within which architecture is done. It identified the tension there can be between characteristics inherent in the physical world and ideas imposed on the world by the mind. The architectural uses of geometry can be discussed in these terms too. There are ways to use geometry that emerge out of the conditions of being, and there are others that may be imposed or overlaid upon the world (by the mind). The latter, termed 'ideal' geometry, is the subject of the next chapter; the present chapter discusses some of the geometries 'of being'.

The word 'geometry', as a subject in school for example, suggests circles, squares, triangles, pyramids, cones, spheres, diameters, radii and so on. These play an important part in architecture. As abstract ideas they belong in the category of ideal geometry – their perfection can be imposed on the physical fabric of the world as a means for identifying place (see next chapter). But geometries emerge from our dealings with the world too. Geometry can derive from an attitude of acceptance of how the world works as much as it can from one of control and imposition. Geometries of being lie at the core of identification of place.

Circles of presence

People and objects introduce geometry into the world just by being. Every body has around it what might be called a 'circle of presence' which contributes to its own identification of place. When a body is in relationship with others, their circles of presence affect each other. When a body is put into an enclosure or cell its circle of presence is also contained and perhaps moulded.

An object standing on a flat landscape occupies its own space but it also exerts concentric circles of presence to which we can relate. If one discounts electronic and radio presence, the broadest of these circles of presence is the visual, described by the distance at which an object is visible. This circle may stretch as far as the horizon, or it might be contained by a forest or a wall. In terms of sound this large circle of presence would be

The Eiffel Tower asserts its circle of presence across the city of Paris.

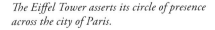

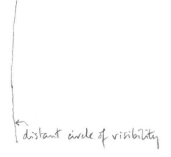

distant circle of visibility

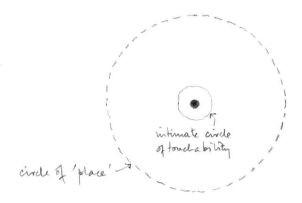

intimate circle of touchability

circle of 'place'

the distance at which a sound emanating from an object is audible; smell, smellable; radio waves, receivable.

By contrast, the smallest, most intimate circle of presence, physically, is described by the distance within which one is able to touch, and perhaps embrace, the object.

The most difficult circle of presence to determine rationally is the intermediate, the one within which one feels that one is 'in the presence' of the object. It might be said that it is this circle of presence that defines and delimits the *place* of the object.

A tree defines one of its circles of presence by the extent of its canopy of branches. A candle, or a lighthouse, describes its circle of presence by the light that it emits. A fire, as suggested in the chapter on *Primitive Place Types*, identifies a place by its sphere of light and warmth. A standing stone, like a statue, exerts itself in the landscape as an assertion of the presence of the person who caused it to be put there.

Any object (such as a tree, a standing stone, the statue of a god) has three circles of presence that may be managed by architecture: the intimate circle of touch- (or perhaps hug-) ability; the distant circle of visibility, which might stretch as far as the horizon; and the less easily determined but nevertheless most important circle of 'place'.

Architecture uses all three – the extensive circle of visibility, the intimate circle of touchability and the intermediate circle of place. Much architecture, from prehistoric times to the present, has been concerned with asserting, defining, amplifying, moulding or controlling circles of presence. It is perhaps in the handling of circles of presence that architecture can be at its richest and most subtle. Circles of presence are rarely perfect circles; they are almost always affected by local conditions and topography. The world is generally so full of objects that their many circles of presence overlap, interfere or maybe reinforce one another in complex ways that are sometimes difficult to analyse. Circles of presence have been manipulated by architecture since ancient times, for various purposes.

A tree defines one of its circles of presence by the extent of its canopy of branches.

A standing stone asserts its circle of presence in the landscape and establishes the place of those who put it there.

A candle (or a lighthouse) describes its circle of presence by the brightness of its light.

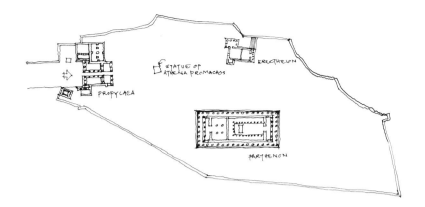

The statue of Athena Promachos asserted the circle of presence of the goddess over the ancient city of Athens.

Most of the buildings on the acropolis in Athens were built during the classical age of ancient Greek culture, the fifth century BC. The top of this rocky hill in the plain of Attica had been a place sacred to the goddess Athena since time immemorial. Such elevated places were sacred partly because they had a clear identity, they were sanctuaries in times of trouble. They also possessed extensive circles of presence – they could be seen (and from them one could see) for long distances across the landscape. The hill of the acropolis retains this circle of presence over modern Athens.

By their architecture the ancient Greeks manipulated the circles of presence of the sacred place of Athena. The extent of the circle of presence around the sacred site was defined partly by the reasonably level area of land on top of the hill, but this was extended and established more firmly by the huge retaining walls that still define the sacred precinct, the *temenos,* around the temples. The plan of this *temenos* is not circular but is a compromise between the circle of presence of the sacred site and the topography of the hill.

The circle of presence of a significant object can be contained and distorted by the enclosure or cell within which it stands.

There were two important statues of Athena on the Athenian acropolis. The giant *Athena Promachos* stood in the open air near to the entrance into the temenos, projecting its own circles of presence over the city, even to ships on the sea some miles away. The other statue was enclosed within the main temple, the Parthenon, which had (and maintains) its

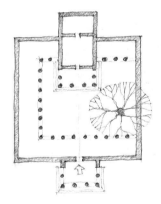

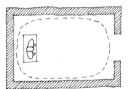

own circle of visibility across the city, and which amplified the hidden presence of the image whilst controlling its circle of place (above) and protecting its intimate circle of touchability, both of which were probably only ever penetrated by priests.

In these ways the acropolis illustrates some of the ways in which circles of presence play their part in architecture. The retaining walls of the *temenos* define the 'circle' of the sacred site; the Parthenon amplifies the presence of the statue it contains; and its *cella* controls and protects the statue's circles of place and touchability.

At Dodona, also in Greece, there is an ancient oak tree. It is said to be an oracle; advice can be interpreted from the rustling of its leaves. The tree is contained within a precinct contained by a wall and 'supervised' by a small temple to Zeus (above). As you cross the threshold of the precinct you enter the circle of presence of the magical tree, and of the god hidden in his temple.

133

Lines of sight

We human beings seem fascinated by the fact that we see in straight lines. This fascination is evident in the way one might vacantly line up the toe of one's shoe with a spot on the carpet, or more purposefully when one sights a distant object with the end of a finger to point it out. The fascination with lines of sight is evident in architecture too.

An alignment of three or more things, one of which is one's eye, seems to possess some peculiar significance. The precise alignment of the sun, the moon and the earth at a solar or lunar eclipse has always been considered a significant event. The builders of Stonehenge appear to have erected the Hele Stone to align the centre of the henge with the sun rising over the horizon on the Summer Solstice (below).

Standing on a pier, we notice when a ship crosses the line projected by the pier out into the sea. Driving through the countryside we remark when a distant feature is exactly aligned with the road along which we are moving. Alignment imparts significance, to both the distant object and the viewer. The 'sight' – the finger tip or the Hele Stone – is a mediating device, like a fulcrum in mechanics or a catalyst in chemistry, that establishes a link

We are intrigued when the landscape appears to contain alignments.

It appears that in ancient times significant buildings were sometimes aligned with sacred mountains.

Reference for alignment of temples and palaces with sacred mountains in ancient Greece: Vincent Scully – *The Earth, the Temple, and the Gods*, 1962.

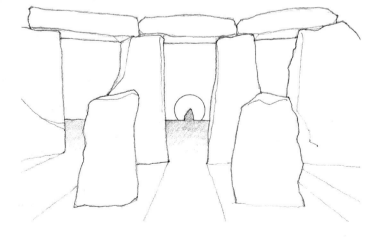

The Hele stone aligned the centre of Stonehenge with the sun rising on the Summer Solstice.

The architect Clough Williams-Ellis followed ancient precedent when he created a line of sight linking his own garden at Plas Brondanw in north Wales with a distant conical mountain called Cnicht (left). Such is the power of this axis that when you first encounter it while wandering through the garden you feel the need to sit down. Williams-Ellis has, in his genteel way, provided a seat.

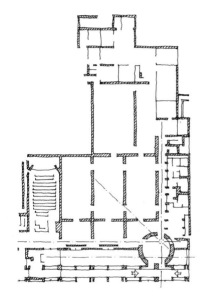

between the viewer and the object. Alignment implies a line of contact – an axis – between oneself and the distant object, exciting in the viewer a thrill of recognition of the linkage (which is even stronger when 'eyes meet across a crowded room').

In architecture conceived as identification of place, a line of sight establishes contact between places. In the ancient world it was one of the ways architects tied places into the world around them, establishing them as fragments of matrices, with particular sacred sites at nodal points. This is a power that is important in the design of religious buildings and places for performance, where engagement between actors and spectators depends on sight. It can also be important in designing art museums, where lines of sight can influence the positioning of exhibits and the routes taken by visitors.

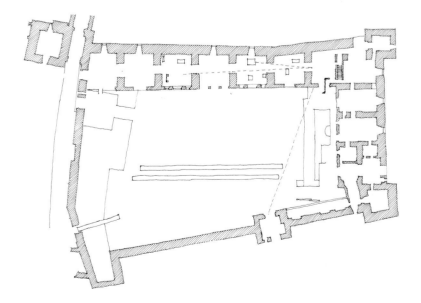

At the museum 'Renewal' in Seattle (1997, above), the architect Olson Sundberg has created sight lines that radiate out from a circular foyer into the galleries and passages.

Reference for 'Renewal' museum:
Architectural Review, August 1998, p. 82.

When he was remodelling the Castelvecchio in Verona, Carlo Scarpa would draw lines of sight onto his plans. Emanating from particularly important points in the building – the entrance gateway, or a doorway between galleries – these would influence his deliberations on the positions of exhibits or pieces of landscaping.

Reference for Carlo Scarpa at the Castelvecchio:
Richard Murphy – *Carlo Scarpa and the Castelvecchio*, 1990.

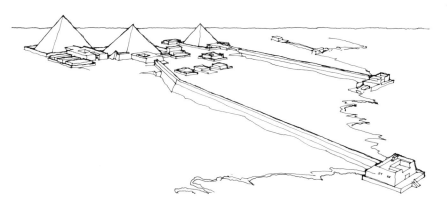

Lines of passage

In the physical sciences, one of the laws of motion is that a body remains in a state of rest or moves in a straight line with uniform speed unless compelled by a force to change that state. This is often a presumption in architecture too. Lines of passage are usually considered to be straight unless diverted by some 'force'. A sensible person usually moves in a straight line between a starting point and a goal unless there is some obstacle that makes this unwise or impossible. In organising the world into places, architecture also establishes lines of passage between those places, using them as ingredients of serial experiences.

The ancient pyramids of Egypt were connected to valley buildings on the river Nile by long causeways (above). Sometimes these were straight; sometimes they had to take

Reference for ancient Egyptian pyramids:
I.E.S. Edwards – *The Pyramids of Egypt*, 1971.

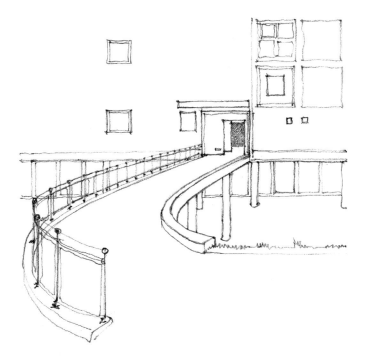

The line of a pathway in the landscape is often a result of people's and animals' tendency to move in straight lines being diverted by changes in the surface of the ground.

In this drawing (left) the goal (the entrance) is clear, but the approach is diverted from the line of sight.

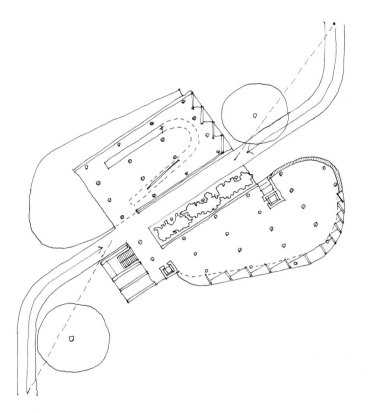

The Carpenter Center for the Visual Arts in Harvard University (1964, by Le Corbusier) can be approached from two diagonally opposite corners of the site. The ramps that rise to the entrances are curved. At the start of either ramp the line of passage to the entrance does not follow the line of sight.

A curved path can provoke curiosity (above).

Sometimes we have too many choices for where to go next (below).

account of local land conditions or perhaps changes in plans during construction, and hence deviated from the direct line.

There is often an interplay between lines of passage and lines of sight. Our natural inclination is that when we see our goal we want to proceed directly to it. Lines of passage are often related to lines of sight but the two are not always congruent. A line of passage can set up or reinforce a line of sight, as when a road aligns with a distant feature in the landscape; but they do not necessarily coincide. Sometimes architecture can make a play of aligning a line of passage with a line of sight as in the nave of a church (see the section on 'Altar' in the chapter *Primitive Place Types*). But sometimes the line of passage deviates from the line of sight, so that a pathway does not take the most direct route between starting point and goal, as in the Carpenter Centre by Le Corbusier (above).

Sometimes a line of passage does not have an obvious goal that can be seen. Interplay between lines of sight and lines of passage can create a sense of mystery in the experience of a work of architecture (right, above).

Sometimes a work of architecture presents a choice of lines of passage, each of which has to be assessed by sight (right, below).

Games played with the interplay between lines of passage and lines of sight can both reinforce the power of architecture to identify place, and orchestrate mystery and suspense, leading people through a labyrinth of spaces.

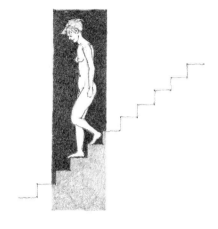

'She thinks of how much more space a being occupies in life than it does in death; how much illusion of size is contained in gestures and movements, in breathing.'

Michael Cunningham – *The Hours*, 1999.

Measuring

The word 'geometry' derives from two Greek words: for earth (*ge*) and measure (*metron*). Measuring the world is essential to life. People measure their environment all the time and in lots of different ways. Measuring with a ruler or tape measure is only one of those ways, and an artificial one. The more immediate way we measure the world is with our own bodies.

We measure distance by walking. We may do it consciously by counting our paces but we also do it subconsciously, merely by walking from one place to another. In connection with walking, we estimate distance or the height of a step with our eyes, and assess the amount of effort needed to cover the distance or climb the step. We estimate the width of doorways and passageways, estimating whether there is space to pass others. We estimate the heights of openings to assess whether or not we must stoop to pass through.

We are conscious of the size of a room and can estimate what it will accommodate. We do this primarily by means of sight but the acoustic of a space can also indicate its size. We subconsciously calculate how the size of a room and the distances between pieces of furniture in it can influence social interrelationships within it. We might estimate the height of a wall to assess whether it could serve as a seat; or of a table to assess its use as a work bench. We literally measure out the length of our own bodies on our beds.

A person stands by a window conscious of the heights of the sill and of the head, and of whether the horizon can be seen. People set the scale of a work of architecture in comparison with their own stature as human beings and with the ways their bodies may move. These

A stairway measures a difference between levels in equal steps.

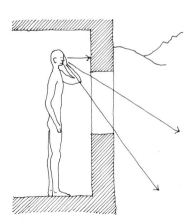

People measure the world with their movement, their bodies and their senses.

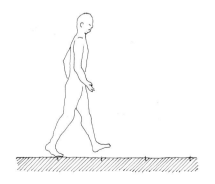

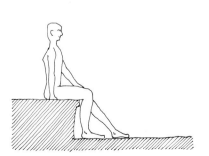

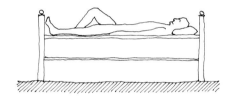

138

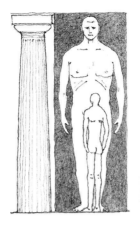

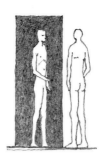

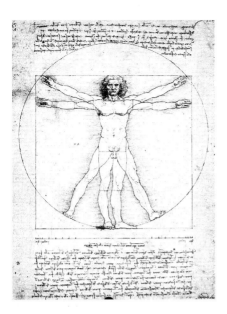

are all transactions between people and works of architecture. People set the measure of the buildings they use but buildings set the measure of the lives they accommodate. People take measure from the works of architecture they inhabit and use their measurements to make different types of assessment. For example, a large doorway exaggerates the status of the occupant and diminishes the status of the visitor (above); a small doorway diminishes the status of the occupant and enhances the status of the visitor; a human-scale doorway puts the occupant and visitor at equal status.

In the late fifteenth century Leonardo da Vinci constructed a drawing (above right) illustrating the relative proportions of an ideal human frame as set down by the Roman writer on architecture, Vitruvius. It suggested that in its ideal form the human frame conforms to geometric proportions and that the measurements of the human frame are tied in with those of nature and the universe. It suggested too that works of architecture should possess the same geometric integrity. In the middle of the twentieth century Le Corbusier contrived a more complex system of proportions relating the human frame to those of other natural creations. Like Leonardo, he used a proportion called the Golden Section. His system, called *The Modulor*, allowed for the different postures the human frame adopts: sitting, leaning, working at a table (below). Earlier in the twentieth century, Oskar Schlemmer, the German artist and dramatist, had recognised that the human frame also measures the world through its movement and thereby projects its measure into the space around it (right). Leonardo da Vinci, Le Corbusier, Oscar Schlemmer (and others) all recognised the potential relationships between architecture and the measure of human form.

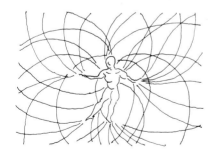

Oskar Schlemmer was interested in the geometry of the human being's occupation of space through movement and dance (above).

Le Corbusier explored how parts of a building might relate to the dimensions of the human form (left).

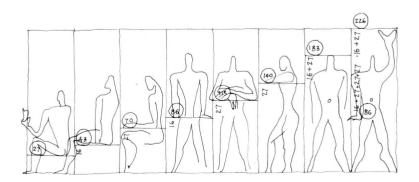

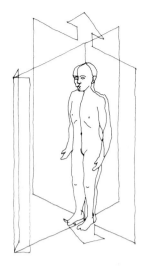 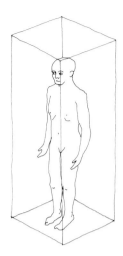 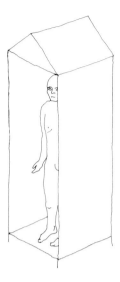

Six-directions-plus-centre

A human being has a front, a back and two sides. Generally speaking, the ground is below, and above is the sky. Each person stands (or sits, or lies) at the centre of its own set of these six directions. These observations seem almost too obvious to bother stating but they are simple truths that have fundamental ramifications for architecture. The six directions condition our relationship with the world, in which each of us is our own mobile centre. They condition our perception of architecture – how we find and occupy places, and how we relate ourselves to other places – and inform the conception of architecture, presenting a matrix for design.

One way architecture can relate to the six-directions-plus-centre is by establishing resonance between an enclosure and its occupant, by making it a place which responds to (or deals with in some way) each of the six directions. An ordinary cell, with its four walls, ceiling and floor, conforms to this. In such places each of us can compare the orientation of our own six directions and the position of our own centre with those of the room, finding places where our six directions are in either formal accord or relaxed interplay with those of the room. By its six sides, a place (a room, a building, a garden) can set out a two- or three-dimensional orthogonal framework, the power of which lies in its ability to provoke in us a sense of resonance and relationship.

In relating to a place that has a front (an in front), a back (a behind), two sides (a left and a right), a top (the above) and sits on the ground (the below), we feel that in some way we are relating to something that is like ourselves and which, to this extent, is created in our own image. We can respond to it through comparison with our own six-directions-plus-centre.

The suggestion of accord between sets of six-directions-plus-centre can be a powerful identifier of place, especially when architecture sets up a centre that a person, the representation of a god in human form or a significant object can occupy. Often in such cases, one of the six directions is dominant, usually the forward: as in the case of a soldier's sentry box, which allows vision to the front while protecting his back and sides from

'We use our eyes for seeing. Our field of vision reveals a limited space, something vaguely circular, which ends very quickly to left and right, and doesn't extend very far up or down. If we squint, we can manage to see the end of our nose; if we raise our eyes, we can see there's an up, if we lower them, we can see there's a down. If we turn our head in one direction, then in another, we don't even manage to see completely everything there is around us; we have to twist our bodies round to see properly what was behind us. Our gaze travels through space and gives us the illusion of relief and distance. That is how we construct space, with an up and a down, a left and a right, an in front and a behind, a near and a far.'

Georges Perec – *Species of Spaces*, 1974.

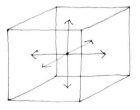

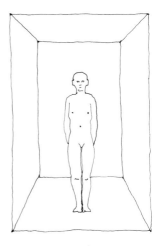

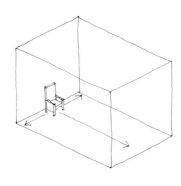

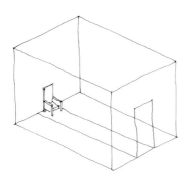

attack, his top from rain or sun and his feet from mud or the cold of the ground. Or as in the case of a throne room, where the position of the throne against one of the four walls rather than at the geometric centre of the room allows the monarch's forward direction to dominate the space (above). Such a manifestation of direction might be reinforced in other ways, maybe by positioning the throne opposite the entrance, or by setting out a path – a red carpet perhaps – that identifies the monarch's route to and from the throne as well as emphasizing the forward direction dominated by the throne (above right).

The architecture of spaces and rooms can respond to the six directions evident in the human form. The six directions are also manifest in the world around. On the ground, where we spend most of our lives, the sky is above and the earth below. But each of the four horizontal directions also has its own character. Each of the cardinal points of the compass relates to the movement of the sun. The sun rises in the east and sets in the west; in the northern (southern) hemisphere, it is at its highest in the south (north) and never enters the northern (southern) quarter.

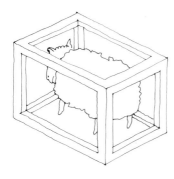

The tank in Damien Hirst's Away from the Flock *forms a three-dimensional orthogonal frame around the sheep. Each face of the tank implies an elevational view of the animal.*

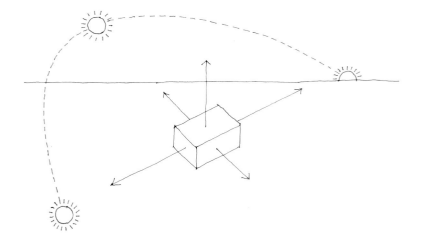

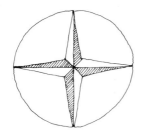

Each of the four cardinal points of the compass, the four horizontal directions of the world, has its own character.

141

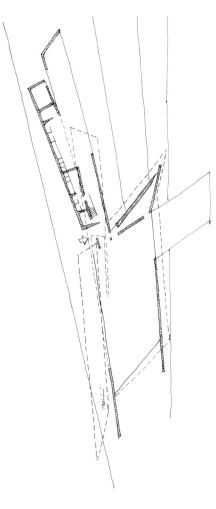

Works of architecture can be oriented to these terrestrial directions as well as to those of anthropomorphic form. In this way buildings mediate geometrically between human beings and their conditions on earth. Any four-sided building on the surface of the earth relates in some way, roughly or exactly, to these four cardinal points of the compass. Any four-sided building is likely to have a side that receives morning sun, a side that receives midday sun and a side to the setting sun; it will also have a side to the north that receives little or no sun. These four horizontal directions have consequences in the environmental design of buildings but they also tie architecture into the matrix of directions that cover the surface of the earth (and which are formally recognised in the grid of longitude and latitude that enables any position on the surface of the earth to be uniquely specified by co-ordinates).

The four-sided building is directly related to the directions on the surface of the earth as it spins through time. Each side has a different character at different times of day. But such a building can be significant in another way too. For if its six directions are considered to be in congruence with those of the earth – its four sides face each of the four terrestrial directions implied by the movement of the sun and its verticality accords with the axis of gravity that runs to the centre of the earth – then the building itself can be considered to identify a centre – a significant place that seems to gather the six directions of the earth into its own and provides a centre that the surface of the earth does not.

In these ways the geometry of the six-directions-plus-centre can be seen to be inherent at three levels of being: in ourselves as human beings; in the original nature of the world on which we live; and in the places we make through architecture, which mediate between us and the world.

The six-directions-plus-centre are a condition of architecture. As such they are susceptible to the attitudes of acceptance and control mentioned in the chapter on *Temples and Cottages*. One may accept their pertinence and influence or one can attempt to transcend them by exploring abstract and more complex geometries or by tackling difficult concepts such as non-Euclidean or more-than-three-dimensional space. Some might argue that subjecting the world's surface to the rule of four directions, or three dimensions, is simplistic; that the movement of the sun through the sky is more complex than the cardinal directions suggest, and therefore that architecture either should not necessarily pay heed exactly to the matrix that the six-directions imply or should look for more subtle indicators for the positioning and orientation of buildings. Others might feel that rectangular form is boring. Nevertheless, the notion of six-directions-plus-centre is useful in analysing examples of

This is the plan of Zaha Hadid's design for a fire station at the Vitra furniture factory in Switzerland. It challenges the authority of the four horizontal directions, at right-angles to each other, by distortion. It does the same with the vertical dimension.

Reference for the Vitra Fire Station:
'Vitra Fire Station', in *Lotus 85,* 1995, p. 94.

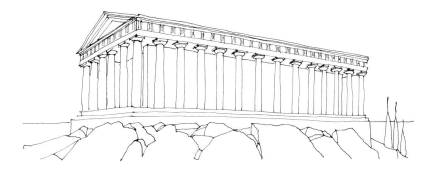

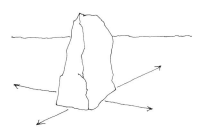

architecture of many kinds and characters. Its power is found in examples that range from the ways directions, axes and grids can be introduced into landscapes to make it easier to know where one is and how one might get from one place to another – even a rough stone, standing like a person, can introduce the six directions into the landscape (above right) – through the vast stock of orthogonal works of architecture, to attempts to escape or test the boundaries of rectangular architecture, as in the works of Hans Scharoun or Zaha Hadid. Though distorted as if by the force of some warp in the gravitational field the four horizontal directions retain their power in the plan of Hadid's Vitra Fire Station (opposite).

Even a simple rough stone standing in the landscape can indicate the four horizontal directions and in so doing begin to impose some order (sense) on the world.

The Greek temple and the six-directions-plus-centre

Many works of architecture relate to the four horizontal directions, to the above and the below, and to the concept of centre, in simple and direct ways. The Greek temple is a particularly clear example (above). The six-directions-plus-centre operate at various conceptual levels even in a building whose form is apparently as simple as this.

First, as an object in the landscape. The building has six faces: one to the ground; one (the roof) to the sky; and four sides, each facing one of the four horizontal directions. In this regard the temple establishes itself as a centre.

Second, as an internal place: the cella of the temple has a floor and a ceiling, and four walls that relate directly to the four horizontal directions implied by the image of the god or goddess who is its occupant and essential reason for being.

Third, in the relationship between the inside space and the outside world: the doorway (the prime link between the two) allows one of the four horizontal directions (that of the face of the deity, which is reinforced by the longitudinal axis of the temple) to strike out from the inside and relate to an external altar and maybe also (as a line of sight) to some remote object of significance – the rising sun or the sacred peak of a distant mountain.

The three ways the six-directions-plus-centre are inherent in the architecture of the temple collaborate to reinforce the role of the temple as an identifier of place. The temple itself is a cell and a marker, but its orthogonal form channels the ways it identifies the place of the sacred image, making it also a centre that radiates its presence outwards.

But there is a fourth way in which this essentially simple building type relates to the six-directions-plus-centre, one that is of special importance in thinking of architecture as identification of place. This has to do with the way the directions of the building relate to those of a visitor or worshipper. Regarding its external form as a body, we are aware (if we

'The intuited form of space, which surrounds us wherever we may be and which we then always erect around ourselves and consider more necessary than the form of our own body, consists of the residues of sensory experience to which the muscular sensations of our body, the sensitivity of our skin, and the structure of our body all contribute. As soon as we have learned to experience ourselves and ourselves alone as the center of this space, whose coordinates intersect in us, we have found the precious kernel, the initial capital investment so to speak, on which architectural creation is based – even if for the moment it seems no more impressive than a lucky penny. Once the ever-active imagination takes hold of this germ and develops it according to the laws of the directional axes inherent in even the smallest nucleus of every spatial idea, the grain of mustard seed grows into a tree and an entire world surrounds us.'

August Schmarsow, translated by Mallgrave and Ikonomou – 'The Essence of Architectural Creation (1893), in Mallgrave and Ikonomou, translators – *Empathy, Form and Space*, 1994.

know the building and are in its presence) when we are at the back, at the front or at either of its sides. Relative to the building, we know where we are. But in addition to that relationship, we are also aware that there are significant places created by the power of the orthogonal geometry of the building; places that may draw us to them. The most important of these is that prominent direction which emerges from the god's statue through the door and strikes out into the landscape. We know when we are standing on this axis and perceive it as special; it excites in us a thrill of connection between our own directions and those of the god.

This powerful axis is established by the architecture of the temple. We are not left as detached spectators but are brought into involvement with the architecture of the building, made part of it. It is exactly the same power, that of the dominant axis, that prompts the practice of nodding reverently as one crosses the axis of the altar in a Christian church or a Buddhist shrine. It is the same power that draws us to stand at the exact centre of a circular space (the Pantheon in Rome, under the dome in St Paul's Cathedral in London or the theatre at Epidavros in Greece). These simple uses of the six-directions-plus-centre are basic, rudimentary and seemingly universally recognised as constituting one of the core powers of architecture.

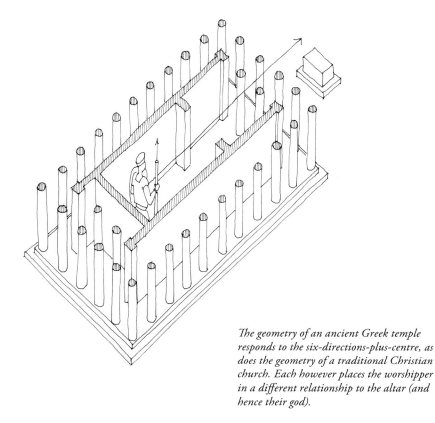

The geometry of an ancient Greek temple responds to the six-directions-plus-centre, as does the geometry of a traditional Christian church. Each however places the worshipper in a different relationship to the altar (and hence their god).

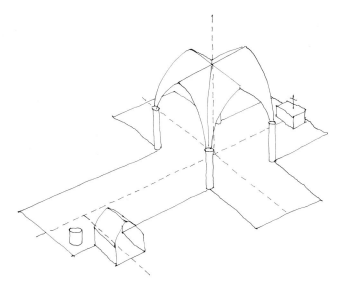

Social geometry

The geometry of social interaction between people is a function of the six-directions-plus-centre that each possesses. Generally we face someone when speaking to them, and sit alongside our friends. In these and similar ways our social interaction is architectural.

When people congregate they arrange themselves in particular ways. In doing so they generate geometries that are social. As a process of identification of place, this is a form of architecture in its own right. Architecture may consist only of people, before it leads to building. But while it consists only of people the existence of this form of architecture is transient.

Works of architecture can respond to social geometries, order them and make their physical realisation more permanent. People may sit in a rough circle around a fire in the landscape. In an inglenook (of an Arts and Crafts house for example) that social geometry is transformed into a rectangle accommodated within the structure of the fabric of the house.

When schoolboys spectate at a playground brawl between two of their number, they form a circle. When there is a formalised bout between two boxers, the area of their battle is defined by a rectangular platform with rope barriers around the edge. Though square it is called a ring, with the

People sitting around a fire form a social circle. An inglenook formalises this geometry of social interaction around a fire. The example below was drawn by Barry Parker *and is illustrated in the book he produced with his partner in architecture, Raymond Unwin –* The Art of Building a Home, *1901.*

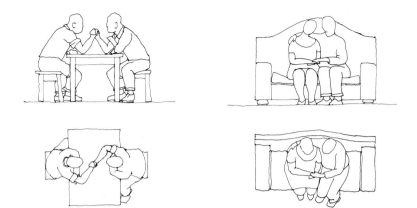

There is a social geometry to the space of confrontation and to that of togetherness.

spectators sitting all around, and the boxers' confrontation is represented in their possession of opposite corners.

The radial arrangement of spectators on the slopes of a valley, watching sports or dramatic performances, was architecturally translated by the ancient Greeks into the theatre in the landscape, with its (slightly more than semi-) circular plan consisting of many tiers of concentric sitting steps.

It may not exactly be an example of 'social' geometry, but the grid layout of graves in a cemetery is a function of the geometry of the human frame and the way the rectangular shape of the space it needs can be tessellated across the land.

People arguing stand opposite each other. When they are friends, they sit next to each other. Both can have architectural manifestations. In British politics, the confrontation of the Government and the Loyal Opposition is physically represented in the benches of the House of Commons (below), which face each other across the chamber with the Speaker (or chairman of the debate) sitting on the axis between them.

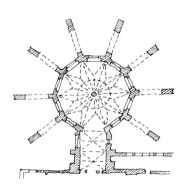

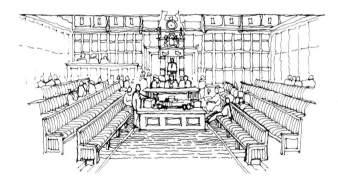

The social geometry of the British House of Commons (left) is a manifestation of the confrontational relationship between the Government and the Loyal Opposition. That of the chapter house of a medieval monastery (above) implies a more consensual approach to making decisions, based in equality.

Some chambers for discussion are designed not for argument and opposition but for collective debate. This is sometimes manifest in their architecture. A chapter house (right) is a meeting room attached to a cathedral or monastery. Often it has a circular or perhaps polygonal plan that, at least architecturally, is non-confrontational and non-hierarchical. Even the central column that supports the vaulted ceiling seems to block direct, diametrical

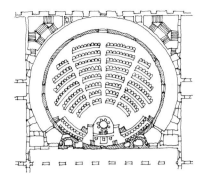

Although the debating chamber of the Finnish parliament was designed, for symbolic reasons, as a circle, its geometry does not easily accommodate the geometry of laying out seats. The conflict between the two geometries is evident in the odd-shaped passage ways around the edge of the chamber.

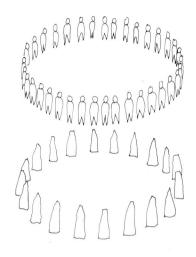

A stone circle makes a people pattern permanent.

opposition across the chamber. It is a moot point whether such architectural arrangements mitigate the behaviour of members of parliament or of chapters. Some countries, nevertheless, have chosen to accommodate their parliamentary debates in circular rather than confrontational debating chambers, if only for symbolic reasons. This, as one example, is the debating chamber of the Finnish parliament in Helsinki (above right), which was designed by J.S. Siren and built in 1931.

The circle is one of the most powerful symbols of human community. Architecturally it seems to speak of people being equal and together in a shared experience. A function of the six-directions implicit in the human form – born of a desire to see everyone else – it is the pattern made, loosely, by the people around their campfire; it is the pattern made by people sitting around a picnic; and it is a pattern associated with conversation. And when there is something specific to watch it is a pattern associated with crowding around some celebrity or spectating at a dramatic or ceremonial event. In the later chapter on *Space and Structure* we shall however see that there can be conflict between this powerful manifestation of social geometry and other geometries of being, notably the geometry of making, which is the subject of the next section of the present chapter.

Many architects, as with the orthogonality of the six-directions-plus-centre, have readily accepted the easy geometries suggested by social gatherings and tried to accommodate them in, or forced them into, the spatial frames of their architecture. Others have attempted a more subtly responsive approach. Though he avoided many other types of geometry in his designs, even the German architect Hans Scharoun accepted the aptness of the circle as a frame for the social event of a meal. In the Mohrmann House, built in Berlin in 1939 (right), the dining area is the only place in the plan that has a regular geometric shape: a circular table is accommodated centrally in a semi-circular bay window between the kitchen and living room. But elsewhere in the plan he has adopted more subtle arrangements that respond, for example, to: the geometry of sitting by the fire looking at the view; or to the geometry of playing the piano whilst also being able to maintain eye-contact with guests; or even to the geometry of sitting talking on the telephone.

The subtleties of relating architectural space to the geometries of social interaction are many. They come into play in the design of any work of architecture intended to accommodate people; that means just about all buildings, gardens, cities....

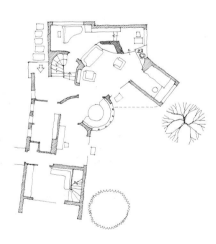

In his design for the Mohrmann House (above), Scharoun recognised the implicit geometry of social interaction by making the dining space semi-circular.

Geometry of making

Many everyday objects have a geometry that is derived from the ways they are made. A clay vase is circular because it is thrown on a potter's wheel; a wooden bowl is circular because it is turned on a wood-turner's lathe; a table is rectangular because it is made of regular shaped pieces of timber. The same is true of building. Often the materials and the way they are put together impose or suggest geometry. And the geometry of building conditions the shapes of the spaces they define. When put together into walls, bricks, as rectangular objects themselves, tend to produce rectangular walls and rectangular openings and enclosures. When using such materials it requires a definite decision to deviate from the rectangular.

The geometry of making is essential to the construction of buildings. In this traditional Norwegian timber house (below), as in many traditional houses from around the world, there is an interplay of social geometry and the geometry of making. Social geometry conditions the sizes and the layout of the spaces, but the shapes of those spaces are also conditioned by the materials available and their intrinsic qualities, and by current building practice. The building is infused with the geometry of making, even though that geometry is not always

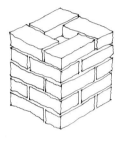

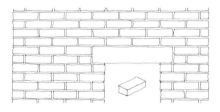

The geometry of bricks conditions the geometry of things that are made from them.

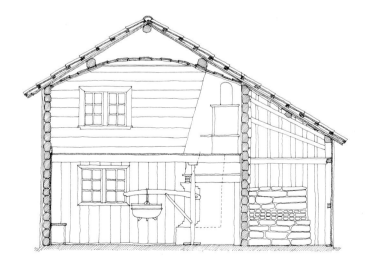

Traditional buildings tend to conform to human scale (measuring), social geometry and the geometry of making. Their architects try to balance the divergent influences of each. This drawing is based on one in:
Tore Drange, Hans Olaf Aanensen and Jon Brænne – *Gamle Trehus*, (Oslo) 1980.

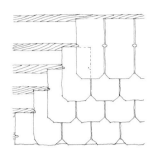

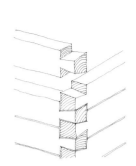

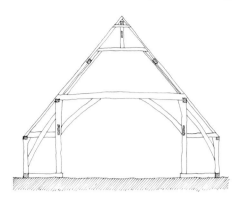

exact and regular. The fabric of the walls and the structure of the roof is influenced by the sizes of timbers available and their innate strength. The sizes of roofing tiles influence the design of the roof. The small panes of the window are conditioned by the sizes of pieces of glass. Even the small portions of masonry are conditioned by the shape of the bricks and the subtle and complex geometries of the stones available. And the bracket that holds the cooking pot has its own structural geometry describing a locus that is part of a circle as it is swung across the fire.

The geometry of making is not so much a power of architecture as a force that conditions building. The force is not active, but lies latent in materials that are available for building and in plausible strategies for bringing materials together into building under the influence of gravity. As such the geometry of making is subject, in architecture, to the range of attitudes mentioned in the chapter on *Temples and Cottages*. In producing an archetypal 'cottage', it may be said, the geometry of making (together with those associated with human scale, behaviour and social interaction) is accepted, whereas in an archetypal 'temple' it (and all or any of the others) might be transcended. Within this dimension architects can adopt any of a range of attitudes to the geometry of making: attitudes that might seek to refine the geometry of making into perfect squares, cubes etc.; or attitudes that celebrate the rough textures and irregular shapes of materials as they are found in nature or subjected only to rudimentary preparation. The Scottish architect Charles Rennie Mackintosh, for example, designed many pieces of furniture. In some of them he exploited the geometry of making, refining it according to his aesthetic sensibility. On the right is a waitress's stool he designed in 1911. It accords with the geometry of making, but this has been refined into a matrix of perfect cubes. There is a constructional geometry too in the shingle and timber buildings designed by the American architect Herb Greene (right, lower), but it is stretched almost to its limit and distorted into animal-like forms. This drawing shows part of his Prairie House built in 1962, on which the shingles are attached to the underlying structure like the feathers of a hen.

The geometry of making includes the geometry of structure, whether it is the timber structure of a medieval tithe barn or the steel structure of a micro-electronics factory. The geometry of structure is said to be susceptible to mathematical calculation, though there seems to be an infinite variety of ways of arranging a structure to span a particular space. Some are said to be efficient if they use material economically and without redundant members; some have an added quality called elegance. Whether there is a direct correlation between efficiency and elegance is a point of debate. The geometry of making

There is geometry to laying slates on a roof and to the ways pieces of timber can be joined together. There is geometry too to the ways in which pieces of material can be put together as a structure.

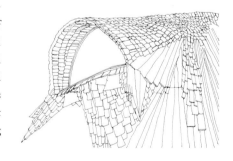

*Reference for Mackintosh furniture:
Charles Rennie Mackintosh and Glasgow School of Art: 2, Furniture in the School Collection, 1978.*

*Reference for the architecture of Herb Greene:
Herb Greene – Mind and Image, 1976.*

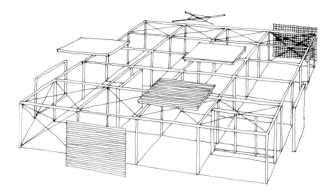

The geometry of making disciplines the dimensional co-ordination of the components of industrialised building systems.

does not apply only to traditional materials such as brick, stone and timber; it applies just as much to buildings with steel or concrete structures and to buildings with large areas of glass wall.

The geometry of making is also the discipline that controls industrialised building systems. Systems consist of standard components that can be made in workshops as a kit of parts to be assembled on site. These parts include structural components and various types of non-structural cladding panels that form the envelope of the building. The dimensional co-ordination that allows standard components to be manufactured in a factory, transported to a site and then put together to make a building, depends on careful and disciplined appreciation of the geometry of making.

The three-dimensional geometry of some medieval carpentry is quite complex. Above is part of the scaffold of the spire of Salisbury Cathedral. The drawing is based on one by Cecil Hewett in his book English Cathedral and Monastic Carpentry, *1985.*

The engineer Santiago Calatrava develops and refines the geometry of structural making in his work. This is a section through his design for the City of Arts and Sciences, in Valencia, Spain, built during the 1990s.

In conclusion to this chapter…. Geometries of being are inherent to our lives. In just about everything we do we measure, align and square things up: travelling; playing games and music; laying tables for meals; constructing poems, machines, buildings; organising our places. Innate geometries exert a strong influence on our dealings with the world. We may ignore or contradict them, we may strive to transcend what they suggest. But often it is sensible to submit to their 'gravitational' attraction. Geometries of being are a benchmark for architecture; we deviate from them only by act of will. To be in harmony with them is to 'go with the flow' and make places relatively easy to build and use. To conflict with them is to make life difficult; but maybe with a transcendent intent that makes such difficulty worthwhile.

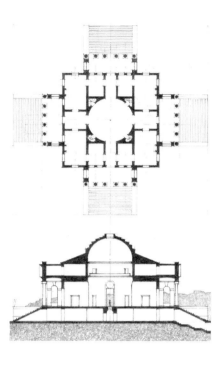

Ideal geometry is not quite of this world. It offers the seductive but unattainable promise of perfection.

IDEAL GEOMETRY

'But in deciding the form of the enclosure, the form of the hut, the situation of the altar and its accessories, he has had by instinct recourse to right angles – axes, the square, the circle. For he could not create anything otherwise which would give him the feeling that he was creating. For all these things – axes, circles, right angles – are geometrical truths, and give results that our eye can measure and recognize; whereas otherwise there would be only chance, irregularity and capriciousness. Geometry is the language of man.'

Le Corbusier, translated by Etchells – *Towards a New Architecture* (1923), 1927, p. 72.

IDEAL GEOMETRY

Leon Battista Alberti, one of the leading architects and architectural theorists of fifteenth-century Italy, began the first of his ten books *On The Art of Building* by asserting that geometry in the design of the appearance of buildings is independent of the materials used in their construction. In so doing he drew attention to the fact that there is another type of geometry applicable in architecture, to be distinguished from what I have called in the previous chapter 'geometries of being':

> 'Let us therefore begin thus: the whole matter of building is composed of lineaments and structure. All the intent and purpose of lineaments lies in finding the correct, infallible way of joining and fitting together those lines and angles which define and enclose the surfaces of the building. It is the function and duty of lineaments, then, to prescribe and appropriate place, exact numbers, a proper scale, and a graceful order for whole buildings and for each of their constituent parts, so that the whole form and appearance of the building may depend on the lineaments alone. Nor do lineaments have anything to do with material, but they are of such a nature that we may recognize the same lineaments in several different buildings that share one and the same form, that is, when the parts, as well as the siting and order, correspond with one another in their every line and angle. It is quite possible to project whole forms in the mind without recourse to the material, by designating and determining a fixed orientation and conjunction for the various lines and angles. Since that is the case, let lineaments be the precise and correct outline, conceived in the mind, made up of lines and angles, and perfected in the learned intellect and imagination.'*

Alberti turned his focus to ideas of 'perfection' as might only be achieved by the educated mind ('the learned intellect and imagination'). Perfection, he suggested, depends on what is here termed, to distinguish it from geometries of being, 'ideal geometry'. Ideal geometry is geometry in abstract, set apart from the physical. It is the geometry of school mathematics lessons. Its elements are the straight line, the circle, the square, the triangle… and their three-dimensional forms: the plane, sphere, cube, cone, tetrahedron, pyramid…. Ideal geometry includes right-angles, axial symmetry and proportions: the simple exact ratios of 1:2, 1:3, 2:3… and more complex ratios such as 1:√2 (one to the square root of two) or that known as the Golden Section, which is about 1:1.618. In its more intricate forms ideal geometry includes the geometry of complex curves and surfaces generated from mathematical formulae (using computers, for example). All these kinds of ideal geometry are used in architecture.

Ideal geometry is geometry on its own terms operating through the human mind in the hermetic realm of mathematics. It is not easy to say exactly *where* ideal geometry

Axial symmetry dictates that one side of the elevation of a building (or its plan), should be a mirror image of the other, irrespective of whether such an arrangement is a sensible way of dealing with pragmatic requirements. The application of ideal geometry generally implies that regular and ordered visual appearance and discipline in composition is more important than practical or social organisation and either overrides the geometry of making or lifts it to a more disciplined level in search of perfection.

* Leon Battista Alberti, translated by Rykwert and others – *On the Art of Building in Ten Books* (c1450), 1988, p. 7.

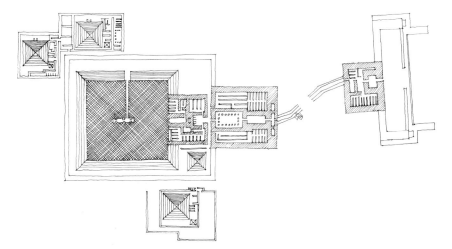

resides, since it cannot be said to belong to the physical world but neither is it merely a conceit of the mind. In the sixteenth century the mathematician John Dee identified architecture as one of the media of mathematics (geometry), having decided that mathematics belonged somewhere in between the real world and the divine.

> *'All things which are and have being are found under a triple diversity general. For, either they are deemed supernatural, natural, or of a third being.... Things mathematical... being (in a manner) middle, between things supernatural and natural, are not so absolute and excellent as things supernatural, nor yet so base and gross as things natural, but are things immaterial, and nevertheless by material things able somewhat to be signified.'**

Architecture has been, through all history since at least the Egyptian pyramids, one of the 'material things' by which 'things mathematical' (geometrical) might be 'able somewhat to be signified'. Ideal geometry is transcendent, seemingly magical, fascinating. It is usually represented on paper or another drawing surface (which Walter Gropius referred to as the '*platonic* draughting board'**) – the sand of a beach, a rock tablet, a computer screen – in a realm of its own. In this it seems an apposite partner to architecture designed by drawing, which, before it is realised through building, also resides in an abstract in-between realm of its own. Ideal geometry can seem to be 'symbiotic' with architecture designed on paper with straight edges, rulers, set-squares etc., or with computer software with its dependence on mathematical formulae.

A matter of imposition

The human mind seems to enjoy ideal geometry and likes to apply it to the world. Since ancient Egyptian times it has been used by surveyors to map land and lay out building work. In the seventeenth century, through the work of Descartes, it became the basis of the method for identifying points in space – the Cartesian Grid. Many maps have a grid (an abstract overlay) of squares by which places can be accurately identified according to west-east and south-north coordinates, which provides a way of making sense of (gives an architecture to) the world. Comparing this way of identifying place by numbers in abstract

* John Dee – *Mathematicall Praeface to the Elements of Geometrie of Euclid of Megara*, 1570. (I have modernised spelling and punctuation in this quotation.)

**Walter Gropius – *Scope of Total Architecture*, 1956, p. 274.
The word 'platonic' refers to the ancient Greek philosopher Plato's philosophy that the world is only an imperfect representation of perfect or ideal essences. (For example, underpinning all the different kinds of dog, there is, not in this world but philosophically, the ideal essence or idea of 'dog'.) In architecture, Gropius suggests, the draughting board (or nowadays it would be the computer screen) is the realm where works of architecture find their perfect 'platonic' form unsullied by the imperfections of realisation (those slightly misaligned bricks and blobs in the plaster) and the effects of reality (weather, wear etc.). On the 'platonic draughting board' all is ideal.

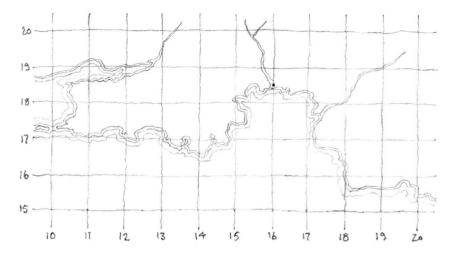

Maps have grids overlaid upon them for idenfying places by coordinates. Rather than identifying the spot marked as 'by the mouth of the river that flows into the large bay', which would be a descriptive method, I can say just 16 18.5, which would allow no confusion. Works of architecture are often designed on similar grids. Computer draughting software provides them ready made because they need them, at a very fine grain, in order to work. The grid invests work designed on it with a sense of order and consistency.

(universally the same for everyone) with the way in which we each identify place in relation to ourselves, illustrates the difference between ideal geometry and geometries of being. The world in itself has no grid; it has been imposed upon it. One might also compare the Cartesian Grid as a way of identifying place with the Songlines of aborigine culture in Australia. With these, people identify place according to mythical stories of the Dreamtime, rather than by abstract coordinates.

Ideal geometry has been used by scientists to theorise about and assimilate the workings of the physical universe, implying that nature itself operates on geometric principles. Some suggest that geometry is the language and therefore a proof of the existence of a 'creator'. Some argue that if geometry is the language by which God designed the universe, it should also be the language by which architects design their buildings and lay out cities. There is something certain, unchanging, and hence reassuring, about the circle and the square. They are dependable. Works of architecture designed using ideal geometry seem to possess a satisfying harmony and sense of rightness; or at least they open up the possibility of 'wrongness' – parts that do not conform to the discipline imposed by the geometry.

The human mind imposes ideal geometry on the world as an overlay, a filter, a frame of reference. Ideal geometry is different from the geometries of being, which (as described in the previous chapter) derive from the world's ontology, i.e. from *being*. As well as emerging from the ways we relate to the world, straight lines, circles, squares, etc. are pure mathematical figures with their own rules and formulae.

In an irregular and changing world the eternal certainty of mathematical figures intrigues the mind. Ascribed an aesthetic or symbolic authority deriving from their apparent possession of rightness, they seem to offer an attainable perfection – as in the *perfect* circle, the *perfect* square, *perfect* symmetry. Architects use ideal geometry to instil their work with a discipline and harmony independent of the geometries of being. The transcendence of ideal geometry over material considerations is considered a touchstone of its nobility. It speaks of a 'higher', more perfect (as Alberti said more 'learned') level of interaction with the world, where the will triumphs over the untidiness and tribulations of mundane reality.

An American architect, Louis Kahn, said that 'A brick knows what it wants to be'. Robert Venturi, another American architect, responded: 'Louis Kahn has referred to "what a thing wants to be", but implicit in this statement is its opposite: what the architect wants the thing to be. In the tension and balance between these two lie many of the architect's decisions.' One of the ways in which architects override 'what things want to be' is by subjecting them to ideal geometry.

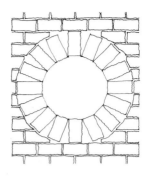
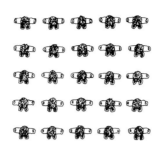
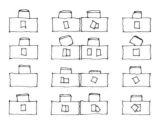

Attitudes to ideal geometry

There are various attitudes to the roles ideal geometry can play in architecture:

* belief that the application of ideal geometry produces beauty and harmony;
* conviction that ideal geometry is 'right' in the sense that it promises perfect form;
* submission to ideal geometry's authority over design decisions;
* use of ideal geometry as an expression of control and the abstract subjection of material (and even people) to an ordering principle that disregards its (their) innate character istics (behaviour patterns);
* dependency on the discipline of ideal geometry, its legibility, predictability and consistency;
* gratitude for the 'ready-made' intellectual structure ideal geometry offers;
* use of ideal geometry as a counterpoint to irregularity, whether within the work or between the work and its context;
* investment of ideal geometry with symbolic or mystical significance;
* relish for the difficulty and cost in realising ideal geometry in physical form, and its expression of power, sacrifice, status;
* playing with ideal geometry, its alignments and coincidences, as a game.

In all these ideal geometry is separate from our phenomenological experience of the world. We can experience walking along a line of passage, being part of a social circle; we sense our selves as centres of our own six directions and the geometry of assembling bricks into an orthogonal wall. But we cannot *experience* a perfect circle or square. We can imagine, see and measure them but they remain apart from us.

It is not easy (does not feel 'natural') to build a perfectly circular opening in a brick wall; bricks have to be cut into odd shapes and, unless great skill is applied, ugly irregular joints can result. Neither would it be easy (or feel 'natural') to fit the circular opening with a window frame starting with straight rectangular pieces of timber; curved pieces would have to be cut from the straight, with substantial wastage. Cutting glass into a circle requires skill too. But is lack of ease a reason for not doing it? Might the achievement be a symbol of will and skill transcending the innate characteristics of bricks, timber and glass?

When soldiers are made to stand or march in geometric patterns, it is a symbol of the discipline to which they are subject. Their individual differences are subordinated to a single geometric unit. Their geometry is a symbol of their power as a fighting force and their obedience to authority.

People argue about whether it is appropriate or not to arrange children's desks in a schoolroom in geometric order. The differences may be practical but perhaps the symbolism, that a child's individuality is subordinated to uniformity, causes more concern.

The military precision with which Parisian park keepers trim their trees into perfect geometric shapes seems to express the humanism of the French attitude to life and a desire to control nature. Their form contrasts with that of trees that are allowed to grow into their own form (opposite).

A purely human contribution

We seem fascinated by geometry because it is special, an aspect of the world that it seems only we human beings can appreciate. Spiders make webs in geometric patterns and bees build combs with hexagonal cells but these forms are functions of the geometry of their making. Only human beings see virtue in making things with perfect geometric forms irrespective of the possible difficulties of making them that way. An irregular line scratched on a wall or in the sand is one of an infinite number of possible irregular lines but a dead straight line, whatever its length or thickness, is always *straight line*. An irregular loop is one of an infinite number of loops but a perfect circle, whatever its size, is a *circle*. It is special, unique. Special too are a square, a composition of squares, a Golden Rectangle.

The incidence of ideal geometry in works of architecture is ancient. Its apparent incontrovertibility has fascinated the human mind for a very long time, as perhaps has the technical challenge of its achievement in built form. The power of the pyramids of Egypt derives in part from the establishment of ideal geometry in the shifting sands of the desert, symbolising permanence in a changing world – the permanence and eternity of death. Whatever else their forms might have meant to those who built them, they stand as emblems of titanic human achievement, intellectual as well as physical, expressed through geometry.

Ideal geometry versus geometries of being

The differences between ideal geometry and the geometries of being are subtle but profound. Sometimes there is confusion about which is which. If for example I build a brick cell in a rectangular form, with each wall a whole number of bricks wide and high, I am working in harmony with what was in the previous chapter called 'the geometry of making' – my rectangular components (the bricks) readily lend themselves to my building them into rectangular walls. But if I decide to make my cell in the form of a perfect cube, perfectly square on each face, then, although I might still be working in accord with the geometry of making, I am introducing an additional factor, that of the desire to achieve an ideal geometric form – the cube. Or, if I decide to build my brick cell as a cylinder with a circular plan, I might do it to accommodate the social geometry (of being) of people sitting in a circle – while compromising the geometry of making, since it is not easy to construct this curved form from rectangular bricks, or I might be driven by a desire for realising the ideal geometry of the perfect circle. In such decisions there is an interplay between ideal

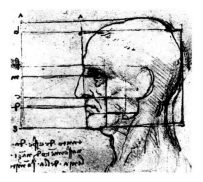

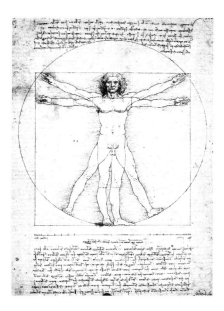

geometry and the geometries of being. Partly because it exists in a realm that stands aloof from the geometries of being, the assertion and achievement of ideal geometry in made form can be an expression of the purely human ability to break free of and transcend natural conditions. In the dimension that stretches from the 'cottage' to the 'temple' (or from the cave to the lunar module), ideal geometry is a characteristic of the 'temple' extreme. Ideal geometry manifests human discipline and aspiration to achieve a perfection of form not found in nature. Ideal geometry is a symbol of humanism: humanity's ability to rise above its conditions, its self-determination. Through the assertion of ideal geometry, human beings impose their will on the world.

An underlying armature of the universe

The relationship between ideal geometry and the geometries of being is confused by the suggestion that ideal geometry is the underlying armature of natural processes and products, such as in the ellipses the planets describe around the sun, the spacing of branches on a tree or the arrangement of human features on a face. Following Vitruvius, Leonardo da Vinci, for example, working in fifteenth-century Italy, made many studies in which he tried to extract the underlying geometric structure of natural form (above). Such observations suggest that ideal mathematical geometry informs the workings and forms of the universe and can be appropriated to inform the creative work of the human mind too. In his book *Architectural Principles in the Age of Humanism* (1952), Rudolf Wittkower explored the ways Renaissance architects used ideal geometric figures, symmetry and ratios in their designs. He also discussed why they believed that such figures and ratios were powerful. One argument was that natural creations, such as the proportions and symmetry of the human frame, the relationships between the planets or the intervals of musical harmony, seemed to follow geometric ratios, and that if the products of architecture were to possess the same conceptual integrity they too should be designed using perfect figures, symmetry and harmonic mathematical proportions. Another argument was that through architecture a geometrical perfection that was only hinted at in natural creations could be achieved in creations of the mind. The application of geometry was seen as one way human beings could improve the imperfect world in which they found themselves. Geometric purity was thus seen as a manifestation of the human ability, or perhaps duty, to make the world better. The result was that architects produced designs for buildings composed using perfect figures, axial symmetry and geometric ratios.

In Renaissance Italy artists and architects tried to determine the ideal geometry inherent in natural forms, particularly the human head and body. They also tried to identify the ideal geometry for architectural elements. In this they were prompted by the first century BC writings of the Roman architect Vitruvius. Leonardo da Vinci made many sketches analysing or determining the ideal geometry of the human form (above) and head (above left).

'… in the human body the central point is naturally the navel. For if a man be placed flat on his back, with his hands and feet extended, and a pair of compasses centred at his navel, the fingers and toes of his two hands and feet will touch the circumference of a circle described therefrom…. And just as the human body yields a circular outline, so too a square figure may be found from it. For if we measure the distance from the soles of the feet to the top of the head, and then apply that measure to the outstretched arms, the breadth will be found to be the same as the height, as in the case of plane surfaces which are perfectly square.'

Vitruvius, translated by Hickey-Morgan – *The Ten Books on Architecture* (first century BC), 1960.

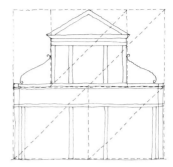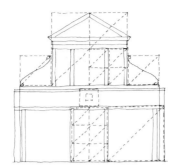

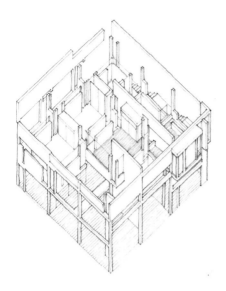

Here for example (above) are two of Wittkower's diagrams of the geometric composition of the façade of the church of S. Maria Novella in Florence, designed by Alberti and built in the fifteenth century. They show that the façade of the building may be analysed as a two-dimensional axially symmetrical composition of squares. These have a role in the design that is independent of the building's geometry of making. The geometry is displayed like an advertisement on the front wall of the church, as on a screen. A direct line of descent can be drawn from this building, with its imposition of a transcendent (non-functional, non-constructional) geometry, through to the late twentieth-century buildings of architects such as Peter Eisenman (Houses I-VI) with their three-dimensional geometric armatures (right) which are worked through with precedence over constructional and functional considerations. (Eisenman's House VI is analysed as one of the *Case Studies* at the end of this book.)

Geometric plans

Many architects have designed buildings in which the accommodation is enclosed within a square plan. This is different from composing the design of a façade as a two-dimensional pattern of squares because it involves the third dimension and perhaps also the fourth – time. A square plan is not usually a result of accepting the geometry of making. A square space is not the easiest to frame with a structure; it requires purposeful intent, derived from something other than mere practicality, to make a plan perfectly square.

Architects may design a square plan for various reasons: maybe for the philosophical reasons outlined above; maybe because a square can seem to identify a still centre that relates to the six directions mentioned in the chapter on *Geometries of Being*; maybe as a kind of game – a challenge to fit accommodation within this perfect but rigid shape.

Architects are always looking for ideas that will give form to their work and direction to their design. Geometric ideas are some of the most seductive. Certainly they are the most readily available. To design within a square plan is an easy idea to grasp (and a way to break through the problem of getting started). But although it may seem a limitation, the square plan is also open to infinite variation.

There are many examples of square plans. They are rare in ancient and medieval architecture (the Egyptian pyramids are an obvious exception, as is the Necromanteion in western Greece, illustrated on p. 214) but in the Renaissance the square became part of the repertoire of design ideas.

Peter Eisenman's House II (one of a series of six designed in the late 1960s and early 1970s), with its complex composition held together on an abstract framework of squares, is in a direct line of descent from Alberti's S. Maria Novella. See also Case Study 9, *towards the end of the present book, which analyses Eisenman's House VI.*

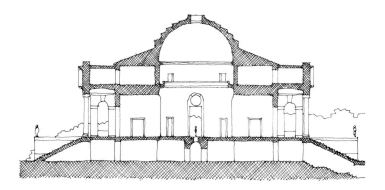

On the right (in the margins of this page and the next) are the plans of the principal floors of two square-plan houses built in England in the 1720s. Mereworth Castle (next page) in Kent was designed by Colen Campbell; Chiswick Villa (this page) in London was designed by Campbell's patron Lord Burlington. Both architects were influenced in the choice of a square plan by the Villa Rotonda designed by the Italian architect Andrea Palladio, built some one hundred and fifty years before the two English examples (larger drawings, this page and the next).

Palladio's plan, the original (below), is the most consistent of the three. It gathers the four horizontal directions (the two main axes at right-angles to each other) into a centre – the focus of the circular hall at the heart of the plan, from which the villa gets its name. (Incidentally, the sides of the Villa Rotonda do not face north, south, east and west but north-east, south-east….) The plan is not just one square but a concentric series of five; the size of each successive one is determined by the radius of a circle circumscribed about the next smallest

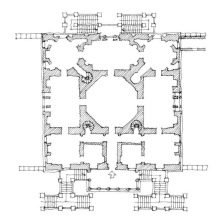

Chiswick Villa

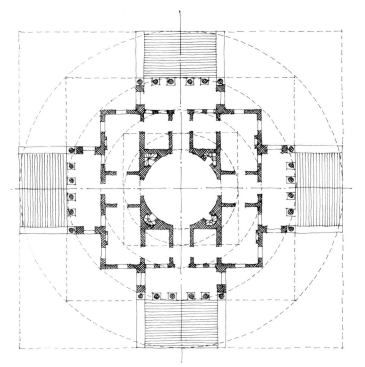

Chiswick Villa and Mereworth Castle, both English houses of the eighteenth century, were designed with square plans, directly influenced by Palladio's Villa Rotonda.

Both the plan and the section of the Villa Rotonda are disciplined according to ideal geometry.

Reference for the Villa Rotonda:
Camillo Semenzato – *The Rotonda of Andrea Palladio*, 1968.

160

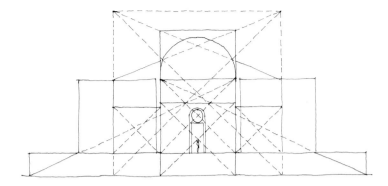

The proportions of the Villa Rotunda seem to be derived from a man standing at its centre. This reinforces its claim to be a temple to the human being.

(below). The smallest circle is the rotonda itself. Each square (except the second smallest) determines the position of some substantial part of the building. The middle square determines the size of the main block of the house; the second largest the extent of the porticoes on each face; and the largest square gives the extent of the steps that lead up to those porticoes. The cross-section through the Villa Rotunda (opposite top, and above) is also a composition of circles and squares, though not such a simple one as in the plan. It is arguable that the geometry of the whole house begins with the size of a human being standing at its geometric centre. The result is a design in which geometry not only decides the form of the building but also symbolises the distinctively human contribution to making the world better, more beautiful and better ordered than it is by nature. The villa becomes a temple to the human being presiding at the centre of the world which it surveys in each of the four directions, with the supra-human world above (symbolised by the dome) and the sub-human world below (symbolised by the servants' quarters in the basement).

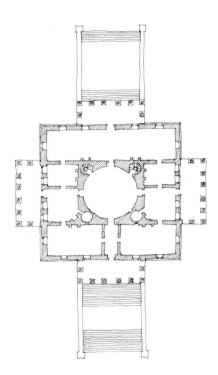

Mereworth Castle

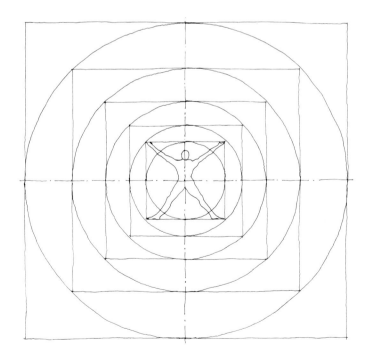

The use of circles and squares as an underlying framework derives from Vitruvius's observation that the human form fits both.

161

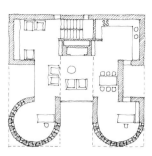

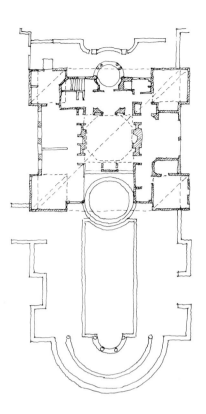

Square plans have also been used by architects designing in the twentieth century. Charles Moore used the square as the basis of his plan for the Rudolf House II (right). As in the Renaissance examples Moore created a central place, which is here the living room, surrounded by subsidiary places: kitchen, dining room, bedroom and so on. Perhaps for practical reasons, the plan is not so neatly arranged as that of Palladio.

The Swiss architect Mario Botta bases many of his designs on geometric figures. He has designed a number of private houses in Switzerland that are often composed of squares and circles, cubes and cylinders. Botta's design for a family house at Origlio (above), which was built in 1981, is a composition of rectangles and circles fitted into a notional square. On each floor he uses the square in a different way. On this floor, the middle of three, the plan is nearly symmetrical, with the living room and fireplace at its heart.

The plan of this house at Riva San Vitale (also by Botta, below) is based on a square too. The house is a tower of five floors built on the sloping bank of Lake Lugano. It is entered across a bridge to the top floor (which is the one shown in the drawing).

In both these houses Botta appears to have used another geometric figure – the Golden Rectangle – to help him in deciding the layout of the plans. The Golden Rectangle is one that has a particular proportional relationship between its two dimensions: the ratio of the short dimension to the long is equal to that between the long dimension and the sum of the two dimensions (below and right). This means that if one subtracts a square from a Golden Rectangle, one is left with another, smaller Golden Rectangle. This ratio, known as the Golden Section, is not a whole number but approximately 1.618:1. In the house at Origlio it appears that Botta used the Golden Section to determine the proportion between the central section and the side sections of the house. In the Riva San Vitale house he seems

Many architects have tried designing houses with square plans.

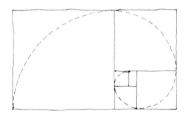

The Golden Section is a special proportion that produces a rectangle in which, if a square is removed, it produces another Golden Rectangle, and so on ad infinitum.

Reference for Botta houses:
Pierluigi Nicolin – *Mario Botta: Buildings and Projects 1961-1982*, 1984.

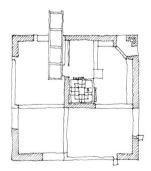

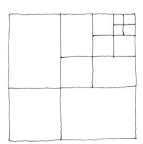

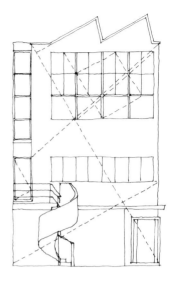

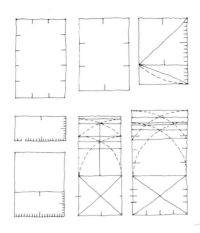

Many architects have used ideal geometry in more mundane ways to give order to their designs. It has been used to give discipline to the arrangement of a plan or elevation irrespective of how they relate to pragmatics and use. Windows and doors, for example, are often given simple geometric proportions that are thought to contribute to their aesthetic harmony. Cesariano produced this diagram of the ideal proportions for doors and windows in 1521 (left).

Through history many architects have used geometric proportions for their windows. The proportions of this window (below) are based on the Golden Rectangle. It is from a 'garden village' house designed by the practice of Parker and Unwin in 1912.

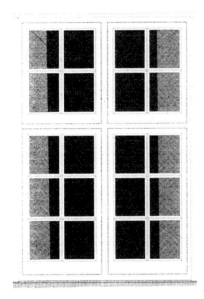

to have used Golden Rectangles in a way similar to that in which Palladio used circles and squares in the Villa Rotonda, like Russian dolls; in this case emanating from one corner of the plan, rather than its centre. The square near the middle of the plan accommodates the stair that connects the floors.

Le Corbusier also used the Golden Section to give geometric integrity to his work. In his book *Vers Une Architecture* (1923), translated as *Towards a New Architecture* (1927), he illustrated his geometric analyses of some well-known buildings and the geometric framework on which he had built some of his own designs. He did not only use the Golden Section, and in some cases his 'regulating lines' (he called them '*traces regulateurs*') make a complex web of lines, the rationale behind which can be difficult to understand. Above is his diagram of the geometric composition of one of the elevations of the studio house that he designed for his friend Amédée Ozenfant, built in a southern suburb of Paris in 1923. Rather like Alberti's S. Maria Novella, the geometry is displayed on the elevation of the house as on a screen. The suggestion is that the underlying geometric arrangement of the elevation, almost like a genetic programme, gives the building a visual integrity it would not otherwise have.

These examples illustrate that the application of ideal geometry in architecture is generally a matter of refinement. Basic architectural elements (defined area of ground, wall, window, door, column, cell etc.), which are instrumental in the identification of place, may be modified by ideal geometry for aesthetic, intellectual or perhaps symbolic reasons. Ideal geometry is mostly concerned with appearances; it can be considered a cosmetic concern. Even when a design seems to begin with the assertion of ideal geometry (as in the ancient Egyptian pyramid or the Villa Rotonda), that geometry is, conceptually, applied to the basic architectural elements of the work, without which it would have no existence. There has been much debate in architectural writing about whether ideal geometry is a touchstone of nobility or a spurious conceit.

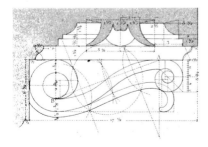

By the nineteenth century, proposals for the geometric construction of architectural elements had become more complex and subtle.

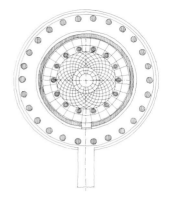

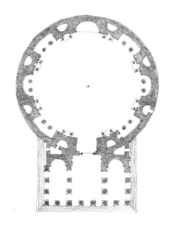

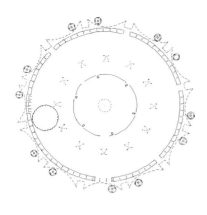

Through history architects have resorted as readily to the circle as to the square for a geometric framework on which to design. Above (as just three examples from many) are the plans of the Tholos (circular temple) at Epidavros, Greece (BC third century), the Pantheon in Rome, Italy (second century AD) and the Millennium Dome in London by Richard Rogers (not to the same scale).

Certainly ideal geometry makes architectural design easier; or at least it gives the architect a crutch or support on which to compose, intellectually, a plan or section. Below left for example is a drawing (by me) following exactly the same geometric game played by Leonardo da Vinci in one of his notebooks (c. 1488) when musing on a design for a 'temple'. And alongside is one of Frank Lloyd Wright's house plans (the Martin Residence, 1904), which has clearly been composed with an underlay, beneath the drawing paper, of graph paper. This technique gives the drawing an integrity that stretches through all the buildings and intervening gardens, holding them together on a shared geometric grid. Ideal geometry lends a plan a sense of 'rightness' because it conforms to a complete and perfect geometrical shape.

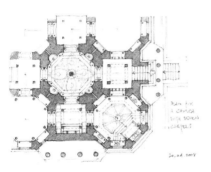

And to show how easy designing over a geometric grid can be, above is a plan I doodled over squared paper during a particularly boring meeting.

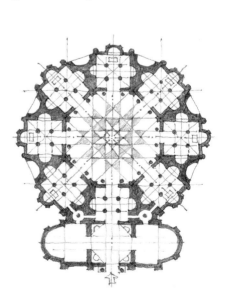

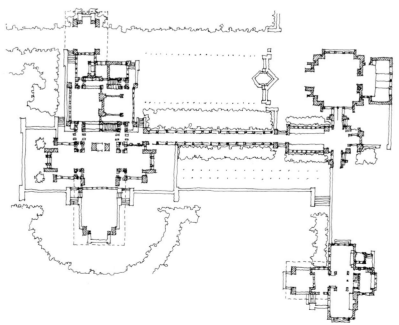

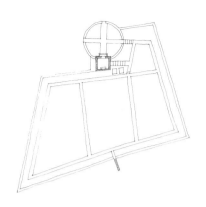

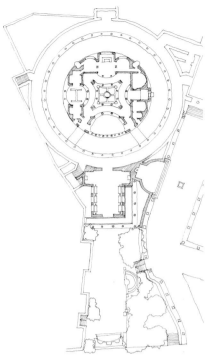

Complex, distorted and overlaid geometries

One might observe that ideal geometry, as well as offering the unattainable grail of (divine) perfection, is defined by its predictable discipline (and hence could be considered boring). Just as music nearly always combines a predictable beat with an irregular melodic line, so too in architecture ideal geometry can be played against irregularity. Protagonists of ideal geometry might argue that this interplay is provided by setting people and their irregular activity against the formal regular frame of geometric buildings or, as in the plan of Wright's Martin Residence, by the counterpoint of trees and vegetation. Others have sought or found the interplay in other ways, either in relation to context or within the work itself.

Sometimes the interplay comes about by reason of a constricted site, which imposes its own irregularity to distort the architect's ideal geometry. Above is the plan of Forsbacka Cemetery by Lewerentz, who allows the distortion of his geometry suggested by the site to reach to the small chapel itself (which, one suspects, would otherwise be square). And on the right, the constriction of an irregular site enriches the formal plan of the Circular Pavilion at Hadrian's Villa at Tivoli, outside Rome.

Many twentieth-century architects have used ideal geometry to give their designs a rational, if abstract, formal integrity. Some, seemingly bored with simple relationships, have experimented with complex arrangements in which one ideal geometry is overlaid on, or contradicted by, another.

In some of the house designs by the American architect Richard Meier, the spaces that result from a complex interplay of orthogonal geometries identify the places of dwelling. This, for example (right), is the site plan of Meier's design for the Hoffman House, built in East Hampton, New York State, in 1967. The idea for the plan seems to have been generated from the shape of the site, which is an almost perfect square (see drawing on next page). The diagonal across the square determines the angle of one of the elevations of one of the two main rectangles on which the plan of the house is based. Each of these two rectangles is a double square. One is set on the diagonal of the site; the other is parallel to the sides of the site. They share one corner. Their geometric interrelationship determines the position of almost everything in the plan. The interaction of the overlaid geometries defines the 'places' of the house – living room, kitchen, dining area, and so on. The complex armature of lines that the geometries of the rectangles create determine the positions of basic elements – walls, glass walls, defined areas, columns. To help in this game the squares are sometimes sub-divided to make the geometry even more complex, and thus identify a greater range of

This plan of the Circular Pavilion at Hadrian's Villa is as reconstructed in the early twentieth century by P.T. Schutze and is included in:
John F. Harbeson – *The Study of Architectural Design*, 1927, p. 216.

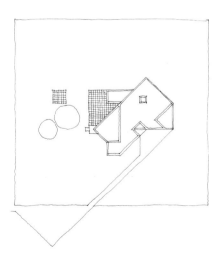

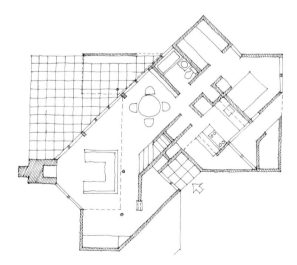

The plan of the Hoffman House, by Richard Meier, is based on two double squares that share one corner. This geometric armature determines many of the decisions about how the places in the plan are organised. In contrast to a simple geometric layout, the overlaid geometries lend the design an intricacy that derives from the interplay between the two grids.

Reference for the Hoffman House by Richard Meier:
Joseph Rykwert (Introduction) – *Richard Meier Architect 1964/1984*, 1984, pp. 34-7.

different places within the armature. The drawing below left shows one interpretation of the geometry that provides the armature of the ground floor of this house. The actual plan is alongside. In this version one of the squares is divided into thirds in both directions, giving nine smaller squares. The positions of the columns set in the glass wall that lights the living room and dining area are determined by the intersections of the third-lines. The fireplace is positioned on the one corner the two rectangles share. The entrance – itself a square – seems to be generated by an interaction of the centre line of one of the double squares with the side of the other, and sits in an axial relationship with the fireplace and the seating in the living room. An alcove in the living room is created by a projection of the middle third of the divided square to meet the corner of the other double square. And so on.

This may seem complicated, and is certainly difficult to follow when explained verbally. If this is the way that Meier progressed his design for this house, which seems plausible, then he was using geometry as the framework for design decision, a hybrid of the geometric armatures for design used by Alberti and Palladio. Geometry is used in this way to suggest formal and perhaps also aesthetic integrity. In his overlaid geometries, Meier adds a further dimension – a layering that produces an intricacy in the quality his spaces.

Meier's geometric overlays may seem complex enough but some other architects have used geometric frameworks even more complex than that in the Hoffman House. One

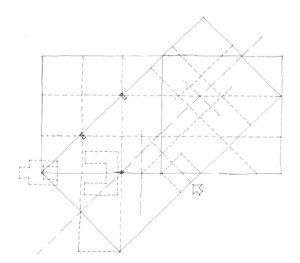

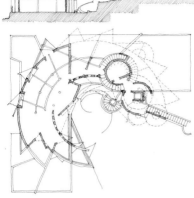

example is an apartment building in the Tel Aviv suburb of Ramat Gan in Israel. Its section and plan are on the right. The architect of this complicated building was Zvi Hecker; it was built in 1991. It is formed of a spiral of fragmented circles and rectangles, with dwelling places disposed in the spaces that result from the intricate geometric overlays.

There are various ways in which architects achieve the complexity born of interplay between regularity and irregularity. Below left is the plan and section of Gino Valle's Casa Quaglia, built in Sutrio, Italy in 1956. Here, by subtraction, a complex composition of walls is framed within a regular square framework. The plan of Alvaro Siza's Bires House (Povoa do Varzim, Portugal 1976) is alongside; it seems to have had a corner ripped untidily from its otherwise tidy orthogonal geometry.

Zvi Hecker's apartment building in Tel Aviv (above) is a spiral of overlaid circles, rectangles and radii.

Gino Valle's Casa Quaglia consists of a fragmentary arrangement of walls and floors under a regular aedicular frame (far left).

Alvaro Siza's Bires House has a 'bite' taken out of one of its corners (near left).

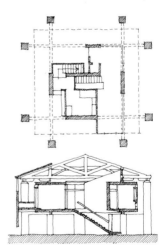

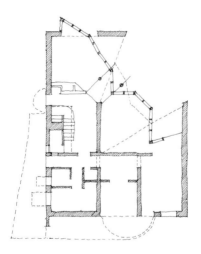

One of many architects who have played with geometry and its distortion in their work is Zaha Hadid. In the 1980s and 1990s she produced a number of designs in which it seemed that some unseen and unknowable force was fracturing and distorting what might otherwise have turned out to be a regular orthogonal building. One of the most celebrated of these designs, and the first to be built, was that for the Fire Station at the Vitra factory near the German border with Switzerland. (It was a celebrated design but also notorious, as it turned out to be unusable as a fire station.) Its plan is at the top of the next page (middle) with, alongside to the right, a plan showing it in the setting of the Vitra factory. You can

Reference for Tel Aviv apartments by Zvi Hecker: L'Architecture d'Aujourd'hui, June 1991, p. 12.

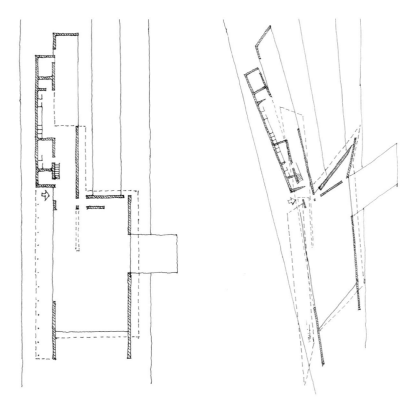

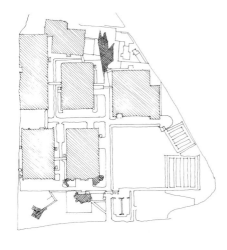

see from this site plan that Hadid's building challenges the orthogonal grid of the factory layout. But the building is challenged within itself too. It is as if that unseen and unknowable force (a black hole maybe) is in operation, disturbing its composure and preventing it from being orthogonal. On the left, I have drawn the plan as it might be if that disruptive force was removed.

In the 1970s the Italian architectural theorist Bruno Zevi drew three diagrams to illustrate how twentieth century Modern architecture had broken open the enclosed box of traditional architecture (below). He was referring back to the early twentieth century work of Frank Lloyd Wright and the De Stijl architects and designers of Europe, as well as to that of Mies van der Rohe (the Barcelona Pavilion for example). It is as if, in the Vitra Fire Station, Zaha Hadid has extrapolated the next step in this historical evolution. My 'rectified' plan seems equivalent to Zevi's third diagram – the composition of opened and shifted planes. But Zevi's planes still obey the discipline of the three mutually perpendicular Cartesian

The Fire Station at the Vitra Factory was built in 1994. It was one of a series of new buildings on the site. Frank Gehry designed the Design Museum built in 1989, and Tadao Ando the Conference Centre (1993). These are indicated at the bottom of the site plan.

Reference for Hadid's Vitra Fire Station:
Aaron Betsky – *Zaha Hadid: Complete Buildings and Projects*, 1998.

Reference for Zevi's diagram:
Bruno Zevi – *The Modern Language of Architecture*, 1978.

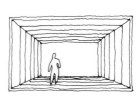

Enclosed box

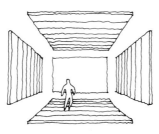

Opened planes

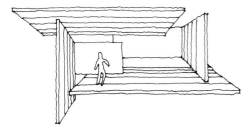

Opened and shifted planes

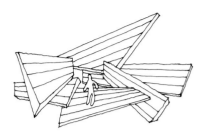

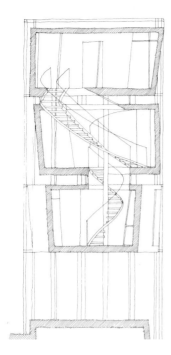

dimensions. Hadid's building has its own diagram (above) in which these too are broken apart. The result is an intentional conflict, rather than an accord, with the 'six-directions' implicit in the human being.

Much of Hadid's work challenges the Cartesian way of ordering (making sense of) the world. Below are the plans of her design for an extension to the Arhotel Billie Strauss in Kirchheim-Nabern, Germany (1995). The section is on the right. Following Le Corbusier's Dom-Ino idea (see the following chapter on *Space and Structure*) the extension stands on pilotis (columns) leaving the ground level clear. But otherwise it refuses to obey the 'rules' of orthogonality, or even consistency from one floor to the next.

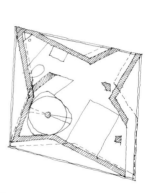

First floor

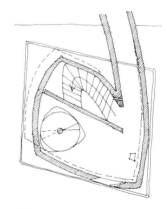

Second floor

Third floor

Parametrics

There are many examples of the ways architects use ideal geometry in both simple and complex ways. It has been one of the most enduring themes throughout the history of architectural design. The increasing use of advanced computer software in architectural design into the twenty-first century has led to more and more sophisticated explorations of the possibilities of generating intricate geometries. Though the forms generated may become more and more complex and subtle, sometimes possessing the genetic integrity of natural forms, the detachment of the relationship with the phenomenological appreciation of place tends to remain the same.

Reference for Arhotel Billie Strauss extension:
Paul Sigel – *Zaha Hadid: Nebern*, 1995.

Nevertheless, the complex geometries made possible using computer based techniques such as parametrics constitute the currently most advanced state of the architectural adventure exploring abstract mathematical geometries that began before the pyramids some five thousand years ago. Parametrics (defined alongside) allows complex amorphous forms (which are all held together on the three-dimensional Cartesian Grid by which the computer works) to be generated by formulae in which when one variable is changed the others also change. So it effectively possible to model warps and shifts instigated by external forces – not just gravity but other morphological forces too. It can produce forms that mimic natural growth, such as in sea shells and trees. This is a technique that it is impossible for me to draw here with my pencil. There are two short movies (April 2008) which show something of the possibility of the technique at:

www.bdonline.co.uk/story.asp?sectioncode=763&storycode=3111007&c=1

These movies illustrate Zaha Hadid's design for the Chanel Contemporary Art Container, a travelling structure, and Foster and Partners' roof for the Smithsonian Institute in Washington DC. Notice that the Foster movie begins with an image of a 'diagrid', the diagonal version of an orthodox orthogonal grid, the quintessential support system for ideal geometry.

* * *

Ideal geometry and its variations, as the evidence suggests, is a seductive area for architects to explore. The use of ideal geometries in architecture is a stimulating intellectual game. Its products can be sensational but distant. It may, as John Dee implied over four hundred years ago, take you half-way to the divine but in doing so it also takes you half-way away from life as it is lived in the real world. A preoccupation with ideal geometry and its sophisticated extensions into computer generated form-making can prioritise beautiful sculptural form over the making of places that are phenomenologically engaging and obscure the genesis of architecture in the identification of place – the profound engagement between human beings and their surroundings. But nevertheless the geometry of squares and circles, Golden Rectangles and more complex formulae will probably always be seen as one of the touchstones of humanism in architecture.

'Parametrics, a method of linking dimensions and variables to geometry in such a way that when the values change, the part changes as well. A parameter is a variable to which other variables are related, and these other variables can be obtained by means of parametric equations. In this manner, design modifications and creation of a family of parts can be performed in remarkably quick time compared with the redrawing required by traditional CAD.'

www.designcommunity.com/discussion/25136.html

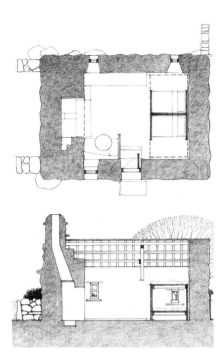

In this cottage, called Llainfadyn, the purpose of the structure of the building is to organise a portion of space, identifying it as a place for dwelling. Structure and space are in symbiosis – a mutually affective relationship. (This small slate-worker's cottage from north Wales is analysed as one of the Case Studies *at the end of this book.)*

Themes in Spatial Organisation 1
SPACE AND STRUCTURE

'After a time, he draws the buggy up to the skeleton of the new cottage. Olympia can see that it will have a stunning view, with only the Atlantic for a front yard…. Most of the cottage has been framed, and there are many places through which one can see the ocean. Olympia begins to imagine fancifully what it would be like to enclose such a house entirely in windows – to have light always, to feel surrounded by sand and ocean…. Together they enter the cottage and move through the rooms that for now exist only in the imagination, rectangular and oblong chambers framed in pine and oak, forming a house that will one day shelter a family. She wonders how such a structure might be built, how one knows precisely where to put a post or a beam, how exactly to make a window. From time to time Haskell murmurs beside her, "this will be the kitchen", or "this will be the sun parlour", but she does not attend him closely. She prefers, for the moment, to think of the house as ephemeral and insubstantial.'

Anita Shreve – *Fortune's Rocks*, 1999, p. 166.

Themes in Spatial Organisation 1
SPACE AND STRUCTURE

Both structure and space are media of architecture. It is by its structure that a building stands. Structure also plays a part in organising space into places. The relationship between space and structure is not always simple and straightforward; it is open to different approaches. One can either choose and allow a structural strategy to define the places one wishes to create, or one can decide on places and force the physical structure of a building to cope with them.

There are thus three broad categories of relationship between space and structure: the dominant structural order; the dominant spatial order; and the harmonic relationship between the two, in which spatial and structural order seem in agreement. In the history of architecture there have been champions of all three relationships, as evident in the examples below.

There have also been protagonists of a fourth category of relationship, in which spatial organisation is said to be separated from structural so that they may co-exist, each obeying its own logic free of the constraints associated with the other.

As we have seen in the chapter on *Geometries of Being*, in regard to the 'geometry of making', structure tends to its own geometries. In the sections of that chapter on 'social geometry' we have seen that objects and people, individually and in groups, can also evoke their own geometries too. In architecture (discounting any imposition of 'ideal geometry') there are vital relationships between these geometries of being. Sometimes they are in tension; sometimes they can be resolved into harmony; sometimes they can be overlaid but conceptually remain separate.

An extra complication is that once a structural strategy is established it can influence (not merely respond to) spatial organisation. The physical structural order of a building can influence the spatial organisation of the life it accommodates.

An important aspect of the art of architecture is to choose a structural strategy that will be in some sort of accord with the intended spatial organisation.

Theatric places in ancient Greece

The way ancient Greek architects evolved indoor theatric places is a good illustration of how spatial organisation can conflict with structural and how such conflict can be resolved by compromises of different types in both. The classic Greek theatre was a geometric formalisation of the social geometry of people sitting on the slopes of a hill watching a performance. Its three-dimensional form was a fusion of social geometry, ideal geometry and the

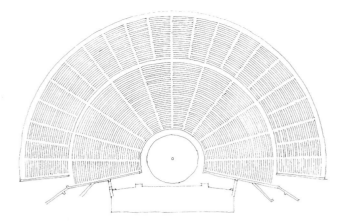

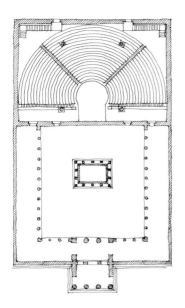

lie of the land. With no roof it did not have to take account of the geometry of structure. In some cases however Greeks wished to create an inside place where lots of people could watch something. This meant having to take account of the geometry of the structure that would hold up the roof. The structures that the Greeks used tended to create spaces that were rectangular in plan; and they could not achieve large spans. Both these characteristics conflicted with the shape of a theatre in the landscape, which was circular and wanted an uninterrupted large space.

In some instances the Greeks' solution was merely to put the 'round peg' into the 'square hole', as in the council chamber at Miletus (top right). Here the circular theatre is enclosed in a quadrilateral cell, leaving corner spaces unused except for stairs back down to ground level. The columns needed as intermediate supports for the roof have been kept to a minimum; the two at the front are to some extent used to help frame the focal space of the chamber but the other two are awkwardly intrusive. A minor concession to the geometry of the seating is made in the way the column bases take their alignment from the seats rather than from the orthogonal geometry of the structure. Almost exactly the same relationship between spatial and structural organisation, but on a smaller scale, is found in the 'new' (late fifth century BC) council chamber built in Athens (middle right). Presumably the two pairs of columns together with the external walls supported principal structural beams along the lines shown in the plan, which then divided the long dimension of the roof into three smaller, manageable, spans.

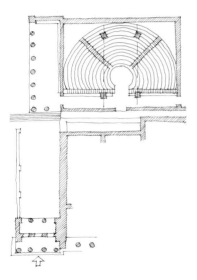

In other examples the shape of the seating is made to fit the rectangular geometry determined by the structure. In the *ecclesiasterion* at Priene (bottom right) the seating has been mutated to the closest rectangular equivalent of the segmental theatre. There is compromise in the structure too, in that the intermediate supports – the columns introduced into the space to reduce the spans of the roof timbers – are not positioned at the 'third points', where they would divide the width of the hall into three equal spans, but have been placed much nearer to the outside walls so that they do not obstruct views from the seats. These neatly identify the stepped side aisles by which members of the audience would reach their seats.

In early buildings with large roofed spaces columns were indispensable. At the top of the next page is the plan of an ancient Egyptian hypostyle hall, from the temple of Ammon at Karnak (late fourteenth century BC). Whatever the space was for, use had to contend with the forest of huge columns, the smaller of which had a diameter of more than three

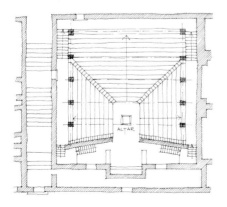

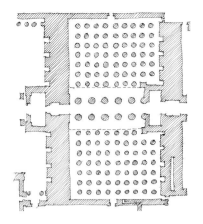 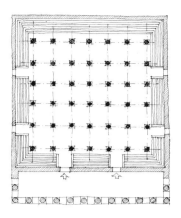

The telesterion *at Eleusis was a hall for performing the 'Mysteries'. Part of the mystery would have been that for the spectators seated around the walls, much of the performance would have been obscured by the forest of columns.*

metres. The ancient Egyptians may have just been impressed by a space filled with huge columns but the same arrangement would be a problem in spaces for performance. This is the case in the *telesterion* at Eleusis (above right), built in the sixth century BC as a place for the performance of the secret Mysteries. It has seats for spectators around the periphery of a square space. Over the performance area is a regular grid of columns to support the roof. These obstructed everyone's view of what was happening on the floor (presumably increasing the mystery).

The next plan – of the *thersilion* at Megalopolis (fourth century BC, below left) – appears to have a similar profusion of obstructive columns, except that at first sight they seem to be scattered irregularly across the floor. If however one superimposes an interpretation of the grid of the roof structure (below right), you can see that the columns were arranged with a particular spatial intent, one that responds to the lines of sight that radiate from a point of focus under the four columns that do make a square on plan. This appears to have identified the place where a speaker would stand (probably open to the light of the sky). The distortion of the grid of columns was a compromise in favour of a spatial arrangement that would allow him to be seen as well as heard.

Through history, many works of architecture have been created under the conviction that structure is the fundamental form-giving force in architecture, and that the geometric order inherent in resolved structure is the most appropriate order for space too. This

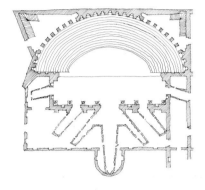

The Renaissance architect Andrea Palladio, wishing to evoke the spirit of the ancient theatres, had to use ingenuity to contrive this oval theatre inside the Teatro Olimpico *(AD 1584) in Vicenza, Italy. In the auditorium the mismatch between the curved seating and the outside walls is masked by an arcade of non-structural columns. (The permanent stage setting includes a sophisticated scene incorporating false perspectives.)*

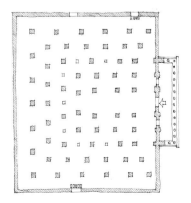 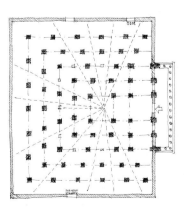

In the ancient thersilion *the structural columns were arranged in a complex pattern for a particular practical reason.*

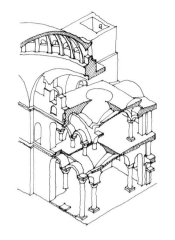

In religious buildings of the past, the structure together with its sophistication and audacity constitute the architecture. Space is structured by the building as an analogy for the way in which the religion structures the lives of its adherents.

conviction possesses symbolic as well as pragmatic power. It was perhaps strongest in the religious architecture of the Romanesque and Gothic periods but it has been the impetus behind many nineteenth- and twentieth-century buildings too, both religious and secular.

In the mosque of Hagia Sophia in Istanbul (right, in section, plan and cutaway axonometric), built as a church in the sixth century AD, the structure *is* the architecture: the spaces it contains are ordered by the pattern of the structure; the places within the building are identified by the structure; the sacred place itself is identified from the outside by the structure of the dome. The whole provides a matrix for worship. (Intriguingly, when the building was converted to a mosque, it was found that the building was not quite aligned with the direction of Mecca, so prayer had to be conducted at a slight angle to the structural geometry, as indicated by the line on the plan.)

This intimate relationship between space and structure is illustrated in medieval churches and cathedrals too. Their places – the sanctuary, chapels, nave etc. – are all identified structurally by resolved stone vaults. The Hagia Sophia and the medieval cathedrals were built in stone but the intimate relationship between structure and spatial organisation they exhibit occurs in structures built of other materials too. The French architect and pioneer in the

section

plan

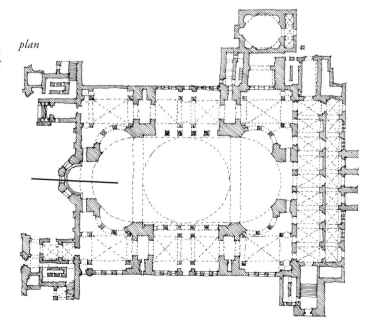

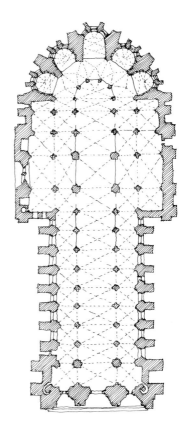

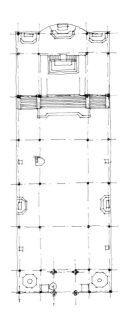

In Rheims Cathedral (left) space is ordered by the structure, the ground plan of which is determined by the 'geometry of making' of the vaults above. In Perret's Notre Dame Le Raincy (right) the space is ordered by the building's reinforced concrete structure. (The drawings are not to the same scale.)

Reference for the work of Auguste Perret: Peter Collins – Concrete, 1959.

use of reinforced concrete, Auguste Perret, translated the structural and spatial clarity of the medieval churches into a structure of concrete. Above (right) is the plan of his church of Notre Dame at Le Raincy, Paris, which was built in 1922. It is a smaller building than Rheims cathedral (thirteenth century, above left), but even so the proportion of the floor area taken up by the structural supports is much less because reinforced concrete is much stronger than stone. The relative distance between the columns in Le Raincy is much greater than in Rheims for the same reason. However, the structural and spatial clarity in both churches is the same. In Perret's church all the places – the position of the main altar, the positions of the secondary altars, the pulpit, the font, and so on – are determined by the spaces defined by the structure.

The space planning requirements of religious buildings are usually fairly simple: the places to be identified can be easily accommodated in the geometric order of structure. But in domestic architecture the relationship between structural order and spatial organisation can be more fraught. The relationship between space and structure in a simple single-cell house is straightforward; all the places to be accommodated are under the shelter of the roof and within the enclosure of the walls. There may be some principal roof timbers, like the simple truss in the example on the right, but these are unlikely to influence spatial organisation in the room below. This room is defined by walls that clearly and inseparably perform the dual functions of enclosure and structural support simultaneously.

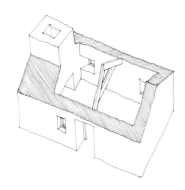

This small cottage has a simple structural order.

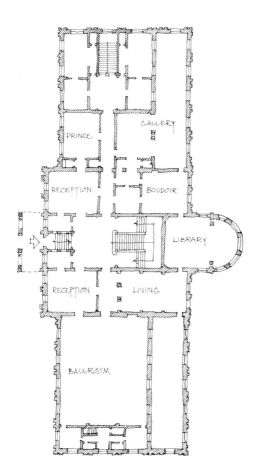

At the other end of the scale of complexity, large houses built of load-bearing wall structures tend to have their spaces organised into many cellular rooms. Probably the heyday for this type of house was during the Victorian era, when many people with newly acquired wealth had large houses built for them. In this plan (right), structural uniformity is compromised by the need for different sized rooms. (Note also how, in its plan, the axial symmetry of the main external elevations relaxes as one moves away from the central axis.)

There are many types of traditional house in which the two functions of enclosure and structural support of the roof are distinguished from each other. In these the roof is supported on a frame of timber, and the spaces are enclosed by non-loadbearing screen walls. These framed buildings may be simple single-cell houses, or they may consist of a number of rooms. In traditional examples the rooms or places within the houses tend to be organised according to the geometric order suggested by the structural frame (below). Here there are small rooms on two storeys set in the two end structural bays, and a larger hall occupying the central two structural bays. Openings too fit into the order of the frame. The walls are filled in with light wattle and daub panels. The plan of this house is a rectangle but timber-frame structures can also have more complex plans.

In a load-bearing wall structure, such as this Victorian house (above), the sizes and shapes of the rooms are conditioned by the ways in which the roof and floors are constructed.

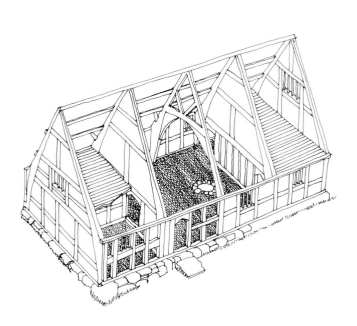

In a timber-frame house (left), the structure determines the spatial organisation.

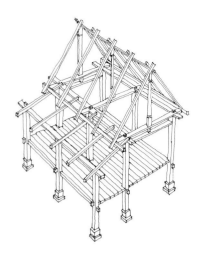

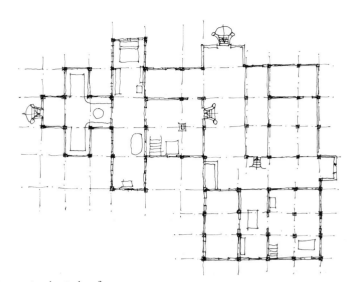

Traditional Malay houses (left and above) are built using a simple timber-frame structure. By processes of addition, they can become quite extensive and comprise many spaces. The places they accommodate tend to be defined by the structural bays, which are sometimes accompanied by changes in level that make platforms.

In the examples given so far, the geometry of structure has suggested that space be organised into rectangles. As we have seen in the section on the 'geometry of making', structure can tend to make circles as well as rectangles. Some houses of all ages have their space organised according to the circular order of a conical roof structure (right).

Some architects, particularly in the twentieth century, have, through their designs for houses, argued that the spaces associated with life are not necessarily rectangular or circular and that dwelling places should not be forced into the geometric plan forms suggested by resolved structures. In Germany during the 1930s, Hans Scharoun designed a number of private houses in which the disposition of places took precedence over the geometric order of structure. Here again (below) is the Mohrmann House, which stands in a southern suburb of Berlin. There are places: for sitting by the fire looking out through a glazed wall into the garden; for playing the piano; for eating; for growing decorative plants. The disposition of these takes priority over the structural organisation of the house. At the same time, Hitler's Third Reich was building ceremonial architecture in

In this traditional Malay house, spaces are defined by the rectangular grid of the timber-frame structure.

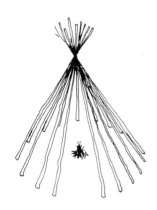

The structure of a native American teepee has an innate conical geometry, producing a circular plan. The geometry of making seems in accord with the social geometry of people sitting around the fire.

Reference for Malay houses:
Lim Jee Yuan – *The Malay House*, (Malaysia) 1987.

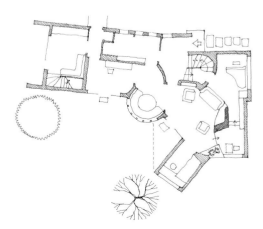

179

Reference for Casa Romanelli:
(Masieri) – *Architectural Review*, August 1983,
p. 64.

Reference for house on Long Island:
F.R.S. Yorke – *The Modern House*, (6th edition)
1948, p. 218.

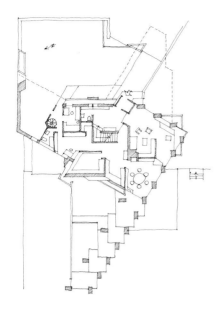

Masieri's design for the Casa Romanelli imposes a complex geometry on the spaces of the house (above).

the grand neoclassical style. Scharoun's approach to planning his houses was born partly of a conscious aversion to the controlling discipline of Fascism and its insistent conviction that the will must triumph.

This house on the right also has a complex plan. It is the Casa Romanelli, designed by the Italian architect Angelo Masieri and executed by Carlo Scarpa in the north Italian town of Udine in 1955. Though, as in the Scharoun plan, the geometry of this house is complex, its spatial organisation is more a result of the overlay of different geometries to create complexity. The disposition of places does not direct the design; rather, accommodation is found for them amongst the walls and columns. Though the structural pattern is complex, it leads while the spatial organisation follows.

Some architects have tried to separate structural order from spatial organisation and place-making. Below is a small house on Long Island, New York, designed by the architects Kocher and Frey and built in 1935. All its accommodation is on the first floor, which stands some two-and-a-half metres above the ground on six columns and is reached by a spiral stair; on top is a roof terrace. Below left is a plan of the structural layout of the main living floor. Although the living place is defined by the extent of the platform, the structure of six columns positioned regularly across the plan makes no suggestion of how the floor should be laid out to make places. The drawing alongside shows how it was laid out; the walls are not load bearing. The movable screens, which give the bed space some privacy, are wrapped around, not another column, but the water downpipe.

The Kocher and Frey house is an example that follows the principle set by Le Corbusier some twenty years earlier in the Dom-Ino idea (right). He suggested that the planning of

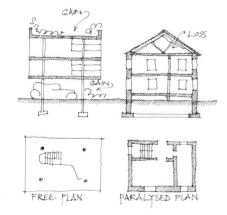

Above is one of Le Corbusier's diagrams arguing the benefits of the Dom-Ino idea in the architecture of house design (below).

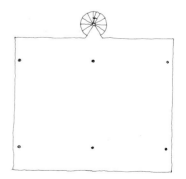

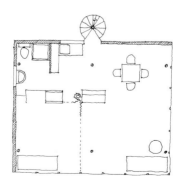

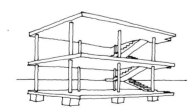

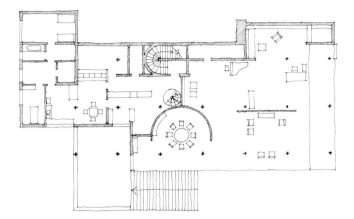

In Mies's plan for the Tugendhat House (left), the partitions stand separate from the structural grid; but the columns help to define places for sitting, dining, studying.

buildings could be freed of the restrictions of structural geometry by the use of columns supporting horizontal platforms. Le Corbusier designed a number of houses using the Dom-Ino idea. Mies van der Rohe also experimented with detaching spatial organisation from structural order. Both however tended to allow structure a part in place identification. Both experimented with space between horizontal planes. To the right are the ground floor plan and structural diagram of the Villa Savoye at Poissy, near Paris, built in 1929. Clearly, as in the *thersilion* at Megalopolis, the structural grid has been distorted. Although the structure does not *determine* places within the plan, Le Corbusier does use it to help in the identification of places. For example: where the columns define the space occupied by the central ramp; where a column picks up the corner of the stair; and where two columns frame the main entrance. There is also a small table and a hand basin attached to a column under the ramp.

In the Tugendhat House at Brno (1931, above), Mies van der Rohe preserved the geometric order of the structural grid of cruciform columns, but he too used the columns to help identify places: two of the columns, together with the curved screen wall, frame the dining area; two others help define the living area; and another column suggests the boundary of the study area at the top right on the plan.

In the Barcelona Pavilion (1929, below), however, Mies van der Rohe was almost totally free of the need to identify places for particular purposes. He managed to create a building in which space is liberated, almost completely, from the discipline of structure, and channelled only by solid, translucent and transparent walls.

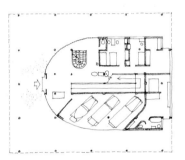

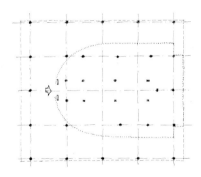

In the Villa Savoye (above), Le Corbusier amended the structural grid to suit the spatial layout.

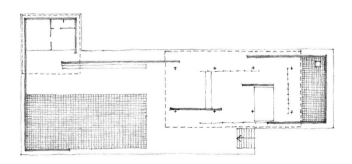

The Barcelona Pavilion (left) is a poetic example of the potential of separating structural order from spatial organisation.

The space of a wood, like that of a cave, is free of the discipline of structural order.

Excavated, folded, warped, amoebic space

The space of a cave is largely free from the discipline of structure too. Excavated from solid matter, which retains its stability through its integrity, the space of a cave is amorphous, neither submissive to nor ignoring the order suggested by constructed structure. Troglodytes, who live in caves in rock that is soft enough, can make new rooms for themselves by scraping the rock away. The space they 'win' need not obey the regulation of the geometry of making, though often it accords with other geometries of being. As long as they have a reasonably level floor to stand on, and enough ceiling height to be able to walk around, the occupants can make spaces any shape they wish.

Space itself can be thought of as a material to be excavated. This small African village (below), comprising a dozen or so houses, each with its own small courtyard, grew by a process of gathering space into rooms by the erection of mud walls. The arrangement of these walls, partly because their material would not be strong enough to support a roof, did not have to follow the discipline of structural order, and so the shapes of the rooms are irregular and free. The roofs of the rooms have their own separate structure of posts, positioned just inside the mud walls. These posts are shown as dots on the plan.

Some architects in the twentieth century have experimented with this notion of space in their designs. One of the most celebrated examples of this is the chapel of Notre Dame

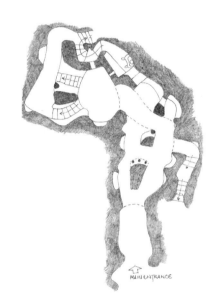

Subterranean architecture does not need to obey the geometry of making. Spaces may be carved out of the rock in any direction, so long as the roof does not collapse. Above is the plan of a grotto at Talacre Abbey in north Wales. (From a survey by William Twigg.)

The plan of this African village (left) illustrates a separation of walls and structure. The mud walls define spaces whilst the timber columns support the roofs.

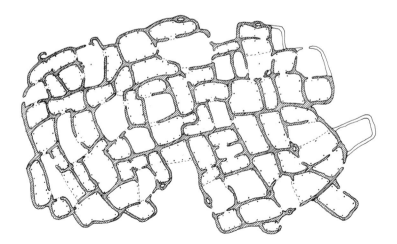

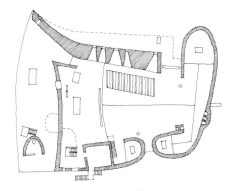

Such modification of structure's relationship with space for aesthetic and poetic reasons has a long and distinguished history. St Paul's in London is a celebrated case (below). The single-hatched parts of this section were added to improve the external composition of the building. Victorian searchers after architectural 'truth' vilified its architect Christopher Wren for this 'deception'.

en Haut at Ronchamp, France, designed by Le Corbusier in the 1950s (above). For poetic reasons it seems Le Corbusier wished to allude to the prehistoric origins of religion by making the interior of the chapel like a cave (or at least like an artificial cave – a dolmen burial chamber). He did this partly by having an irregular floor, an overbearing roof (like the capstone of a dolmen), and by making it appear that all openings (doors and windows) are like crevices in, or perforations of, thick rock. He also did it by rejecting the ordering of space suggested by structural discipline. Just as the structural integrity of a cave is not evident in its form or the shape of its space, so the plan of the Ronchamp chapel does not indicate the way its roof is supported: its necessary structure is concealed within the walls. Far from such irregularity being a manifestation of the 'cottage' attitude, it is an assertion, in the interests of poetic expression, of the transcendence of architecture over the dictates of gravity, material and structural order. It is born of heroic intent rather than submissive response.

Such heroic transcendence of the geometry of physical structure informs buildings such as Frank Gehry's Guggenheim Museum (right) in Bilbao, Spain, too. In this building most of the interior spaces are the non-orthogonal reciprocals of the building's exuberantly non-geometric sculptural form.

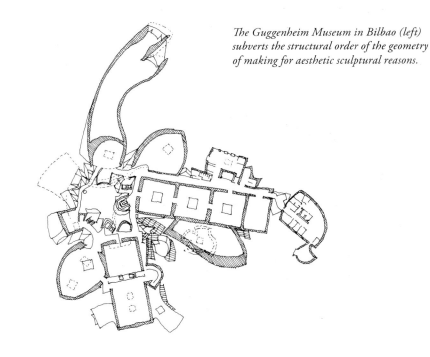

The Guggenheim Museum in Bilbao (left) subverts the structural order of the geometry of making for aesthetic sculptural reasons.

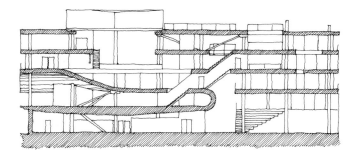

In their design for the VPRO office building, architects MVRDV try to 'warp' space by bending floor planes back on themselves (left).

Relaxing adherence to forms and orders suggested by structure and the geometry of making may be exploited for dramatic aesthetic effect – in the sculptural form of buildings and the intricacy of spatial experience – or to experiment with ideas that challenge orthodox notions of the relationships between space and structure.

In the VPRO office building in The Netherlands (1999, above), MVRDV architects have explored the idea that space may be 'warped' or 'folded' by the moulding of ceilings that become floors, and floors that distort the convention that they should be horizontal.

And in this cinema in Dresden (below) architects Coop Himmelb(l)au have exaggerated the distortion of orthogonal and structural geometry in ways that undermine trust in the reliability of one's own six-directions-plus-centre.

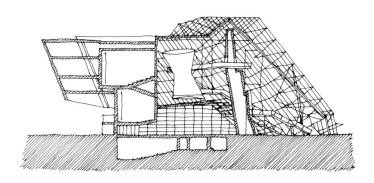

These lavatories in Japan (above), designed by Shuhei Endo, are accommodated within the twists of corrugated metal sheeting.

Reference for lavatories in Japan:
(Endo) – *Architectural Review*, December 2000, p. 44.

Control of complexity is made possible by the calculating power of computers that can cope with complex irregular three-dimensional forms and provide the information needed for their construction. Computers can also be used to generate complex forms formulaically, as in the work of architects such as Greg Lynn, and to create virtual architectures that exist only within their cybernetic space, which therefore need take no account of gravity or material characteristics. In 1999–2000 architects Asymtote produced the Virtual Guggenheim Museum, the internal (virtual) spaces of which (existing only inside the computer) were subject to none of the usual constraints presented by the conditions of the physical world. The shapes of these 'spaces' can also change in the same way an amoeba can change its form:

> http://www.guggenheim.org/exhibitions/virtual/virtual_museum.html

Reference for the MVRDV building in Hilversum, The Netherlands:
Architectural Review, March 1999, pp. 38-44.

Reference for the Coop Himmelb(l)au cinema in Dresden:
Architectural Review, July 1998, pp. 54-8

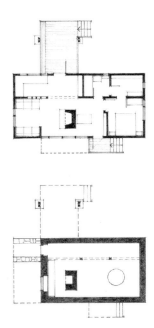

In many buildings, space is organised using parallel walls. It is easy to put a roof on parallel walls. They also resonate with our four horizontal directions.

Themes in Spatial Organisation 2
PARALLEL WALLS

Themes in Spatial Organisation 2
PARALLEL WALLS

One of the simplest, oldest and yet most enduring of architectural strategies is based on two straight parallel walls. This strategy is found in prehistoric architecture and continues to be useful. Architects have explored its possibilities right into the twenty-first century, developing variants and hybrids. It is unlikely that its potential has yet been exhausted. The obvious attraction of this most uncomplicated arrangement is its structural simplicity – it is easier to span a roof between two parallel walls than any other form. But although it is simple, the strategy of using parallel walls is not without its subtleties. As with many ancient forms of architecture these subtleties may have aroused a sense of wonder in the minds of those who first used them, a wonder we have lost only through familiarity. The causes of that wonder are still available for rediscovery and use in design.

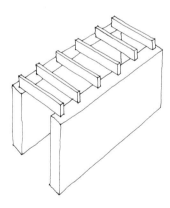

In the chapter on *Geometries of Being*, and in particular the section on the 'six-directions-plus-centre', it was said that terrestrial architecture relates, in some way or another, to the earth, the sky, the four horizontal directions and the idea of centre. The strategy of parallel walls relates particularly to the four horizontal directions. Its power lies in its control over these directions, in definite ways that can be used to create a sense of security, direction and focus. Protection is provided by the roof that shelters the 'inside' from the rain or the sun, but also by the side walls, which limit the directions of approach to two – 'front' and 'back' – or, with the addition of a non-structural rear wall, to one – 'front' – making this simple building like a cave. The sense of direction, or dynamic, is

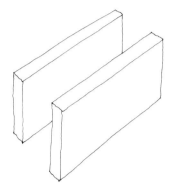

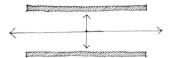 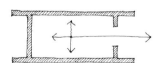

created by the long shape of the space between the walls. The line of direction can run either way, straight through between the walls, or culminate within the building, terminated by a back wall (below right). These characteristics of the parallel wall strategy are to be found in some of the most ancient buildings on earth. In the nineteenth century the archaeologist Heinrich

Parallel walls define a space that is simple to roof (above).

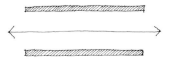 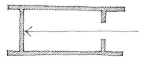

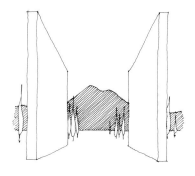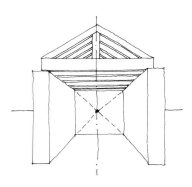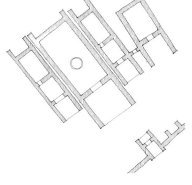

Schliemann discovered a city thought to be the ancient city of Troy, made famous by the stories of Homer. Some of the houses he found there were based on the simple form of two parallel walls (above right). The gateway, or propylon, was formed of two parallel walls too, extending the experience of transition from outside the city wall to inside. Although the houses of Troy would have had focuses in their hearths, they do not appear to have taken advantage of the focusing power of parallel walls. This comes about by combination of the line of direction, the convergence of perspective lines and the frame created by the walls with the roof above and the ground below. Vincent Scully, in his book *The Earth, the Temple, and the Gods*, suggested that the ancient Greeks used the sense of direction and focus created by parallel walls to relate their buildings to sacred sites on the peaks of distant mountains.

The evolution of ancient dolmens (below) shows the discovery of parallel walls as a structural and a spatial strategy. Some early examples are without regular form (below left); balancing a huge capstone on the tips of a few standing stones seems to have been achievement enough in itself. Later examples illustrate experiment with regular orthogonal layouts (below middle) with parallel walls. It seems a particularly human development from the amorphous cave, born of structural order (the geometry of making) and producing architectural effects that add to the ways places can be identified. The parallel wall strategy

The plan of each of these Trojan houses seems to have begun in the mind of their architect as a pair of parallel walls; this is evident in the way the back and entrance walls are set in from the ends of the side walls. The largest of the houses seems to have been the most formal, with a single room that has a hearth. The other smaller houses have two rooms, made by cross walls. Notice that the doorway into the back room in each case is off the axis of the house to increase its privacy. These back rooms were probably sleeping rooms. Notice also that the architects of these houses did not see the possibility of using one side wall to serve two houses. Except in one instance, where the gap is large enough to use the space as a pathway (with its own entrance), there is unusable dead space between the houses.

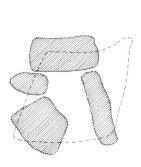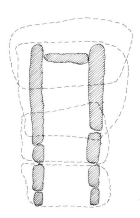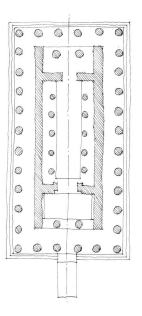

also underlies the architecture of: the Greek temple (right), from which the axis set up by the parallel walls strikes out into the landscape; the Romanesque basilica (top of opposite page), in which the perspective of the walls focuses the axis on an altar at the sanctuary end; and the Gothic church (bottom left of opposite page), which identifies the place of the

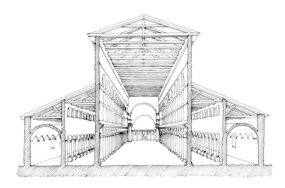

altar in a similar way but with a more sophisticated vaulted and buttressed roof structure. Through the developing sophistication of the basic parallel-wall strategy, with the addition of columns externally and internally (making peristyles, or naves and aisles), and later the insertion of windows for letting in light and buttresses for strengthening, one can see that the grand Christian Gothic cathedral is a direct descendent of the pagan religious and domestic buildings of prehistory and of the houses and temples of the ancient Greek and Roman world.

In the twentieth century, architects have experimented with parallel walls as a basis for spatial organisation in ways that sometimes transcend the pragmatic. Their interest has been in what parallel walls can do as basic architectural elements. Some have challenged the orthodox ways parallel walls are used. The next three examples are all churches. In the first, the architect uses parallel walls in an elemental but still traditional way. In the other two, variations are explored, in both cases for poetic spatial reasons. When Michael Scott designed a new church at Knockanure in Ireland in the 1960s (below right) he reduced the parallel-wall strategy to its most basic form: two walls, spanned by a beamed roof, with the altar and cross at the implied focus. A wall inside the entrance screens the central axis.

The parallel wall strategy underlies the basic spatial organisation of the ancient Greek temple, the early Christian basilica (above) and the Gothic cathedral (below left).

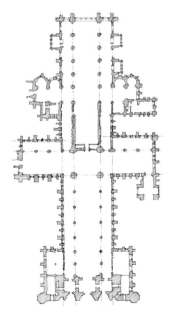

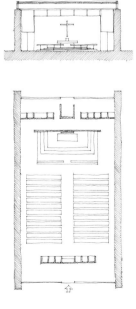

The use and development of the parallel wall strategy can be traced through thousands of years of architecture (far to near left) from the ancient burial chamber or dolmen, through the Greek temple and Gothic cathedral, to the modern church.

Reference for Knockanure church:
(Scott) – *World Architecture 2*, 1965, p. 74.

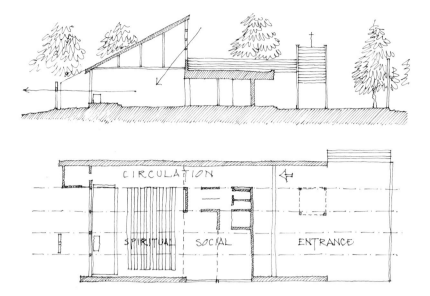

The parallel walls of the Student Chapel at Otaniemi frame the transformation of one's view of nature, from mundane to sacred.

Reference for Finnish churches:
Egon Tempel – *Finnish Architecture Today,* 1968.

In the Student Chapel at the University of Otaniemi near Helsinki in Finland (above), two parallel walls are used to channel a progression from a secular to a spiritual view of nature. The chapel was designed by Kaija and Hiekki Siren and built in 1956–7 on a low hill amongst pine and birch trees. The special place of the church in the woods is identified by the two flank walls, and the implied movement through the building is from right to left on the plan and section. Progress through the church is controlled by cross walls. The plan defines five zones along this route. The first of these is the world through which one approaches the church. The second is the courtyard, entered from the side and partially enclosed by walls and screens of basket work woven from twigs. Inside the courtyard there is a bell tower, which acts like a marker. From the courtyard one passes through to the chapel itself, which is the fourth zone, past the third, which is a club-room and overspill space for the chapel. The fifth zone, into which one cannot progress, is the transformed nature one sees through the totally glazed end wall of the chapel. The focal cross stands outside the building amongst the trees. The 'nib' housing the vestry helps to separate the nature through which one approached the chapel from the nature one sees from one's pew – the setting of the cross.

A number of Scandinavian architects in the late 1950s seem to have experimented with the parallel wall strategy. The next example is a cemetery chapel at Kemi (right, also in Finland) designed by Osmo Sipari and built in 1960. Here the two parallel walls are triangular in section, and the ceremonial axis of the cross and catafalque has been turned through 90 degrees to run across rather than with the longitudinal grain of the parallel walls. The entrance too, which relates to the cross, is in one of the walls rather than through one of the open ends of the parallel wall plan. There are two other significant walls in the plan: a third parallel wall that runs from within the chapel out into the garden; and one at right-angles to the parallel walls, which connects the gate into the cemetery grounds to the main door of the chapel.

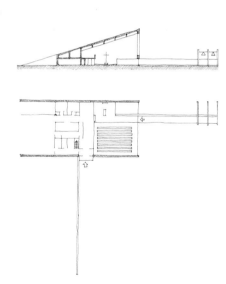

This cemetery chapel (above) was designed by Osmo Sipari. Its place is defined by two parallel walls, in this case at right angles to the ceremonial axis, which is accentuated by a long wall that accompanies the entrance route. Another wall, parallel with and between the two main walls, starts inside the chapel and leads mourners out into the memorial garden.

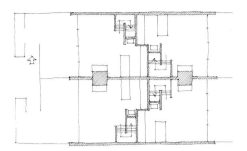

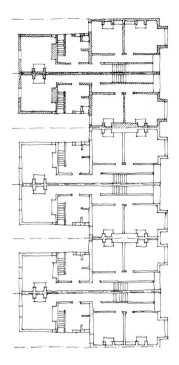

The parallel wall strategy has been used in house design too. Because it allows extended repetition, it is the basis of the terraced house (right), in which the place of each dwelling is identified between two party walls. These party walls, though concealed from view, are the primary elements in the spatial organisation of the row of houses.

Craig Ellwood, an American architect, put two dwellings between each pair of party walls in this group of four courtyard apartments in Hollywood (1952, above). The central wall accommodates the fireplaces. The cross wall is more complex in its layout, making places for the kitchen/dining space and the stairs to the upper floor.

The low-cost house below was designed by Charles Correa for a hot climate. The use of parallel walls means that it can be repeated almost endlessly. The plan incorporates places for the activities of life and has a tiny patio open to the sky. The irregular section allows private upstairs sleeping accommodation, above the cooking and eating areas. Ventilation through all spaces is allowed by the screen walls at the ends of the house, together with openings in the roof.

In these examples of houses using parallel walls, each dwelling unit was accommodated between its own pair of walls. In the next two examples a single house occupies a number of intramural spaces.

The parallel wall strategy is the primary organisational principle of the terraced house.

Reference for terraced houses:
Stefan Muthesius – *The English Terraced House*, 1982.

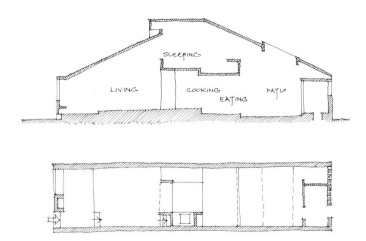

This low-cost house (left) was designed for repetition made possible by adopting the parallel wall strategy.

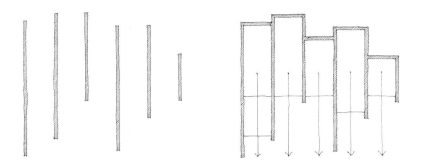

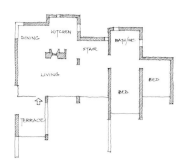

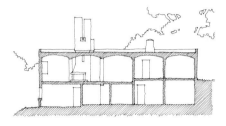

The diagrams and drawings along the top of this and the opposite page illustrate a house in Switzerland designed by Dolf Schnebli built in the early 1960s. The section through the house shows that its structure is composed of five barrel vaults supported on six walls. These walls form the structural order and the basis of the spatial organisation of the house. In the ancient tradition, each of the spaces between the walls is given a single directional emphasis by one end being closed with a cross wall. The other end is visually open but sealed against the weather by a glass wall. The places of the house are disposed within this matrix of parallel walls. Some are accommodated between walls (the bedrooms for example); some stretch across more than one bay of space, necessitating the removal of some portions of the walls from the structural diagram. The hearth is positioned as an additional place identifier, across the structural grain. There is a terrace, also defined by the walls.

The next house also uses more than one bay of space in a parallel-wall plan. It is a summer house on the coast of Attica, Greece, designed by Aris Konstantinidis. In this plan (right) the implied direction runs across the grain of the parallel walls, from top to bottom on the drawing. The house stands on the coast. The three walls are used to create four zones. First there is the approach zone; then the living zone, which accommodates the living room, dining room, kitchen, bedroom and also the car port; then a shaded terrace; and finally the fourth zone, which is open to the sea. In this house a reinforced concrete roof is supported on rough stone piers. The hearth divides the living from the dining places; the roof-pier by the entrance has been turned through ninety degrees to allow access for the car.

The parallel-wall house below was designed by Norman and Wendy Foster with Richard Rogers. The sense of movement from entrance to terrace is with the grain of the walls, which run down a sloping site. Here there are three zones created by the four walls.

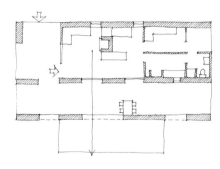

Konstantinidis's design for a summer house (above) is a composition of parallel walls, but with the view to the sea perpendicular to the grain they establish.

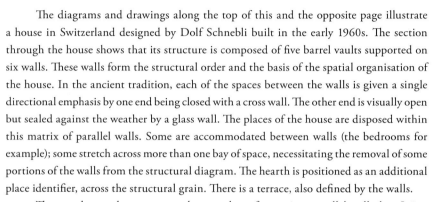

Reference for Lichtenhan house by Dolf Schnebli:
World Architecture 3, 1966, p. 112.

Reference for Greek summer house by Aris Konstantinidis:
World Architecture 2, 1965, p. 128.

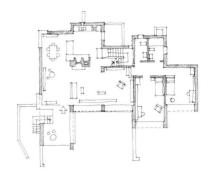

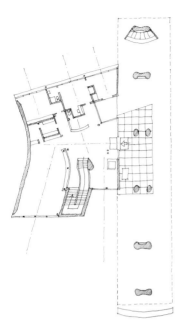

Some architects have experimented with parallel walls that are not straight, or with layouts in which a parallel-wall strategy has been distorted, for particular effect. The drawing on the right is the plan of the ground floor of a student residential building in the City University, which lies in the southern suburbs of Paris. It was designed for Swiss students by Le Corbusier, and built in 1931. It is called the Pavillon Suisse. The rectangle of dotted lines indicates the block of accommodation, which is lifted off the ground on massive columns. This block thus also forms a large 'porch' that protects the entrance into the building. As one goes in there is a reception desk in front and to the right. Behind that there are the private quarters of the director and an office. Past the reception desk is the common room. And to the left there is a lift and the stair that leads up to the student rooms. The plan of this part of the building is not rectangular. Its furthest extent is defined by a convex curved wall; and the stair seems to wriggle its way upwards rather than having a straight flight. At first the plan does not appear to conform to the parallel wall strategy. One can however reinterpret the plan as an orthogonal layout (right, below). This shows that the subtleties of Le Corbusier's plan seem to have derived from distorting a parallel-wall layout. The drawing shows the ground floor of the Pavillon Suisse straightened out. In this version the block of student accommodation forms one of the parallel walls, and the wall at the left of the plan the other. Between them are other walls, framing the stair and the entrance, and dividing the rooms of the director's flat and office. By comparing this straightened version with Le Corbusier's own plan, one can see what he gained by deviating from the parallel grain. This is an example of a subtlety of layout doing more than one thing at once. One effect is that there is more space for the private accommodation. Also the curve of the wall tends to turn the lines of sight of the private accommodation, and of the common room, away from the block of student rooms. In addition the reception desk is turned more towards the entrance, and the stair is given a more sculptural curved form in which lines of passage interact with lines of sight. Finally, Le Corbusier takes advantage of the curve to make a bench seat, along the glass wall of the entrance to the common room, more sociable.

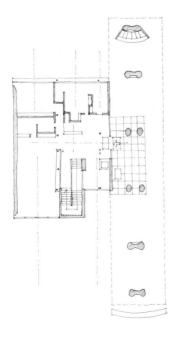

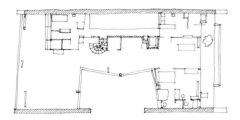

Le Corbusier's interest in manipulating the parallel wall strategy is evident too in the house he designed at 24 Rue Nungesser-et-Coli in Paris (1933, left).

193

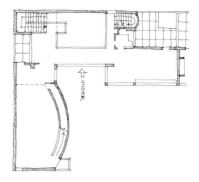

Le Corbusier tried concave as well as convex deviations from the parallel. Earlier than the Pavillon Suisse, in the early 1920s, he designed a house for a Monsieur La Roche. It stands at the end of a *cul de sac* in northwest Paris. On its first floor (above left), supported above the ground on a short wall and three columns, he designed a gallery, in which Monsieur La Roche could display his collection of paintings. This room has one straight wall and one that is, from the inside, concave. Along the curved wall there is a ramp leading up to the next floor. The curve of the wall and ramp make the room more of a place to stop; it lies on a route – a *promenade architecturale* – that begins outside the house and finishes on a roof terrace, passing through the triple-height hallway, up the stairs, into the gallery, up the ramp to the library on the second floor, and out onto the roof terrace. The curved wall plays a part on the outside too; as well as making the building more sculptural it tacitly helps guide visitors to the front door.

In a temporary sculpture pavilion in Sonsbeek Park near Arnhem in the Netherlands, built in 1966, Aldo van Eyck distorted the parallel-wall strategy in another way. Conceptually, he began with six simple parallel walls on a defined area of ground (below left). Built of simple blockwork, they were about 3.5 metres high and 2 metres apart with a flat translucent roof. These walls set up a pattern of movement through the pavilion. He disrupted this plan (below right) with openings and semi-circular niches, to create places for the exhibits, to allow more routes through the pavilion and to open lines of sight across the grain of walls, resulting in a complex frame for sculpture and people looking at it.

Richard MacCormac, in his design for a new library building at Lancaster University, dedicated to John Ruskin, has adapted the parallel-wall strategy by curving the walls together at the ends to exaggerate their effect of enclosure (right). Inside, more parallel

In this plan for a small house at the Bristol building exhibition in 1936, the architects Marcel Breuer and F.R.S. Yorke curved one of a set of parallel walls, in a way similar to Le Corbusier in the Pavillon Suisse (but maybe without the subtlety).

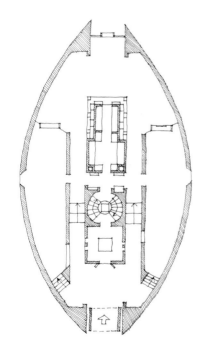

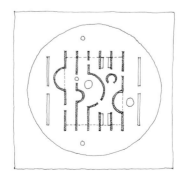

The curved 'parallel' walls of the Ruskin Library (above), by Richard MacCormac, are like a pair of cupped hands protecting their contents.

Reference for the library at Lausanne-Dorigny:
Institut de Théorie et d'Histoire de
L'Architecture – *Matiere d'Art*, 2001, pp. 78-81.

Reference for the Beyeler Art Gallery:
(Piano) – *Architectural Review*, December 1997,
pp. 59-63

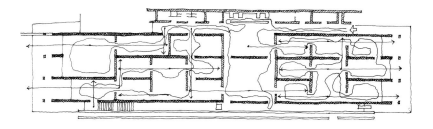

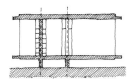

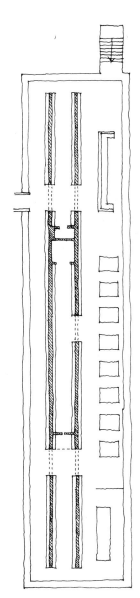

walls form an internal 'temple', protected by the 'hands' of the curved walls, and channel movement through the building.

Two building types are particularly dependent on wall surfaces: the library and the art gallery. This small library at Lausanne-Dorigny, Switzerland, designed by Patrick Devanthéry and Inès Lamunière, and built in 2000 (right), is structurally and spatially dependent on two parallel walls. The floor and roof are cantilevered from them and the inside spaces are organised around the surfaces they provide for the bookstacks.

The Beyeler Art Gallery in Basle, Switzerland, designed by Renzo Piano (1997, above) is also organised around parallel walls. Four walls, supporting a translucent roof, form the core of the gallery, with subsidiary walls helping to organise the secondary spaces. The spaces between the principal parallel walls are divided into galleries by cross walls. Openings in the walls are not spaced regularly but create a labyrinthine route by which visitors can explore the exhibition. (The routes people take are like lines of melody on the framework of a music stave. This is a good example of how an interplay with regular geometry, mentioned in the chapter on *Ideal Geometry*, may be provided by people rather than within the work itself.) The openings in the walls also frame views through from one space to another and from inside to the landscape outside. This form is consciously reminiscent of that of the ancient Greek temple. Piano has even added the columns detached from the ends of the principal walls.

The architectural possibilities of parallel walls are far from exhausted. Architects seem able to find endless variations on this basically simple theme. The internal spaces of the Myyrmäki Church in Finland (below, designed by Juha Leiviska, 1984) occupy a 'forest' of parallel walls arranged informally alongside a railway embankment in the town of Vantaa.

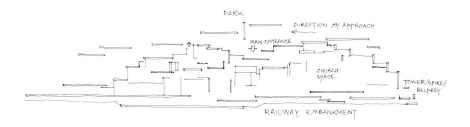

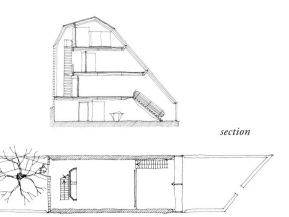

section

plan

Future Systems architect Jan Kaplicky has designed a small house in Islington, London (1994, above right) on the basis of two parallel walls. The stepped section of the house is partly heated by sunshine coming through the south-facing sloping glass wall.

The Swiss architect Peter Zumthor is interested in using materials and putting them together in fresh ways. His design for the Swiss Pavilion at the Hanover Expo in 2000 (below) is an intricate composition of parallel walls of stacked timber (which could be re-used after the exposition). With these he created a maze, which he wanted to be a resonator of sounds and smells. Music performances were held in the small 'clearings' amongst the stacks of wood.

Jan Kaplicky's house in Islington uses the parallel-wall strategy in plan. Variation comes in the section, which has one large, sloping, south-facing glass wall, to catch warming sunshine.

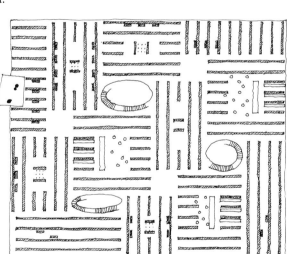

The Swiss Pavilion at the Hanover Expo (left), designed by Peter Zumthor, was a maze composed of parallel stacks of timber arranged in two directions. It was as if space had been woven like threads in fabric, with 'knots' at the various meeting places.

The parallel wall strategy is a sensible and economical way to organise space. Sometimes architects deviate from it seemingly for no better reason than to be different. Often however it provides the foundation for subtlety and variation. The Mothers House in Amsterdam, designed by Aldo van Eyck (1980) is a case in point. The plan is illustrated, from one of the pages from my notebooks, in an earlier chapter – *How Analysis Helps Design* (see p. 16). You can see from the drawing that the accommodation at the rear of the building is divided into five small flats. These are defined by parallel walls, but van Eyck subtly varies each of these party walls to give every flat its own particular spatial identity.

Reference for the Swiss Pavilion by Zumthor: Institut de Théorie et d'Histoire de L'Architecture – *Matiere d'Art*, 2001, p. 120.

Reference for the Islington house by Kaplicky: Progressive Architecture, July 1995, p. 31.

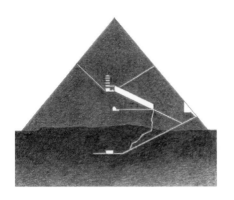

Architecture has always been about levels in relation to the ground and the sky. 'Up' and 'down' have connotations that are symbolic, poetic and emotional. The experience of being high, on top, above is different from being low, underground, beneath. And both are different from being on the ground.

Themes in Spatial Organisation 3
STRATIFICATION

'Verticality is ensured by the polarity
of cellar and attic… it is possible… to
oppose the rationality of the roof to the
irrationality of the cellar. A roof tells its
raison d'être right away: it gives
mankind shelter from the rain and
sun…. We "understand" the slant of a
roof…. Up near the roof all our thoughts
are clear. In the attic it is a pleasure
to see the bare rafters of the strong
framework. Here we participate in the
carpenter's solid geometry.
As for the cellar, we shall no doubt find
uses for it…. But it is first and foremost
the dark entity of the house, the one that
partakes of subterranean forces. When
we dream there, we are in harmony
with the irrationality of the depths.'

Gaston Bachelard, translated by Maria
Jolas – 'The House. From Cellar to Garret', in
The Poetics of Space, 1958, pp. 17-18.

Themes in Spatial Organisation 3
STRATIFICATION

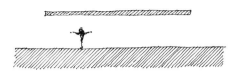

Human architecture would no doubt be different if we could fly freely in three dimensions. Because we walk and are held down by gravity our lives mainly take place on flat surfaces and our architecture is concerned with the planning of floors. With this limitation in movement, human life and architecture tend to deal primarily with the two horizontal dimensions. Architects tend to accept, and sometimes even celebrate, this emphasis by designing buildings in which movement and places are organised between horizontal planes of platform and roof.

The German architect Mies van der Rohe celebrated the horizontal emphasis of human life in many of his projects. Below is the plan of a 'Fifty-by-fifty' (foot) house he designed in 1951 but which was not built. The house is elemental; it consists of a square flat roof over a paved area. The roof is supported in the most minimal way possible on four columns, one in the middle of each side of the square. The walls are completely of glass. All the spaces of the house are contained between these two horizontal planes and the glass walls do not obstruct lines of sight in the horizontal dimensions. It may be said that the Fifty-by-fifty house is a building of one stratum. It controls and organises a particular portion of the land's surface at ground level; it has no changes of level – no pits or platforms; there are no upper floors or cellars excavated out of the earth.

At the top of the next page (left) is the section through a part of a small house designed by the Italian architect Marco Zanuso and built near Lake Como in 1981. It has three strata, each with its own character. Imagine being in each. There is the ground level stratum, which

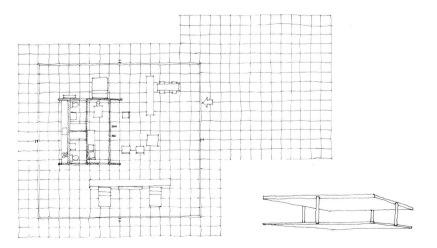

In contrast to Mies's 'Fifty-by-fifty' house, the Marquis of Bute, who was probably the richest man of his generation, had his 'Summer Smoking Room' on the topmost floor of the Clock Tower at Cardiff Castle. Here he was above the mundane world (but could get 'higher' according to the substances he smoked) and could see as far as the docks some few miles away, which were the source of much of his wealth. The alterations that were done to the castle for him during the mid nineteenth century were designed by William Burges. Burges created 'special worlds' at the top of each of the castle's five towers, whilst in the basement is a vaulted cellar. The towers are ladders from the 'depths' to the 'heights'. One is topped by a small cloistered garden open to the sky.

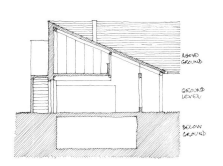

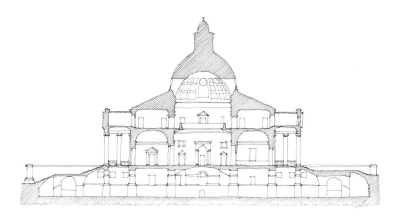

has easy access to the outside; it has a stratum under – a cellar excavated from the earth that has characteristics of darkness and coolness; and a stratum above – a sleeping gallery, which is more private, secluded from the ground floor and with a sloping ceiling because it is directly under the pitched roof. Stratification is more about the differences in experience it provides at the different levels of a building than it is about appearance.

Above right is a grander house (not to the same scale), in Kent; it too has three main strata. This is a section through Mereworth Castle, designed by Colen Campbell and built in 1725. It has a lower level that is partly above ground but has some of the characteristics of a cellar – an undercroft with ceilings vaulted to carry the weight of the floors and walls above; cool and not well lit. The most important level is the one above, with the grandest rooms. This is known as a *piano nobile* – 'noble floor' – which suggests that some sense of nobility was attached to its being above the level of the ground. There is a stratum of rooms above the noble floor but you can see that this layer is penetrated to allow a dome over the space at the centre of the house, which suggests an unattainable stratum above all others. Consider how different it would have been to spend most of your life on the 'noble floor' than as a servant in the undercroft.

Many less grand buildings are stratified in similar ways. Below left is an agricultural laboratory designed by a Swedish architect – Fredrik Blom – in 1837. It has a ground floor with its entrance (and which at the far side becomes a first floor because of a change in ground level); it has a cellar, which seems excavated from the ground and has a structure appropriate to carrying the weight of the building above; it has a middle floor that has its own particular character – separated from the ground but not in the roof, and with what appears to be a

The stratification of Mereworth Castle in Kent is very similar to that of Palladio's Villa Rotonda outside Vicenza, on which it was modelled.

Below middle: the strata of a building can often be seen in its elevation, but their different characters can also be experienced inside the building. The ground floor is accessible from outside; the upper floors are separate from the ground, perhaps more aloof and private; the character of the top-most floor is affected by the geometry of the roof and perhaps by the availability of light from the sky.

Below right: in this part of the library of Uppsala University there is a lecture theatre on the topmost level. In masonry structures it is easier to support large spaces over small ones than vice versa; *the walls or columns of the smaller spaces can support the floor of the large.*

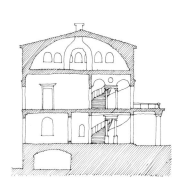

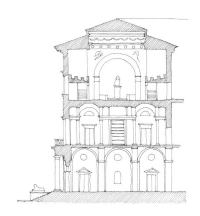

balcony on the roof of the porch; and it has an attic where the shape of the space is affected by the geometry of the roof structure – in this case the triangular section of the roof has been translated into a curved ceiling. There is similar stratification in this farmhouse (above left) designed by Giovanni Simonis. The levels are linked by the sets of stairs, the angle of which seems to relate to the pitch of the roof. Notice too how each floor has a different relationship with outside: the upper-middle floor for example has a protruding balcony which could take you outside at a high level to survey the landscape, while the attic and cellar are much more enclosed, hemmed in by the structure of the building.

Such variations can be used to enhance the poetic experience of a building, as in the house in India shown at the bottom of the page. Entered at a middle level, you look down into a small high courtyard, complete with fish pond and mango tree; but you may also go up to the roof where you are amongst the leaves of the high coconut palms.

In the 1920s Le Corbusier radically re-evaluated the stratification of buildings. In his 'Five points towards a new architecture' (1926) he declared that buildings could have gardens on their roofs and open ground floors, suggesting that by these devices, rather than subtracting ground area from the landscape, buildings would in effect double it (above middle). In place of a closed attic would be a terrace open to the sky; in place of a cellar, a space open for free movement under the house. An unstated, but probably intended, consequence of this was that some Le Corbusier's houses, like those of Palladio three hundred years earlier, have a *piano nobile* (see the Villa Savoye on p. 203). Le Corbusier also experimented with the interrelationships between the levels in buildings. In a small house for a site in Carthage, Greece, designed in the 1930s (top right), he made interlinking single- and double-height spaces. The roof terrace is shaded against the strong Greek sun by an additional roof.

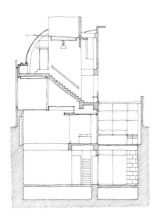

The Gotoh Museum in Japan (above, 1990), by David Chipperfield, has an intricate section that reaches up from deep in the ground to a lightweight roof structure.

Stratification is a central ingredient in the Ramesh House in Trivandrum, India, by Liza Raju Subhadra (below, 2003). Entering at the middle level you may descend to the courtyard shaded by the mango tree or ascend to the roof amongst the palm leaves.

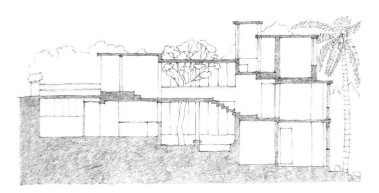

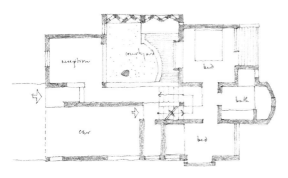

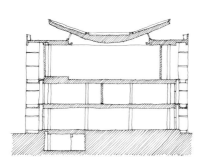

Le Corbusier's section through the Millowners' Association Building (right) takes advantage of the freedom of the uppermost floor.

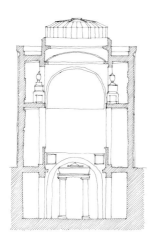

In the *Unités d'Habitation*, some large apartment blocks Le Corbusier designed after World War II, the dwellings interlock with each other across the section of the building and around a central access corridor. The drawing below is through only a small portion of a block (which was designed to accommodate some 1600 people together with community services). You can see that each apartment stretches across the whole width of the building and has a double-height space looking through a balcony out to the surrounding countryside. But each is different because of the interlocking section; one has its smaller rooms upstairs whilst the other has them downstairs.

Le Corbusier also recognised the freedom in the manipulation of space and light that an architect has on the top floor of a building. A lower level is restricted in that its 'roof' is usually also the floor of the level above and the possibilities of allowing light in directly from above are severely limited. On the top floor these restrictions do not apply (the 'above' is no longer hampered by the 'below' of a floor above); there is more opportunity for moulding space in the vertical dimension and using light from above. In the Millowners' Association Building, Ahmedabad (1954, above), Le Corbusier follows the structurally sensible convention that a large space is supported by the walls of smaller spaces below. This also allows the large space – the discussion chamber – to be lit from above, through a convex roof (with the same freedom from the restrictions of floor above as the dome over the central hall of Mereworth Castle).

Associated with the 'temple' attitude to the identification of place (discussed in the chapter *Temples and Cottages*), is the idea of creating levels above the ground – worlds above the mundane. The stage for performance is an example of this, on which actors play imaginary parts in a make-believe drama; so is the *piano nobile*, on which gentry may

By using rooflights and openings in floors, John Soane created spaces where light from the sky could penetrate into the lowest stratum. In some parts thick glass floors allow light to filter down through the levels. This is a section through part of his own house; a place where he kept his large collection of sculpture and architectural fragments.

Reference for John Soane:
John Summerson and others – *John Soane* (Architectural Monographs), 1983.

In this part-section through Le Corbusier's Unités d'Habitation *(below) two apartments overlap. They have double as well as single height spaces. They also enjoy light entering from both sides of the building.*

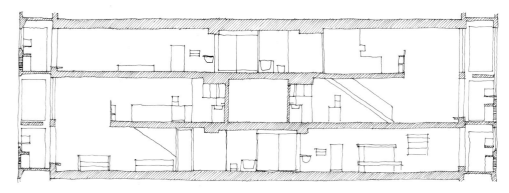

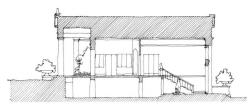

think of themselves as above the *hoi polloi*. At the Schloss Charlottenhof, a villa built in 1827 in the extensive grounds of the Sanssouci Palace at Potsdam (near Berlin, above), Karl Friedrich Schinkel designed a terraced garden raised approximately three metres above the flat landscape around. The garden is at the same level as the main level of the house. The lower levels of the house were for the servants. The ascent to the noble level is by a pair of staircases in the entrance hall. In this way the house is used as an instrument for elevating the inhabitant, and visitors, from the ordinary ground level to a higher plane.

Schloss Charlottenhof (above) has a garden raised above the general level of the park in which it sits. The house itself provides the transition to this higher level.

    In the Villa Savoye (below), Le Corbusier created three main strata: a ground floor accommodating the entrance hall, the servants' quarters and the garage; the first floor with the living and sleeping rooms, and with an open terrace enclosed within the almost square enclosure of walls; and a level above with a solarium for sunbathing. The three levels are linked by a ramp at the core of the house, along which one may climb from the ground to main floor and from there on to the roof. Here too the house is used as an

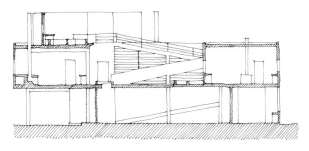

instrument to lift you from the ground level to a higher plane, that of the living spaces and the terrace. But Le Corbusier takes you a step further than Schinkel did at Schloss Charlottenhof. He takes you to a level higher than all the rest, open to the sky.

    The usual stratification seems to be inverted in this house by Robert Venturi (right) which may be interpreted as something of a playful counter to Le Corbusier's precepts for sectional design. In contradiction of Le Corbusier's route through the Villa Savoye, with its culmination under the open sky, the top floor of Venturi's design is made to feel like a cellar with its deeply recessed windows and vaulted ceiling. In contrast to the smooth horizontal floor scape under the Villa Savoye, Venturi gently mocks Le Corbusier by allowing the steeply sloping site to maintain its profile within his house, providing steps that lead out into the woods. The house is entered at mid level, from above, so one may go down to the ground but up to the 'cellar'.

Sometimes the usual stratification can be inverted. In this house by Robert Venturi the attic is vaulted, as if it is supporting weight above, and the lowest floor follows the irregular geometry of the ground. The main entrance is at mid-level, over a bridge.

Reference for Venturi:
Andreas Papadakis and others – *Venturi, Scott Brown and Associates, on Houses and Housing*, 1992.

Reference for Schinkel:
Karl Friedrich Schinkel – *Collection of Architectural Designs*, (in facsimile, 1989).

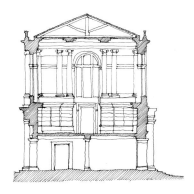

The library of Trinity College in Cambridge (left) was designed by Christopher Wren and built by 1684. Wren followed the precedent of earlier college libraries by putting the library on the first floor, in this case over an open loggia.

Libraries

The library is a building type that in many instances has a particular stratification. Traditionally libraries were built on a floor above ground level: to avoid damp (in days before damp proofing of walls); to increase security for the valuable books; and possibly also because their large spaces could be built over smaller rooms. The Bibliothèque Ste Genevieve in Paris (right, above), designed by Henri Labrouste, and built by 1850, is on the first floor. The library has a steel vaulted ceiling and is supported on columns and the walls of cellular rooms beneath. The library hall itself is reached by passing through the columned ground-floor hall, under the books, to a pair of staircases at the rear of the building where one turns to face the opposite direction and then enter.

In the Bibliothèque Ste Genevieve there is a sense that physically rising to a level above the ground is equivalent also to rising to a higher intellectual level. This was evoked by Gunnar Asplund, the Swedish architect, when he designed the Stockholm City Library (right, below) built in 1927. Here you enter up a staircase that emerges almost in the centre of the circular, and very high, library hall. The hall is lit by a ring of high windows, which create rectangles of sunlight that slowly track across the white walls. The book-stacks are on three tiers around the circumference, each with its own walkway.

To enter the Bibliothèque Ste Genevieve you pass under the library to ascend stairs at the rear of the building.

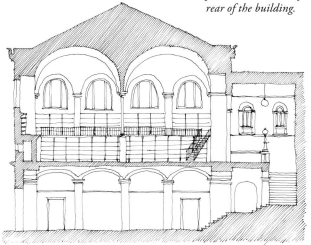

Asplund's Stockholm City Library is entered up a stair that emerges almost at the centre of the circular library hall with its very high ceiling.

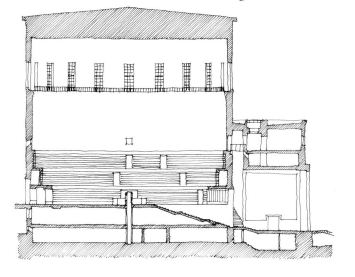

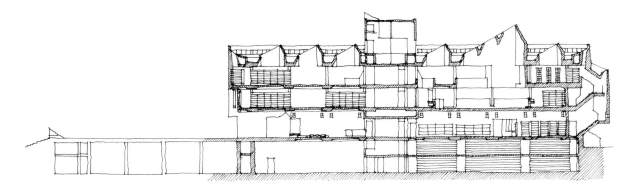

The Cranfield Institute Library is a fairly small university library designed by Norman Foster and built in 1992 (right). It too has book-stacks on the upper floors, with the smaller spaces – a lecture theatre and some seminar rooms – on the ground floor. Similar to Labrouste's library, this is a metal-framed building with vaulted ceilings. Like Asplund's it has a staircase that rises through each floor. The number of columns is doubled on the lower floors to take the extra weight of the books. At the other end of the scale is the Berkeley Library at Trinity College, Dublin (above), where you rise from the entrance into cavernous spaces built from *in situ* reinforced concrete and lit through grand roof lights.

The new National Archive in Paris was built in the early 1990s (below), designed by Stanislaus Fiszer. Its section shows a number of aspects of stratification. It has three principal strata, each of which has two levels. The entrance level has a central atrium with a ramped stair that takes library users up to the higher levels. The offices and administration are also in this stratum. The lowest stratum, below ground, contains storage rooms. The upper floors are large and take advantage of the possibility of being lit through the roof. On various levels Fiszer has used changes in ceiling height to help identify different places, especially to suggest separation between peripheral and central zones (this is done by suspended ceilings that conceal services), but it is only in the top stratum that he has the freedom to vary the sizes of the volumes of space significantly. The reading room, lit by the sloping roof-light, is flanked by two levels that accommodate bookstacks, computers, etc.

The dimensions of stratification can be pragmatic, aesthetic and poetic. They can be dramatic, ludicrous or subtle. A simple building can express the difference between space

The Berkeley Library in Trinity College, Dublin, by Ahrends, Burton and Koralek (1967, above) has its main book stacks and study spaces on the upper floors lit through impressive roof lights.

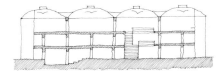

The Cranfield Institute Library has twice as many columns on the lower floors as on the top floor, to carry the heavy load of the books. As in the Bibliotheque Ste Genevieve the top floor has a barrel vaulted roof. Filtered light comes through its ridges. The lecture room is on the lowest floor to take advantage of the possibility of excavating the ground for the raked seating.

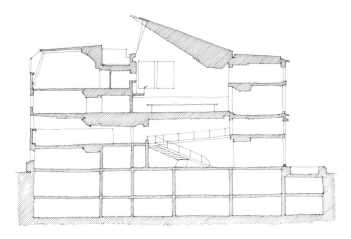

The National Archives building in Paris has three strata, each of two floors. The lowest is below ground, and houses the stores. The middle stratum accommodates the entrance concourse and offices. The reading rooms, bookstacks and computer facilities are in the top stratum where ceilings are free from the constraints of a floor above and light can be admitted from the sky.

205

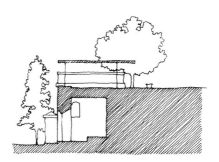

One of the most direct ways in which stratification can be poetically expressive is to set up a dichotomy between heavy and light, between dark and light, between ignorance and awareness, between superstition and enlightenment. This is a small glass pavilion in the French countryside, designed by Dirk van Postel and built, on a stone base that was once the abutment of a bridge, in 2002.

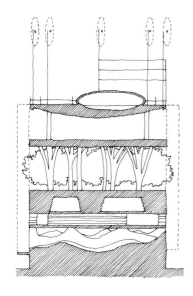

that is embedded in the earth or heavy masonry, and space that is open to the horizon, thereby alluding to the associated poetic ideas of ignorance and knowledge, superstition and enlightenment, earthiness and nobility.

In a few of their designs, the architects MVRDV have used the stratification of buildings in ways that challenge orthodox expectations. In their design for the Dutch Pavilion at Expo 2000 in Hanover, for example, (right) they created a 'layer cake' of different types of landscape into the different floors of the building. There was 'cave' layer, a layer of flowers, a layer of forest… and on the roof, a layer dedicated to the wind.

Stratification can be gentle and subtle too, coming into play at the smallest of scales. In his design for a shelter for some Roman archaeological remains at Chur in Switzerland, Peter Zumthor creates a distinctive entrance (below), constructed as a steel box incorporating steps that do not touch the ground. As you step up they give slightly. Like an air lock, the steel box transports you on to a level that floats just above the remnants of the distant past. Architectural stratification is not just about spatial organisation; it is about the subtle and dramatic orchestration of people's experience of their relationship with the ground, the subterranean world and the sky.

Each floor level of the Dutch Pavilion at Expo 2000 in Hanover had a different spatial character (above). On the ground floor its architects, MVRDV, created the amorphous space of the cave, and on the third floor that of the forest. On the roof, as the culmination of this spectrum of landscapes, are some wind turbines.

In his shelter for Roman archaeological remains at Chur in Switzerland (left), Peter Zumthor uses architectural stratification to make the present float above the past.

Reference for the glass pavilion:
(van Postel) – *Architectural Review,*
September 2002, p. 58.

Reference for the Dutch Pavilion:
(MVRDV) – *Architectural Review,*
September 2000, p. 64.

Reference for the Roman archaelogy shelter:
(Zumthor) – *Architecture and Urbanism,*
February 1998.

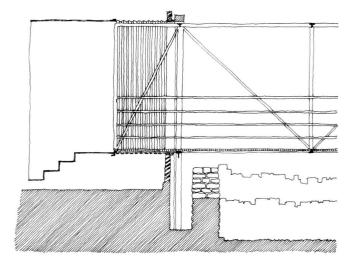

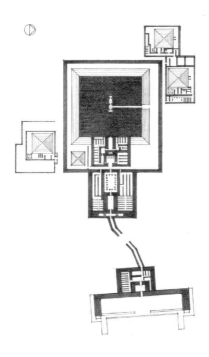

An ancient Egyptian pyramid complex can be interpreted as a transition from life into death. There is a hierarchy of places from the river to the desert. The heart of the complex is the tomb of the pharaoh. The point of symbolic transition is the place where the mortuary temple meets the base of the pyramid.

TRANSITION, HIERARCHY, HEART

*'You began by following a gently winding
path to the left of which there rose up, very
gradually, with an extreme nonchalance even,
a slight declivity that was oblique to start with
but which slowly approached the vertical. Bit by
bit, as if by chance, without thinking, without
your having any right at any given moment to
declare that you had remarked anything like a
transition, an interruption, a passage, a break
in continuity, the path became stony, that's to
say that at first there was only grass, then there
began to be stones in the middle of the grass,
then there were a few more stones and it became
like a paved, grassy walkway, while on your
left, the slope of the ground began to resemble,
very vaguely, a low wall, then a wall made of
crazy paving. Then there appeared something
like an open-work roof that was practically
indissociable from the vegetation that had
invaded it. In actual fact, it was already too
late to know whether you were indoors or out.
At the end of the path, the paving stones were
set edge to edge and you found yourself in what
is customarily called an entrance-hall, which
opened directly on to a fairly enormous room
that ended in one direction on a terrace graced
by a large swimming pool.'*

Georges Perec, translated by Sturrock – 'Species of
spaces' (1974), in *Species of Spaces and Other Essays*,
1997, pp. 37-8.

Themes in Spatial Organisation 4
TRANSITION, HIERARCHY, HEART

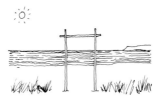

Once some students built a doorway from three pieces of timber on the beach. They were amazed at its powers: to divide one place from another; to frame a view of the place beyond; and to provoke a frisson in those who passed through it. (For further discussion of the powers of doorways see my book Doorway, Routledge, 2007.)

Experiencing products of architecture involves movement. One passes from outside to inside, or through the serial stages of a route. Even in a simple enclosed space it is not possible to look in all directions simultaneously, so one moves around.

One might tend to think of a place as somewhere one stops – a market square, a living room, an operating table. These may be called static places, or perhaps nodes. But the pathway taken to get from one static place to another is a place too. We might call this a dynamic place. Dynamic places play an essential part in the conceptual organisation of space.

Dynamic and static places have characters that derive from the basic and modifying elements by which they are identified. The character of a static place may be affected by that of the dynamic places that lead to it; and the character of a dynamic place might be affected by that of the static place to which it leads. The experience of a corridor that leads to a cell in which there is an electric chair is affected by one's awareness of the place to which it leads. The experience of the burial chamber at the heart of one of the ancient Egyptian pyramids is affected by the nature of the route by which one reaches it – penetrating the mass of the pyramid.

Even in quite mundane examples, transitions form part of the experience of works of architecture. The door of a house is a significant interface between the public and the private realm. Many religious sites have some form of gateway that marks the entrance: the lych gate of an English churchyard; the propylon through which one enters the temenos of

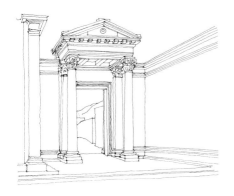

A porch not only marks an entrance, it also identifies a place of transition between outside and inside.

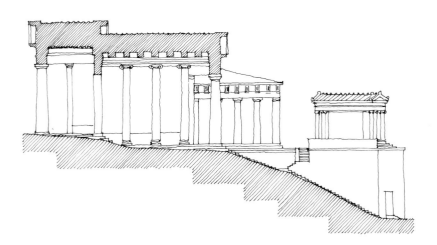

The propylon *is a building through which one must pass to reach the* temenos *(sacred precinct) of a Greek temple. On the left is a section through the propylon on the acropolis in Athens; it stands at the western end of the temenos, marking its entrance (above). It provides the transition from the everyday (lower) world into the sacred (upper) world of the temples.*

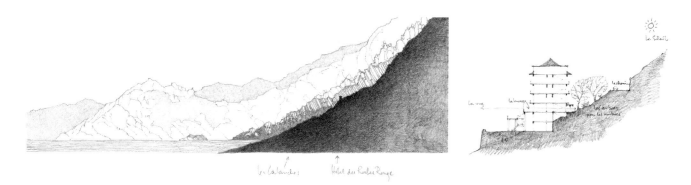

a Greek temple; the gates and forecourt of a Chinese temple. All contribute to the effect that a static place – the hearth of a house, the altar of a temple – is set apart from the rest of the world.

Transition is an essential element in our dramatic experience of the world. Transition places are important in the ways static places relate to each other. They play a part in the relationship between a place and its context.

Often there is a sequence or hierarchy of stages between one static place and another. When entering dwellings, for example, one usually has to pass through a number of different zones of increasing privacy. Sometimes this hierarchy or serial experience of places culminates in a place that is conceptually at the core of the work of architecture – its heart. This is the plan of the palace of Tiryns in Greece (right). It was a hilltop citadel built more than 3000 years ago. If one begins at the top of the drawing one can trace a path through a hierarchy of places leading up to the most important, the king's throne room – the megaron. From the entrance court, itself surrounded with thick walls, one would have passed into a long and narrow passage, through a couple of gateways, and then to a smaller court where there was the first of two formal propylons. Passing through this, one would have entered another courtyard, and then through the second propylon into the innermost

Transition is an important component in the drama of architectural experience. This hotel (above) is on the west coast of Corsica. You approach from the shady side. But entering, and passing through the hotel, you emerge on a terrace with a magnificent panoramic view of the sea, the rocky coast and the sunset.

At the ancient Palace of Tiryns in Greece (below) you have to pass through a number of transitions to reach the megaron at its heart.

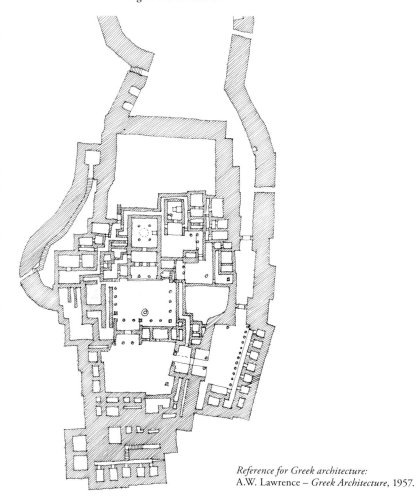

Reference for Greek architecture:
A.W. Lawrence – *Greek Architecture*, 1957.

courtyard, which seems to have been cloistered. Off this courtyard was the megaron itself; but to reach its hearth and the throne one still had to pass through a porch or portico and then an anteroom. This was not the shortest distance from the entrance to the throne – the route is a spiral that changes direction twice during its course. Perhaps the route was made tortuous to lessen the slope of the climb up the hill; but it also made the heart of the palace seem much more deeply embedded in its body and allowed the creation of a number of transitions, each of which could be defended in the event of enemy incursion.

Transitions, hierarchies and hearts can be found in less dramatic works of architecture too. The drawing on the right is the ground floor plan of a house Ernest Gimson designed for himself at the end of the nineteenth century. It was built in the Cotswold village of Sapperton. The main entrance to the house is from the right-hand side of the drawing, from a village lane. The heart of the house may be said to be the hearth in the hall (living room), which is the largest room in the plan. To reach the hearth from the lane one passes first between two bushes (like sentinels), through a gate set in a waist-height wall, into a small entrance court, along a stone path flanked by flower beds, through an arch into the stone porch (there are some steps down into the garden alongside it), through the front door, which is set in a very thick wall (that actually supports a fireplace on the floor above), and into the living room. If the lane is 'public', then the entrance court is 'semi-public'; the porch is 'semi-private' and the living room is 'private'. This sequence of places and transitions creates a hierarchy from the public realm to the privacy of the interior. Each stage in this hierarchy is accounted for in the architecture Gimson gave his house. (One passes through a sequence of places when entering by the back door too: through a wall into a back courtyard, where there is an open-sided shed whose roof is supported by two columns; the back door is tucked under this shed roof.)

At around the same time, Frank Lloyd Wright was designing the Ward Willits House, built in Highland Park, Illinois in 1902 (top). As in the Gimson house, the heart is the hearth that in Wright's design lies right at the core of the plan. In this example the hierarchy of places between the public realm and the private includes the motor car. The route begins in the bottom right-hand corner of the plan. The car drives up to and under the *porte corchère* that projects out from the house over the driveway. Emerging from the car, under the shelter of the roof, one climbs three steps onto a small platform that leads to the front door; passing diagonally across the small hallway one climbs some more steps and then turns sharp left into the main living room. The hearth, in a sort of inglenook, is behind a screen that hides it from the entrance.

The transition from public to private in Wright's Ward Willits House (above) begins at the road, leads up the drive to the porte corchère *(to the right in the plan), up some steps, in through the front door, diagonally across the hall, up some more steps, around the side of a screen, and finally to the fireplace at its core.*

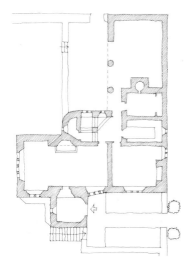

To reach the hearth of Ernest Gimson's house (above) you pass from the public roadway, through a semi-public garden, into a semi-private porch before entering the private realm of the sitting room.

Reference for Gimson's house:
Lawrence Weaver – *Small Country Houses of To-day*, 1912, p. 54.

Reference for Aalto summer house:
Richard Weston – Alvar Aalto, 1995.

Reference for President's Chapel, Brasilia:
Albert Christ-Janer and Mary Mix Foley
– *Modern Church Architecture*, 1962, p. 77.

COURTYARD

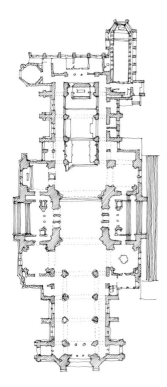

elevation

plan

Transitions and hierarchies of place extend the passage from the public realm to the private. Often, as in the case of the Ward Willits house, an architect avoids the most direct route so that the person approaching and entering a house, or other place of seclusion, can be led through a progressive sequence of experiences.

Transitions also provide a buffer between one place and another, particularly between an inside and the outside. This may have practical benefits, such as when a draught lobby helps to insulate the inside of a building from a cold outside but they may also have a psychological effect too, such as the calming contrast between a busy street and the quiet interior of a church.

In 1953 Alvar Aalto built a summerhouse on the island of Muuratsalo (top left). Its plan is a square enclosed by high walls. The living accommodation is ranged along two sides of the square, leaving a square courtyard. This courtyard creates a transition between the interior of the human dwelling and the nature that surrounds it. The opening in the courtyard sets up a line of sight along the shore of the lake in which the island sits.

Transition, hierarchy and heart do not only apply to the architecture of dwellings. They are used in works of architecture with different purposes. They may be modest and simple, or grand and complex.

Above right is an elevation and a plan of the chapel of the President's Palace in Brasilia, Brazil, designed by Oscar Niemeyer and built in 1958. Its plan is very simple but also subtle. The first basic element of the architecture of the chapel is a flat platform supported on stilts; this defines the circle of place of the chapel. The altar stands on this simple platform, which is approached across a flat bridge. The altar is hidden from view and protected by a white wall that curves around it and rises to a pinnacle surmounted by a cross. This defines the more intimate circle of presence of the altar. The transition from the outside to the inside of the chapel is simple but it includes various stages: crossing the bridge onto the platform; approaching the chapel; and going in, which must be like entering a shell – entry is progressive rather than immediate and the modifying element of light, which also enters through the door, washes progressively more dimly on the curving wall.

The *Opéra* in Paris is a grander example of a transition from the everyday world to that of (in this case) operatic make-believe. It was designed by Charles Garnier and built in 1875. The section has been simplified to show only the major internal spaces. The heart of the *Opéra* is of course the auditorium – the tiers of seating and the stage. The transition

The President's Chapel in Brasilia has a simple but subtle entrance transition (above).

In his plan for Liverpool Cathedral, Sir Giles Gilbert Scott created a hierarchy of spaces between the outside and the sanctuary, designed to set the altar well apart from the everyday world. Like all medieval cathedrals, this building is a manifestation of transition from the secular world to the sacred.

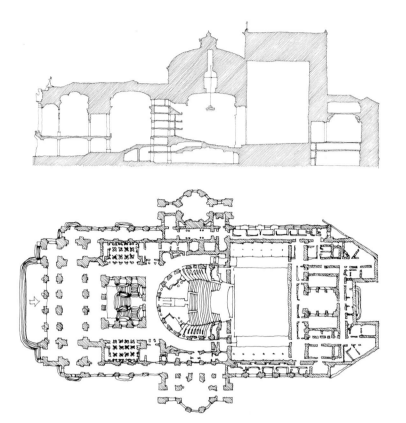

In the Paris Opéra *there are two sequences of transitions from the street to the make-believe world of the stage. One is that taken by the audience, who have a chance, before the performance and during the intervals, to show off their expensive clothes in the large foyers. The other is that taken by the actors/ singers who enter by the stage door and transform themselves in their dressing rooms before emerging on the stage as different characters. The two converge at the magical interface between the auditorium and the stage – the proscenium arch.*

is from the world of the city outside to a place where one is in the presence of the magic, or make-believe, of opera or ballet. The first stage in this transition is the flight of steps at the entrance, which immediately raises one onto a plane above the everyday. The second is the entrance through the thick walls into the first lobby. From here one can see through to the second lobby, where there is the grand staircase. This space is richly ornamented and brightly lit. It is like a stage itself, on which the audience can display themselves in their special clothes before going into the auditorium for the performance. The proscenium arch is the ultimate transition, the one on which the illusion of another world depends.

Transitions in architecture have often been used as metaphors for interfaces between different worlds: between the public and private; between the sacred and secular; between the real and the make-believe; between the world of the living and the world of the dead. Transitions and hierarchies are also used in relation to ceremonies. Ceremonies of initiation or of departure often take place along routes that are identified architecturally. The plan of the pyramid illustrated on the title page of this chapter is effectively a diagram of the ceremonies the body of the dead pharaoh went through before being interred within the pyramid. The barge bearing the body would have moored by the valley temple (at the bottom of the plan) where it would have been prepared and embalmed. It would then (maybe weeks later) have been carried along the long causeway to the mortuary temple at the base of the pyramid where more ceremonies would have been performed. Subsequently it would have been carried around to the northern entrance where it would have been carried through a passageway into the heart of the pyramid.

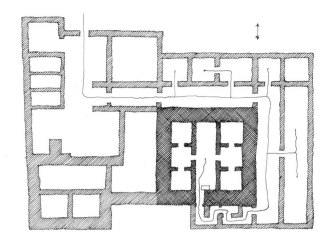

The ancient Necromanteion (left) has a transitional route that wraps around the central sanctuary. The route culminates in a short labyrinth at the entrance to the square building, which was said to be a place where one could meet inhabitants of the Underworld.

'Before I can send you home you have to make a journey of a very different kind, and find your way to the Halls of Hades and Persephone the Dread, to consult the soul of Tiresias, the blind Theban prophet, whose understanding even death has not impaired.'

Homer – *The Odyssey*, c.700 BC

The Necromanteion (above) in western Greece reputedly dates back at least to the time of Homer (see the quotation right). It was a place where people came to talk to the dead. But before they were allowed (by the priests) to meet the departed they had to undergo rituals of preparation (designed to make them more suggestible) that took several days. First they were taken to a series of rooms where they were fed hallucinogenic foods. Then they were ritually bathed. Finally they were taken through a small but disorientating labyrinth (which can be seen on the plan) before being allowed into the sanctuary proper. The thick-walled perfectly square building (aligned, like the pyramids of ancient Egypt, with the cardinal points of the compass) was built over a large vaulted chamber, said to be the home of Hades and Persephone (the Underworld). Remains of mechanisms have been found at the site, which suggest that it was once fitted with machines that could conjure 'ghosts' for the (by the time they reached the sanctuary) confused visitors to consult. Presumably the priests charged large sums of money for facilitating access to the dead. In this building the heart is the square sanctuary but it is protected physically by the sequence of transitions wrapped around it and by the disorientating rituals.

On a related theme, the Danteum (right) was designed in the 1930s for Mussolini by the architect Giuseppe Terragni. It was never built, but intended as a celebration of Dante's *Divine Comedy*. It consists of a sequence of spaces representing: the forest in which the poet finds himself at the beginning of the poem, the Inferno, Purgatory and the Imperium. The visitor would have been able to wander through these spaces, climbing the stairs, and end in Paradise. (Notice Terragni's use of the Golden Rectangle.)

The experience of transition and hierarchy in space, and their culmination in the heart of a building (or garden or city), is one of the most powerful dimensions on which architects may orchestrate people's experience. This is the dimension of time and memory; but it is also the dimension of emotion. Transitions and their resolution in architecture, as in music, have strong effects on how we feel, how we behave and even who we are. They may make us feel exposed and on show; they may take us into refuges where we feel safe; they may take us on journeys of discovery or lead us to dead ends.

'Nel mezzo del camin di nostra vita…'

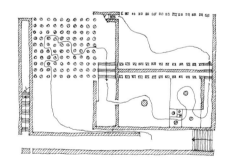

The Danteum (above) was to have been a built representation of the setting of Dante's Divine Comedy.

Reference for the Danteum:
Thomas L. Schumacher – *The Danteum*, 1993.

POSTSCRIPT

'Hesiod seems to be on the right track in putting Chasm first in his system. At any rate, the reason he says 'First came the Chasm, and then the broad-breasted Earth' is presumably because the first requirement is that there should be space for things. In other words, he shares the common belief that everything is some-where – that is, in some place. And if place is like that, then it would be truly remarkable and prior to everything, since that which is a prerequisite for other things to exist, but whose exist-ence does not depend on other things, is bound to be primary. The point here is that place is not destroyed when the things it contains are destroyed.'

Aristotle, translated by Waterfield – *Physics* (c.340 BC), 1996, p. 79.

POSTSCRIPT

The framework for analysing architecture this book offers is not comprehensive. Many themes remain to be identified and explored; many more to be invented. Architecture is a creative activity; it depends on minds making sense of their surroundings and coming up with ideas for how the world might be changed, organised differently according to various criteria and attitudes. In any creative activity there is an interplay between originality and the adoption and re-interpretation of ideas that have been used elsewhere. Even the most original of architects exploit ideas others have used before them.

Le Corbusier, for instance, who is often counted as one of the most original architects of the twentieth century, employed innumerable ideas borrowed from others: from the elemental, such as floors, walls, doors and roofs, to the more sophisticated, such as the parallel-wall strategy, stratification and transitions. In many cases his originality may be characterised as a re-interpretation and inventive re-use of existing ideas rather than the invention of new ones.

But in studying the products of intellectual creativity, in which one might find (in different examples) similar responses to similar challenges, or borrowed ideas, one must also celebrate the contributions of the imagination, which sometimes breaks free of any established canon of ideas. This book focuses on the canon of ideas encountered quite often in looking at works of architecture. In doing so it does not seek to undermine the role of imagination in architecture but rather to provide a foundation for it.

I am aware of some themes I have not had room to include in this book and know there is more work to be done on many of those that have been included. Each of the chapters, each of the basic or modifying elements, could be the subject of its own extended study. My own book *An Architecture Notebook: Wall* (Routledge, 2000), which was published a few years after the first edition of *Analysing Architecture*, deals with the powers of walls in a great deal more detail than has been possible here but still does little more than scratch the surface. Likewise with *Doorway* (Routledge, 2007), which only begins to open the way into the many dimensions of this apparently simple and rudimentary element of architecture. There is also more to do on, for example, the multifarious ways geometry contributes to identification of place; the subtleties of the parallel-wall strategy have not been exhausted here; there is work to be done on understanding the concept of 'place'; and so on.

The purpose of this book has been to open a field of research rather than to provide a complete account of it. The parallels that spring to mind are with the fields of linguistics and musicology, where the underlying structures of language and music – both creative activities – are studied.

This book has dealt with some of the underlying organisational strategies of architecture rather than with stylistic appearance. As the many books on architecture that deal with them testify, the historical styles of architecture are not without interest and significance. But this book has shown there is a 'common language' of architecture on which architects working in different styles draw. Many of the architectural ideas illustrated in this book have, in the course of history, been clothed in various styles, from the bare and simple to the highly intricate and ornamental. The parallel-wall strategy, for example, is the underlying organisational principle shared by buildings of many different styles. It was used by the ancient Egyptians, Minoans, Trojans, Greeks, Romans and others; by Medieval, Renaissance, Victorian Gothic, Victorian Classicist, Arts and Crafts, Modern architects; as well as in Middle Eastern, Indian, Chinese, Japanese, South American buildings. Even so, the parallel-wall strategy retains its own powers, independent of the style.

*   *   *

The key that let me into this field of research was the realisation that architecture is, before all else, identification of place. This was discussed in detail in the first chapter but, although it is not always mentioned, it can be seen to underpin all the others too. The purpose of basic elements is not just to be themselves but to identify place; the effects of the different attitudes associated with the 'temple' and the 'cottage' are to identify place in different ways; the power of the six-directions-plus-centre is that they identify place; the purpose of organising space – by structure, by parallel walls, into stratified layers, or into hierarchies with transitions and hearts – is to identify place.

This provides a key to architectural design as well as analysis. If one thinks of architecture as designing (or styling) 'buildings', one designs in one way; if one thinks of it as identifying places, then one designs in another. With identification of place in mind, the focus of attention shifts from tangible form to inhabitation. In the latter, a 'building' is seen not as an end in itself, but as a means to an end. This is not a new thought, but it remains a significant (and sometimes overlooked) one. It can be found in varying degrees of clarity in most of the texts included in the list of supplementary reading given at the end of this book.

It is a thought that seems to require re-statement from time to time, because it can be elusive and also because it can easily be lost beneath a mound of seemingly more pressing concerns. The practice of architecture is so beset by constructional, contractual and commercial pressures that this silent and seemingly undemanding core of its 'reason for being' can often be ignored.

Throughout history, other factors have helped push 'architecture as identification of place' down the list of priorities. These are in addition to the common tendency for people to find it easier to think in terms of the tangible – such as buildings – rather than the intangible – such as places.

First is the suggestion, implicit in a lot of writing, that the word 'architecture' can be reserved for a special class of building. This is stated explicitly in Nikolaus Pevsner's famous assertion, 'A bicycle shed is a building; Lincoln Cathedral is a piece of architecture'.* To think like this might be satisfactory for an architectural historian, because it relates to a quality as perceived, but it only confuses definition of the *activity* of architecture.

In thinking of architecture as identification of place one is on firmer ground. Both the bicycle shed and the cathedral are works of architecture in that they are constituted of elements composed to identify places, though they may be of different character and quality: the shed identifies a place for storing bicycles, the cathedral a place for worship. The people responsible for both are 'architects', though one may be in some way better at it (or more qualified) than the other. Thinking of architecture as identification of place, everyone is to some degree an architect. Setting out the furniture in a living room is architecture; so too is laying out a city; or making camp on a beach. The difference is one of degree, and at different scales there are different levels of responsibility.

The legislative bodies in some countries rule that the responsibilities of building – in that they involve technical expertise as well as contractual problems and spending large sums of money – should only be handled by people with particular qualifications that make them professionals. In some cases, the United Kingdom included, the title 'architect' is protected by law. But there is another justification for architecture being a profession, which can also be better understood by thinking of it as identification of place. It is architects who, by definition (whether or not they are legally entitled to the name), organise the world into places for life and work. This is a responsibility on a par with that borne by those involved in medicine, law or religion. There is a level where everyone deals with their own concerns (as in health, disputes and spiritual belief) but there are also levels where matters can be complex and require the education, experience and commitment of people who accept professional responsibility.

A second factor that has pushed 'architecture as identification of place' down the intellectual agenda has been a conscious fascination, in some strands of architectural theory,

* Nikolaus Pevsner – *An Outline of European Architecture*, 1945, p. xvi.

with its contrary – the idea of 'place-less' architecture. There is not space here to follow this strand in detail but it was recognised and described by Oswald Spengler in his book *The Decline of the West* (1918) as a preoccupation with 'the infinite'. It was evident too in Mies van der Rohe's interest in 'universal space' and it has been brought to realisation in many 'anti-street' urban developments during the middle two quarters of the twentieth century. In 1931, the Swedish architect Erik Gunnar Asplund gave a lecture in which he illustrated one such development, declaring triumphantly that 'PLACE GIVES WAY TO SPACE!'

The third factor that has worked against 'architecture as identification of place' has been technology. This is partly because people tend to focus more on how buildings are built than on what they do in identifying places, but also because many primitive place types have been made redundant. The 'hearth', for example, is no longer an essential place in many homes; heating tends now to be provided by a boiler perhaps kept in a cupboard and warmth distributed through pipes and radiators. From its heyday in the time of the pharaohs, the 'tomb' has plummeted to almost total irrelevance in the repertoire of architecture. The 'market place' was superseded by the shop, but even that is under threat from tele-marketing and the Internet. Most significantly perhaps, the pulpit, the look-out and the stage have been overtaken by television, which allows politicians to preach into people's living rooms, viewers to see great distances (even to the moon and outer planets of the solar system) and performances to be watched from almost anywhere.

Related to this is the enormous increase in the prevalence of the framed image. As was shown in the chapter *Architecture as Making Frames*, the two-dimensional image of a work of architecture, set within the four sides of a frame, does not allow one to experience it as a place or series of places. This is true of a painting or a photograph, a film or a television image. Even if the picture presents the illusion of three dimensions, even if it includes movement, the frame diminishes the experience of place. Nevertheless these images are perhaps the most common ways the products of architecture are viewed; there are only a limited number of buildings that each of us can actually experience; the vast majority – especially those which architects are urged by critics in the press to emulate – are seen as framed images. This has the effect of reinforcing the perceived importance of visual appearance in works of architecture (and even pictorial composition), further undermining the importance of identification of place.

It is probably true to say too, that architects involved with large projects worry more about whether the roof will leak (or similar matters to do with the performance of the fabric of a building) or whether they will lead their client into some expensive legal battle

Reference for Asplund:
E.G. Asplund – 'Var arkitoniska rumsuppfattning', in *Byggmästeren: Arkitektupplagan,* 1931, pp. 203-10, translated by Simon Unwin and Christina Johnsson as 'Our Architectural Conception of Space', in *ARQ (Architectural Research Quarterly)*, Volume 5 Number 2, 2001, pp. 151-60.
(In this version the declaration is translated as 'The enclosed room gives way to open space.')

(against themselves perhaps) than about whether they are making good places; at the least such worries must seem more immediate and have more potential to give architects personal problems, if not spoil their lives. Concerns about construction, about performance, about legal and contractual matters, can easily occupy all an architect's time, leaving none for issues that can readily (but wrongly) be disregarded as worthless, namely those to do with identification of place.

The architecture of hearths, tombs, shops, schools, libraries, museums, art galleries, meeting rooms, places of work, offices… all are challenged by developments in technology that complicate and confuse issues of place. But this is not to say that the idea of place is no longer relevant. Architecture, like language, is always changing; new types of place emerge while others become redundant. Architecture now has to take account of types of places that were not pertinent until the relatively recent past: places for televisions, for computers, for skate-boarding; airports; cash-dispensing machines; motorways. But there are also many primitive place types that remain relevant: places to sleep, to cook, to eat, to walk, to grow plants, to meet people, and so on.

*   *   *

These are all matters that indicate something of the nature of the theoretical ground on which the present book stands. But its main purpose has been to show that architecture, its products and its strategies, can be subject to analysis within a consistent conceptual framework. This is not to say that the whole framework is understood nor even that the framework is finite in its extent. Nor is it to say that all the themes that have been described and discussed in this book are relevant to every work of architecture that has ever been, or applicable to every new work of architecture that will be proposed.

It is apparent that different movements in architecture through history, and different individual architects, have had different preoccupations. Within the creative field of architecture different themes may be given different weights, independently or relatively. One architect or movement may concentrate on the relationship between space and structure, another may stress the ways social geometry influences the organisation of buildings, giving the ordering power of structure a lower priority; one may exploit the powers of the six-directions-plus-centre where another may see them as best subverted; one may seek to concentrate on the modifying elements of architecture – light, sound, touch – where another may be more interested in the formal powers of the basic elements – wall, column, roof. Some of course are most interested in the image their work commands in the press. The permutations are endless.

Architecture is a matter not of system but of judgement. Architecture, like writing plays, composing music, framing laws, or even scientific investigation, is subject to drive, vision and interest. It is a creative activity that accommodates differing and varying views on the interactive relationship between people and the world around.

Architecture is, because of this, also a political and a commercial field. It is political in that there are no 'right' answers and 'wrong' but answers that find favour and those that do not; 'favour' lies with those who have the most powerful voice. It is commercial in that the products of architecture have to survive in a consumerist market – a new building is like a newly launched product; whether it succeeds or not depends on whether or not its 'customers' 'like it'. And this leads into the debate about who architecture's 'customers' are.

Despite the unnerving complexity of the ways it can be done, and the uncertainty of the conditions within which it is done, architecture as a creative activity *is* susceptible of reasoned understanding. By analysis of examples, its powers can be understood and assimilated for use in design.

If one considers architecture not in terms of material *things* (objects, buildings) – not as a catalogue of formal types or a classification of styles or technologies of construction – but in terms of *frames of reference for doing* (which is another term for the themes explored in this book), then it is possible to build a framework for analysis that is consistent yet not restricting; one that allows the creative mind to learn from works of architecture of the past and to generate ideas for the future. Architecture should not be limited by classifications that deal only with what *is* or *has been*; there will always be potential for new ways of identifying places. Architecture's vitality depends upon invention and adventure. But any field of human endeavour – music, law, science – needs a base of knowledge that can be presented to students of the subject as a foundation upon which they can build and develop. Architecture is no different.

CASE STUDIES

'It is evident that the raw material at the disposal of the artist has been constant (from a realistic standpoint) since the beginning of time: the natural world, accessible to the senses of sight, sound and touch. But it is equally evident that the uses to which man has put this common stock are so infinitely various that he has, in fact, disintegrated this public world, as one might call it, into as many private worlds as there are minds to perceive them. In a sense, of course, we all of us do this; out of our limited experience we create a limited universe adapted to our understanding and suited to our needs. We know this, and we accept it without imagining that our private world is interesting to anyone but ourselves. But the artist starts from the assumption that others want to share in his private world, and he proceeds to communicate it to them by means of his art. In so doing he creates a myth. Such a myth is an act of faith: it is meant to be understood as reality, never as an "artistic" fiction; it is not a parable or an allegory.'

Roger Hinks – *The Gymnasium of the Mind*, 1984, p. 13.

Case Studies – INTRODUCTION

The following ten *Case Studies* are included for various reasons. First, they provide a way of drawing together the threads of the analytical exploration of architecture offered in the preceeding chapters by analysing individual examples according to a number of the analytical themes identified. Second, they represent an opportunity to evaluate the applicability of the analytical method implied in the preceding chapters. (In this I think it is important not to treat the preceding chapters as a 'checklist' for analysis but more as prompts that can help to draw out the intrinsic underlying architecture of any example.) Third, they illustrate unexpected congruences between buildings which at first sight might appear very different. This, to some extent, supports the observation that there is a 'common language' of architecture underlying and underpinning superficial differences in the styles and appearances of buildings. Fourth, some of the cases studied illustrate the ways in which architects have used their own analyses, of buildings they have encountered or studied, to inform their own design work. This supports the claim made at the beginning of this book that all architects can benefit (increase their versatility and fluency in the 'common language' of architecture) from analysing the work of others, especially through drawing. And fifth, these *Case Studies* offer me the opportunity of doing some more drawings and showing you some more buildings.

Case Study 1 – IRON AGE HOUSE

  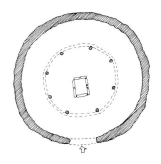

In the Iron Age houses were generally circular in plan, with conical roofs thought to have been of thatch supported by structural frames of rough hewn timber. This example has been reconstructed on its original foundations within a hill fort, called Castell Henllys, in west Wales. As such its construction and internal layout is partly the result of informed speculation on the part of the archaeologists studying the site. Nevertheless its plausible reconstructed form illustrates some fundamental architectural strategies, which retain as much potential in the identification of place now as they would have had thousands of years ago.

The round house at Castell Henllys is a fireplace encircled by a wall and sheltered by a conical roof. The ring of columns help to support the roof, but also divide the space of the house into a central area and a periphery of secondary spaces.

Reference for Castell Henllys:
www.castellhenllys.com/english/castellhenllys.htm

Identification of place

Conceptually the house 'begins' with the hearth, encircled by a wall and roof that enclose its circle of presence and protect inhabitants from the weather (right). The circular plan does not seem to have derived from an interest in the ideal geometry of a 'perfect' circle but may be construed as rather the least artificial way of separating out a place from everywhere else – an inside from an outside. It is as if the fireplace has been encircled by a wall in the same way as one might circle a paragraph in a newspaper with a red pen, to mark it out and distinguish it from the rest of the page. It is the same arrangement as the henge (or circle of standing stones), which may have had an altar rather than a fireplace at its focus. The house has no windows – the only light would come in through the doorway. In its darkness this house would primarily be a refuge from the outside world, a sheltered bed place, a datum by reference to which its inhabitants would know where they were – at home or abroad in the world.

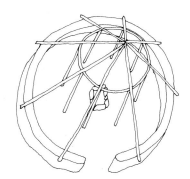

Social geometry and the geometry of making

The circular plan also accords with the social geometry of a group of people living together around the fire. At Castell Henllys a similar round house has been reconstructed as a 'council chamber' (right), with a circle of benches, backing against the circle of columns supporting the roof, arranged around the central hearth. Such an arrangement suggests a strong harmony between building plan and social use.

This harmony becomes stronger when one considers the geometry of making. The circular plan lends itself well to a conical roof (middle right). It is difficult to decide whether the conical roof produced the circular plan or whether it was a solution to the problem of

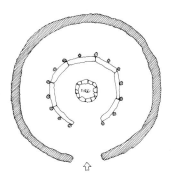

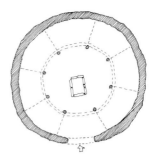

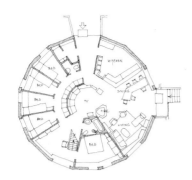

putting a roof over a circular plan, so well do they go together. Structural timbers (the roughly finished trunks of slender trees) are arranged rather like the poles of a teepee. Because of their length, these timbers need extra support at about their midpoint to stop them sagging. This is provided by the inner circle of columns, which support a ring of timbers that also support additional rafters not shown in the drawing. (They also suggest the position of the circular bench in the so-called council chamber.)

Space and structure

The spaces within the round house too are arranged in a way suggested by the inner circle of structural columns but different from in the council chamber building. Here they imply a division of the peripheral space into eight segments, one of which is taken by the entrance, forming a transition from outside to in (above middle). In the Castell Henllys reconstruction the other segments are each allocated to different purposes; one to storage; four as bedrooms, with partitions between; and two together as an open-plan kitchen area (above right). Above the bedrooms a loft has been constructed, with its floor supported on the roof timbers and the inner ring of supporting columns (see section, below right). This loft is reached by a ladder. As in the council chamber there is a strong harmony between the structural order of the house and the internal arrangement of space.

Elements doing more than one thing

Various components of the house can be seen to do more than one thing: the doorway gives access but also provides light and air; the walls keep out the weather but may also have been used as surfaces for painting; the roof timbers hold up the roof but would probably have had things hanging from them. But perhaps the component doing the most things is the inner ring of columns. It can be seen to be (architecturally) doing at least five or six things all at once: helping to support the roof; supporting the loft; dividing the periphery into eight segments each with its own purpose; and reinforcing the circle of presence and social geometry around the fire. Possessions, such as shields and skins, are hung from them too.

This is a simple, maybe primitive, house but nevertheless it illustrates some significant architectural powers – the power to define, enclose and protect; the power to frame social life and relationships – and demonstrates a strong resonance between life and form.

The arrangement of spaces in this twentieth century house (above) is almost identical to that in the round house at Castell Henllys. The Engstrom House was designed by Ralph Erskine and built on Lisö Island in Sweden in 1955. Instead of being conical and constructed of a thatched roof supported on a timber framework, Erskine's house is hemispherical, and made of curved steel sheets supported on a steel structure. The Engstrom House has sixteen instead of eight segments, and is also a little larger than the house at Castell Henllys. Nevertheless it is similarly organised around an almost central hearth (plus television), surrounded by segmental bedrooms divided by radial partitions, and with an open-plan kitchen.

Reference for the Engstrom House:
Peter Collymore – *The Architecture of Ralph Erskine*, 1985, pp. 68-9.

This section through the round house shows the upper level with its access ladder.

Case Study 2 – ROYAL VILLA, KNOSSOS

This perspective drawing shows the place of the throne separated from the main hall by the steps, low wall and columns.

Archaeology often provides clearer examples of the fundamental spatial powers of architecture than is evident in more recent buildings. The upper drawing on the right shows the inside of a building known as the Royal Villa near the ruins of the ancient Minoan palace of Knossos on the island of Crete. It is much smaller than the main palace and set apart, cut into a slope of the rocky landscape. The Royal Villa was built some three and a half thousand years ago (maybe a thousand years before the original Iron Age house in *Case Study 1*). The lower drawing is a plan of the villa, partly reconstructed by early twentieth-century archaeologists.

It is not known what the building was for nor exactly how it was used. Although it may be interpreted in various ways, the architecture does provide some clues. In some cases buildings seem to have been designed to accommodate particular ceremonies and rituals. It is clear, for example, that the central space of the Royal Villa – the megaron – which is almost symmetrical about a central axis, juxtaposes a focus – the alcove in the western wall where fragments of a throne were found – with a hall for people to gather. This is a classic form, which in variation is found in ancient (even more ancient than Knossos) Egyptian temples, in churches and mosques, and in many other buildings for ceremonies and formal proceedings. Notice how it differs from the circular form of the 'council chamber' as reconstructed by archaeologists at Castell Henllys; where its social circle suggests broad equality (maybe the chief sat opposite the doorway). The layout of the Royal Villa clearly suggests the dominion of a single person who would have sat upon the throne.

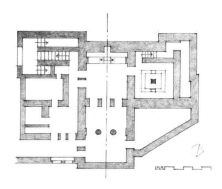

The plan of the Royal Villa illustrates how the arrangement of architectural elements reinforces the emphasis on the throne as the focal point of the composition.

Identification of place

The Royal Villa gives a good illustration of how architecture identifies place; in particular, how architecture provides a point of reference and sets down the spatial rules for a particular form of relationship, either between a high status person and suppliants, between a cult object and worshippers, or between the master of ceremonies and the participants in some ritual. In the case of the Royal Villa, archaeological interpretations seem to agree that the building was an instrument for aggrandising one person – maybe King Minos himself but probably (since the villa is away from the main palace) one of his nobles or a high priestess of the palace – and managing the interaction between this person of power and lesser citizens wanting some case to be judged or some prayer or petition to be heard. The building could be a shrine, a court for hearing legal proceedings or even a wedding chapel(!). Its formal layout would lend itself to any of these ceremonial activities.

Reference for the Royal Villa at Knossos:
J.D.S. Pendlebury – *A Handbook to the Palace of Minos at Knossos*, 1935.

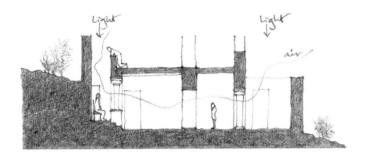

Basic and modifying elements

The building uses a very simple vocabulary of basic architectural elements: the wall, path, doorway, roof, platform, column. In fact one of the columns seems to have been special; it is set in the centre of what has been termed by archaeologists the 'pillar crypt', which is the square room to the right, in the plan, of the megaron. Encircled (or 'ensquared' rather) by a channel with two cists or small tanks set in the floor apparently for the collection of liquid, the column is thought to have had ritual significance; other pillar crypts have been found in Minoan architecture. Otherwise the most interesting basic elements are: the platform which lifts the throne onto a higher level, separated from the hall by a low wall with two columns holding the roof above; and the other two sets of two columns that define layers of space between the entrance and the throne. The parallel wall strategy is used throughout (except in the diagonal wall in the bottom right-hand corner of the plan, which may have defined a yard with no roof) because of its structural simplicity. The perspective of the parallel side walls of the megaron helps focus attention on the throne.

Although clarity of sound in this building is likely to have been important – so that the judge, king or priestess, could hear the supplicant – the building is so small and there would have been little extraneous noise (perhaps a goat or two) that this would not have been a problem. Some archaeologists however believe that the opening above the throne was to allow concealed advisers on the upper floor to help the judge in his or her deliberations (see the sketch section above). There are other instances of buildings with similar purposes having a conduit for sound from a place of concealment (in ancient Maltese temples for example) and politicians to the present day keep their advisers ready at hand.

The main modifying elements managed by the Royal Villa are light and ventilation. Archaeologists believe that the opening over the throne admitted light as well as sound, so that the judge on his, or the priestess on her throne would have been illuminated from above. Some accounts also suggest that the outermost part of the hall, outside the pair of circular columns, was a light well screened by a wall from the landscape. Various factors come into play in interpreting this part of the building. Like many later Greek temples, the throne room is oriented to the east, towards the sun rising over the mountain on the other side of the valley; whether this morning sunlight was important within the Royal Villa is not known. Also, a supplicant standing in the outermost part of the hall would be better visible to the judge on his throne if lit from the sky. Of equal importance is the through ventilation that would be provided by openings at both ends of the megaron.

On the left is a rough section through the lower part of the Royal Villa. The upper floors are only partly shown (they do not survive). It illustrates how openings towards the sky might have provided light in specific places as well as air to ventilate the megaron. (It also shows an adviser whispering to the king!) The high wall at the right is archaeologists' speculation. If it were not there or much lower than shown, the character of the megaron would be very different. As it is, the interior is enclosed and perhaps claustrophobic. If it were lower or not there, the king on his throne would have had a view of the landscape. Other instances, such as that shown on p.111, suggest that the relationship between high status apartments and the landscape was important for Minoans. They enjoyed a view through one, two or even three sets of columns.

Maybe the 'Royal' Villa was where one of the Minoan snake priestesses held court or performed sacred rites. Maybe the pillar crypt was where the snakes were kept. The truth of these speculations is less important to architects than to archaeologists. For architects, it is more important to understand the grammar of buildings such as the Royal Villa, and how it may be used.

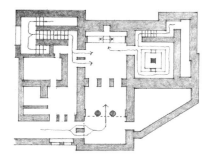

Transition, hierarchy, heart

The Royal Villa has a very clear heart – the focus of the throne and the space just in front of it. All routes within the building culminate at this point (above). There appear to be three – two from upstairs and one from outside. Some interpreters of this building suggest that because the villa is built into a slope, the main entrance for those living in it was on the upper floor (the middle of three). Apartments above might have caught some breeze in the hot Cretan summers. One of the two routes from upstairs comes through the pillar crypt; the other, down a grander stair (a single flight becomes double at a half landing), enters from a wing that contains ancillary accommodation, maybe a bath and a latrine. One interpretation of this arrangement is that the judge descended from his personal chamber by way of the pillar crypt where he was prepared for the reception of supplicants or petitioners, maybe by a ritual (involving foot-washing in water contained in the floor channel or perhaps, more gruesomely, sacrifice, with blood collected in the cists). Meanwhile, the supporting priests or officials would have processed down the other stairs. Supplicants probably waited outside, or in the passageway, before being admitted for their audience. It is noticeable that they were not allowed to enter on the axis of the judge, but came in from the side. Double doors were set in each of the three openings between the rectangular columns, but it is likely these were only intended to close up the megaron when not in use rather than employed for dramatic effect.

Like the board of a game, this small building is a clear example of how architecture can set the rules of the relationships between the various players in a ceremony: the judge and the supplicant; the judge and his or her advisers. It is the architecture that establishes and reinforces relationships between the people involved. It is the architecture that also sets the tone and atmosphere considered appropriate for the ceremony.

In The Brothers Karamazov *(trans. Magarshack) Dostoevsky describes a scene in which an 'elder' of a monastery comes to the veranda of the hermitage to listen to the concerns of a group of women:*
'About twenty peasant women crwoded… near the wooden veranda built on to the outer side of the hermitage wall. They had been told that the elder would at last be coming out and they had gathered in expectation.… On appearing on the veranda, the elder at first went straight to the peasant women, who crowded round the three front steps leading to the low veranda. The elder stood on the top step, put on his stole, and began to bless the women who clustered around him. They pulled a "shrieker" towards him by both hands. As soon as she caught sight of him, the sick woman suddenly began hiccuping, squealing in an absurd fashion, and trembling all over as though in a fit of convulsions. Putting the stole on her head, the elder read a short prayer over her, and she at once fell silent and calmed down.'
The architecture of this scene (below) is similar to, but perhaps less formal than, that of the Royal Villa, with the elder emerging from an interior to stand on a raised platform, at the top of a short flight of steps, to bless those who have come for reassurance. Such scenes are common to cultures across the world and seem to have ancient ancestry. In the Royal Villa however the 'judge' did not emerge onto the platform but had to ascend to it from the general level of the hall.

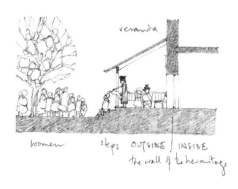

Case study 3 – LLAINFADYN

Llainfadyn is a small house that has been removed from its original location and re-erected in the Museum of Welsh Life at St Fagans, near Cardiff. It was first built in the eighteenth century as a quarry worker's dwelling near the village of Rhostryfan in north-west Wales. Nowadays it is enjoyed by visitors to the museum, who appreciate the stimuli it offers to their various senses whilst believing that they are seeing something of how people lived in the past. At first sight the house appears to be a very simple building, but its architecture has some subtleties, such that it has been used a number of times as an example in the preceding chapters of this book. (A drawing of its interior is on the title page of these *Case Studies*.)

Identification of place and basic elements

One of the most powerful, and most incontrovertible, ways of identifying a place is to enclose it with walls topped by a roof, separating it from everywhere else. Imagine what it feels like to pass from an open landscape into the interior of any small cell. Outside one is exposed to the sky, the weather, light from the sun, other people; inside, one is protected, insulated, sheltered. Cells are ubiquitous, so much so that their powers are hardly acknowledged consciously. The ways walls compartmentalise life into rooms, and roofs shelter it, are

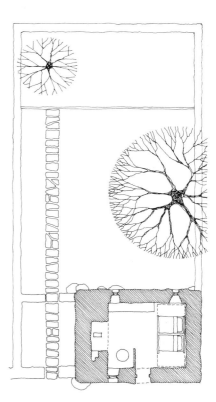

The architecture of Llainfadyn includes the cottage and its plot of ground defined by walls and hedges (above).

The chimney stack with its smoke from the fire below is the marker of a place where someone lives.

231

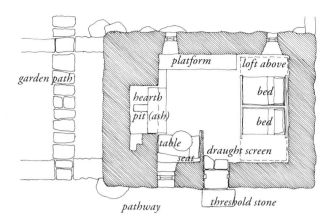

largely taken for granted; but cells constitute one of the strongest ways a mind can amend its conditions to the benefit of its body and well-being. Prehistorically inspired by caves, womb-like cells are refuges from the world. The walls of Llainfadyn are particularly powerful. They are very thick, and built of huge stones (right, lower drawing). The doorway is small, the windows tiny with broad splayed jambs. Outside, the walls' appearance of strength is impressive. Inside, one feels their protection.

Around the side and back of the house walls and hedges assert possession of its immediate territory – its garden, used for growing food. Outside the door there is a pathway, its width defined by a field wall and hedge. The house as a whole stands as a marker of the place where someone lives. Its chimney, emitting wisps of smoke from the wood fire, marks the hearth within. Inside the house there are many types of platform: beds on which to sleep, tables on which to prepare and eat food, seats on which to sit, shelves for storage and display, and a low slate platform to keep wooden furniture off the damp floor. The fire is in a large niche in the thickest wall, and has a small pit to collect the ashes. A thin slab of slate stands by the doorway as a draught screen. The bedrooms are formed by the beds themselves, two box beds positioned side by side, with boards on top making a loft above.

Modifying elements

Light is the element by which we see buildings, but it is also the element by which we can see what we are doing when we are in them. Sunlight on the whitewashed boulder walls of Llainfadyn accentuates their sculptural quality, but this aesthetic effect is unlikely to have been intentional. The mind that conceived this house was probably more concerned with practicalities: letting sufficient light into its interior to be able to live, without losing excessive amounts of heat, and using openings of a size the available materials would allow. In Llainfadyn the combined effect of these three practical concerns produced a layout in which two small windows have been positioned to light the area of greatest activity around the fire, with a third in one of the bedrooms. The general light level inside the house is low, but on good days the door could be left open to admit more light. At night there would have been light from candles to supplement light from the fire. The absence of electric light is important to the character of the house.

The source of heat in the house is of course the fire in the hearth, which is the focus of the main room. Its heat is contained in the space by the walls, and (especially around the fire) stored in their stones. The smell of wood-smoke pervades the interior and surroundings

The plan of Llainfadyn follows the geometry of making. Even though it would have been difficult to build vertical stable walls with such large round and irregular boulders (that is why the walls are so thick), it is relatively easy to put a roof over a simple rectangle of walls.

The walls of Llainfadyn are built of huge irregular boulders, which means that to be stable the walls have to be very thick.

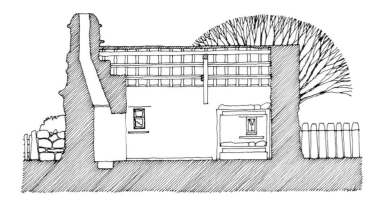

A section through the cottage shows the large hearth, with the two levels of sleeping places at the other end of the living space.

of the house. The size of the space of the house balances the constructional capabilities of available materials (especially for the roof), the practical need for sufficient room to live and the capacity of the fire to warm that space. The scale of the house is human; the doorway is just the right size to allow a person to pass through it easily, neither aggrandising nor humbling. The spaces within are neither generous nor mean, but sufficient to accommodate the activities intended.

Hard-wearing smooth surfaces are provided where necessary: the threshold stone at the doorway; paving around the hearth; the seats, tables and shelves. The beds have soft mattresses and warm bedding.

There are various dimensions to the element of time in Llainfadyn. In its original location and inhabitation one's experience of the house would have changed with the time of day, with different activities, the weather and the seasons. In its artificial setting it changes with the weather and seasons, but is only accessible when the museum is open, during the day time. It is not possible to do anything in the house except look at it. One cannot even sit down; one certainly cannot sleep there to wake in morning, add wood to the fire and prepare food. As a museum exhibit the house is presented as it was two hundred years ago. It has a clock that tocks, marking time, as if it has stood still.

Elements doing more than one thing

In architecture, elements are used for what they do as well as for their appearance. In unpretentious buildings like Llainfadyn the practical purposes of elements were probably the main concern, and little if any conscious consideration was given to the luxury of aesthetic appearance. Nevertheless, in some cases, as well as possessing an unselfconscious beauty, such buildings display skill and subtlety in the way elements are composed to organise space into places. This skill may have derived from working directly with materials and allowing spaces to evolve over time in response to use, rather than by designing through the abstraction of architectural drawing and with the expectation that a building should be perfectly organised when first completed. Such skill and evolutionary amendment through time produces a directness and immediacy of relationship between the places made and the life they accommodate.

In Llainfadyn elements (basic and modifying) work at various levels, and in varying combinations, to establish its component places. The coherence of the orchestration of its elements within the unified whole is an important aspect of its quality as a work of

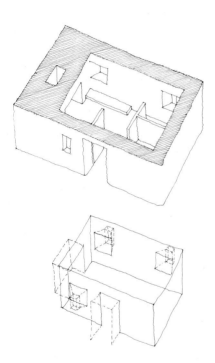

The spaces within the walls – windows, hearth, doorway – are places in their own right: places to store belongings, to dry wood for the fire, to greet a visitor or shelter watching the rain.

233

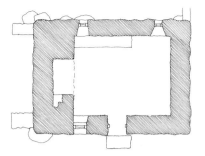 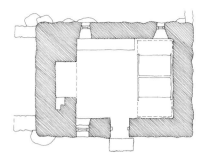 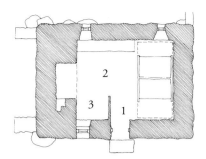

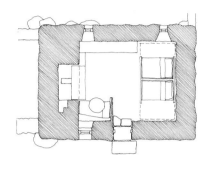

architecture. The outer walls constitute the main fabric of the house and enclose its inner space, but they also contribute to the place of the hearth, the place of the table alongside and the two bedrooms.

The thickness of the wall around the doorway makes the entrance into a place in itself, almost a porch (though in its original location the house also acquired a small timber porch, which was not included in the museum reconstruction). It is at the doorway, as well as the windows, that one becomes aware of the massiveness of the walls.

One of the key elements in the house is the draught-screen by the door. Generally the space inside the house is disposed into places in economical and intriguing ways. Rather than using walls to compartmentalise it into rooms in what has become the orthodox way of organising houses, places within the house are defined by the furniture and by simple elements. The basic space of the house is a simple rectangle (above left), with the doorway halfway along one side and the fire at one end. There are also the two windows at the fireplace end of the space and the single window at the colder end. The two beds positioned at the cooler darker end of this rectangle of space effectively divide it into four rooms (above middle): the two bedrooms (only one of which is lit by a window); the loft above them; and a main living space. In this arrangement the doorway now enters into the corner of the main living space, justifying its position halfway along the house as a whole. Next, in the conceptual organisation of this space, the draught screen is introduced to the left of the doorway as one enters (above right). This simple device, as well as screening the draught from the door, effectively divides the main living space into three zones. It creates an entrance zone (1), which means that when entering one reaches almost the exact centre of the dwelling before feeling that one is fully 'inside', and can turn to the left and see the fire; the darker of the two bedrooms is entered off this entrance zone. The draught-screen also creates a general-purpose space (2), in which many of the activities inside the house would take place; the second of the bedrooms and the loft are accessed from this space. And third, the draught-screen creates a small space to sit by a table alongside the fire (3). This space, shown in the drawing on the title page of these *Case Studies*, is also lit by one of the windows. This small place is the heart of the house.

Like the Royal Villa at Knossos, Llainfadyn establishes a framework of spaces, internal and external. Here, rather than formal religious or judicial ritual, the architecture frames daily life and its more mundane rituals: getting up in the morning; cooking; eating; welcoming visitors; mending things; going to bed.

The draughtscreen alongside the doorway does more than one thing. As well as sheltering the interior from draughts between the doorway and the fire, it implies a division of the internal space of the cottage into three: an entry place or lobby; a place to sit around a small table; and a general purpose place in front of the fire.

Case study 4 – *IL TEMPIETTO*

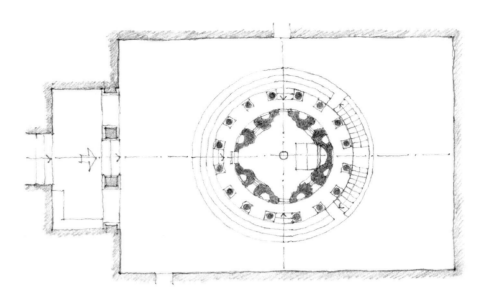

Il Tempietto *sits in its own small courtyard. Its section (below) shows it has three main levels.*

Hidden in a courtyard alongside a church on a hill overlooking Rome is a small circular chapel designed by Bramante and built in the early years of the sixteenth century. It is known as *Il Tempietto* – the small temple – and is one of the first buildings in Rome designed in the Renaissance style derived from ancient classical precedents.

Identification of place

Il Tempietto does not merely identify a small place of worship, it stands as a marker and memorial to one of the most symbolically significant places for the city – the spot where St Peter, Rome's patron saint and founder of the Roman Catholic Church, was reputedly crucified upside-down. That the chapel is screened within its courtyard, hidden from the city, seems to reinforce its poignancy, and express some guilt that human beings can do such things to each other.

Ideal geometry

Apart from the vocabulary of ornamentation derived from ancient Roman precedent, the touchstone of Renaissance architecture was a fascination with ideal geometry. We would probably like to know the exact geometry that Bramante constructed as the framework for the design of *Il Tempietto*. But this is not possible without the actual drawing he produced. And it is likely that he, in doing that drawing, was forced to compromise. There would necessarily be parts where the geometry just could not be exact. As Plato would have predicted, it is just not possible for the precision and perfection of mathematical, ideal geometry to exist in this real world. Our attempts to attain it in drawn or built form are condemned to failure.

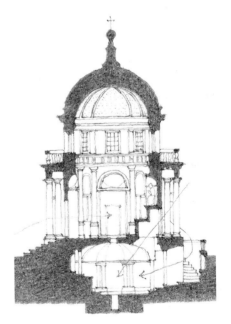

Reference for Il Tempietto:
Robin Evans – 'Perturbed Circles', in *The Projective Cast: Architecture and its Three Geometries*, 1995.

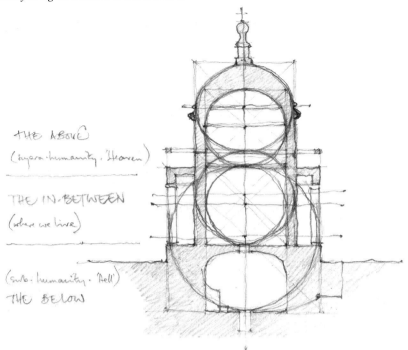

THE ABOVE
(supra-humanity, 'Heaven')

THE IN-BETWEEN
(where we live)

(sub-humanity, 'Hell')
THE BELOW

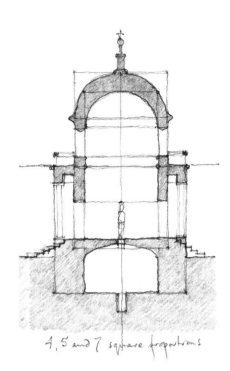

4, 5 and 7 square proportions

The drawings above and alongside show some of my attempts to identify the underlying geometry of this building. I am not sure which might be closest to the truth, but this does not really matter since it is not the precise geometry Bramante used that is at issue. It is sufficient to know that he did follow Alberti's prescription (quoted at the beginning of the chapter on *Ideal Geometry*) and paid attention to the 'lineaments' of his building, composing them according to a framework of squares and circles in plan, elevation and sectional drawing – cylinders and spheres in the building itself.

There are various ways in which one can interpret the underlying ideal geometry of Bramante's design. But it is clear that he used the perfect forms of the square and circle, cylinder and sphere.

Stratification

It is possible to analyse this building according to the various themes outlined in this book, but perhaps the most significant is stratification. When you visit this building, if it is open, it takes you a moment to realise that there is a hole in the floor of the chamber with the altar. You look down through it and see there is another chamber below – a crypt – and in its floor is a hole reaching into the ground. Gradually it occurs to you that this is meant to be the actual hole into which St Peter's cross was planted. The building has three 'strata': the level of the chamber with the altar, up a few steps from the courtyard level; the level of the crypt with the hole of the cross; and the level of the cupola or dome. The last is obviously the stratum of heaven above; the lower chamber is the stratum of the horror of St Peter's crucifixion; and the middle level is left in-between – the level of humanity on earth.

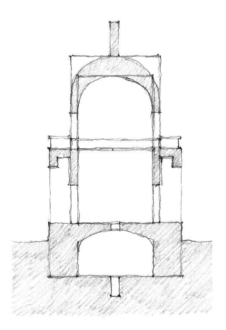

When you leave the chapel and walk around to the back, you find the steps down to the lower chamber, which is visible through a barred door, usually locked. This chamber is lit through an opening above its doorway. Examining the section through Bramante's building (see p. 235), you see the clever way in which he hollowed out the altar in the chamber above to allow this opening.

Case Study 5 – FITZWILLIAM COLLEGE CHAPEL

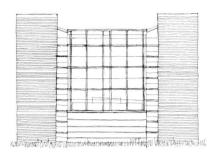

Elevation

The small chapel at Fitzwilliam College in Cambridge, UK, was designed by the British practice MacCormac Jamieson Prichard, and built in 1991. The chapel has been attached to the end of a wing of the existing college accommodation (designed by Denys Lasdun in the 1960s). It faces a large tree (which was already there) almost in the centre of the rectangular college grounds. The circle that outlines the plan of the chapel identifies a place that enjoys a particular relationship with this tree. The purpose of the building was to establish a place of worship. It has done this by cupping the place between two brick walls curved around like protecting hands; these form a cylinder that contains the chapel.

Basic and combined elements

The principal architectural elements of the chapel are wall, platform, aedicule, focus, cell, column and glass wall. The platform is the main floor of the chapel (see the section, on the next page). Being raised it makes the chapel interior feel apart but, because of the glass wall that faces the tree, not separate from the land outside. On this platform is the aedicule – which seems to be composed of four pairs of columns arranged at the corners of a square. The columns in each pair are structurally separate: the inner four columns support a central square flat roof; the outer four support a secondary pitched roof that spans between the outer walls and the roof of the aedicule. The internal focus of the aedicule is the altar, a simple table covered with a red cloth. Below the platform there is a crypt-like meeting room totally secluded from the outside world. Its floor level is slightly lower than that outside. Within this meeting room, and enhancing its crypt-like quality, the structural supports of its ceiling, which align with the columns of the aedicule in the chapel above, appear as heavy masonry piers – battered as if to suggest they need to spread a heavy load – providing a strong and visible foundation. The ceiling of the crypt is convex, like the hull of a boat.

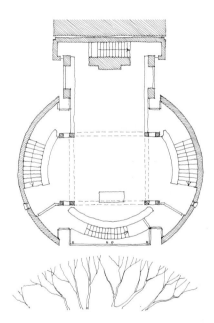

Plan of main floor

The platform, the aedicule above with its altar and the cell beneath are all enclosed and protected by the two curved side walls, arcs of the circular plan. The open end, between these two walls, is the large clear glass wall through which the tree can be seen.

Though there are many subtleties, the building makes simple and direct use of these elements. Each seems to fulfil its timeless purpose: the walls enclose and protect; the platform raises a special place above ground level; the aedicule frames a specific place – that of the altar, which is the focus and heart of the building; the cell separates a place from everywhere else; the columns act structurally, bearing the loads of floor and roof, but also help to define space; and the glass wall allows in light and is for looking out.

References for Fitzwilliam College Chapel:
Peter Blundell Jones – 'Holy Vessel', in *Architects' Journal*, 1 July 1992, p.25.
'Dreams in Light', in *Architectural Review*, April 1992, p.26.

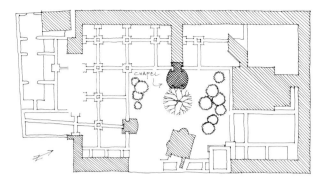

Modifying elements

In the morning, sunlight streams into the chapel from the east through the branches of the tree and the large window. In both the chapel and the crypt there are narrow perimeter roof-lights that allow light to wash down the walls: softly on overcast days, and with a pattern of sharp shadows when the sun shines. With the changing light and slowly moving sun patterns the interior is never quite the same twice. At night the lights inside turn the chapel into a lantern or lighthouse. By contrast with the harsh purple brick on the outside, the colours inside are soft and warm. This image of a warm interior is further reinforced at night when the inside lightness contrasts with the dark.

Elements doing more than one thing, and using things that are there

The platform is a floor and a roof; the glass wall allows a view out and makes a lantern at night. The aedicule defines the main chapel space and the place of the altar, but it also helps to create four subsidiary spaces: the place of the organ (at the rear of the chapel); the places of the two stairs that curve up from the entrance below; and the place of the priest's stair up from the crypt. The inner walls, which are the boundaries of the crypt and which define all three stairs, also form the bases of circumferential seating in the chapel.

   As in any building there are many other things doing more than one thing at once: the spaces between each pair of columns accommodate the vertical radiators; the organ is housed in a wall that also contributes to the enclosure of the chapel and defines the place of another stair.

   The chapel uses the end of the existing wing as an anchor; it uses the tree as a companion. But it also uses, and exploits, the place between the two, which previously lay dormant. It sits within a large landscaped quadrangle, which is an outside room. The chapel gives the quadrangle a focus it did not have previously.

Primitive place types, and architecture making frames

The chapel identifies a place for an altar together with its associated place for worshippers. There are many precedents for such primitive places being bounded by a circle or aedicule; here it is both. The chapel sits in the frame made by the other college buildings and their gardens. The circle of the building itself is a frame for worship. Within, the seating on the

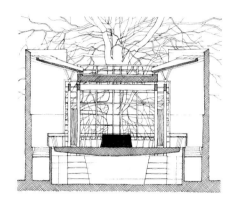

This section is drawn facing the tree. You can see the platform (which has a curved under surface) supporting the aedicule in the chapel above, and supported by the piers in the meeting room below. The altar stands on the platform in front of the large east-facing glass wall. You can also see the gaps at the perimeter of the roof and around the edge of the platform floor, which allow light to wash down the walls of the chapel and the meeting room.

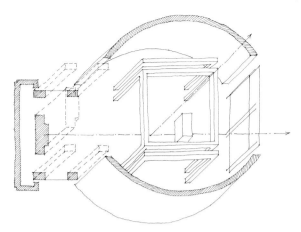

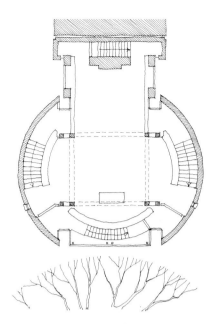

Plan at chapel level, showing the square aedicule and the four subsidiary spaces it helps to make: the place of the two stairs from the entrance; the place of the priest's stair rising under the glass wall from the meeting room beneath; and the place of the organ at the rear of the chapel.

circumference is a frame within that frame; the aedicule is a frame within a frame within a frame; the altar is a frame within a frame within a frame within a frame, like Russian dolls. The glass wall frames a particular view of the tree, as an abstract picture, but also makes a link between the internal space and nature outside (rather like the Student Chapel at Otaniemi where the cross is an external focus).

Temples and cottages

Architecturally as well as in purpose, the chapel is a 'temple'. The aedicule stands on a platform above the natural ground level. The form of the chapel is geometrically disciplined; its materials are carefully finished. And although it is attached to an existing building and relates to the tree, it does not submit to either. The building's one submissive characteristic is perhaps its use of bricks that match those of the older building.

Circles of presence and six-directions-plus-centre

The chapel creates its own circle of presence, which houses the altar with its circle of presence, and which responds to, and exists within, the circle of presence of the tree. Through these overlapping circles one may carry one's own.

Inside the chapel the six directions are defined by the six sides of the cubic geometry of the aedicule. The lateral directions are blocked by the side walls. The direction to the rear loses itself in the area of the organ; the down direction is the floor and the crypt beneath (see the Villa Rotonda by Palladio, as well as Bramante's *Il Tempietto – Case Study 4*), the presence of which one is reminded of by the stairwells.

The two directions that hold greatest importance in this chapel, as in most traditional religious buildings, are the up and the forward. The forward passes through the altar and the glass wall to the tree and the rising sun beyond. The vertical up (the *axis mundi*), though not strongly emphasised by the architecture of the building (there is no spire, or vault, or cupola – nor holes in the floor and ground), is simply implied by the coincidental axes of the cylinder of the outer walls and the cube of the aedicule. This centre, together with the four horizontal directions, is recognised, but undemonstratively indicated, by a faint cross of pairs of parallel lines inscribed across the ceiling of the aedicule.

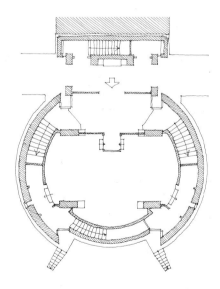

Plan at 'crypt' level, showing the entrance, and the four piers which support the floor of the chapel.

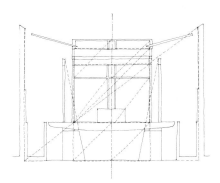

The form of the chapel seems to hang on an armature of geometric shapes and volumes. In the plan you can see a pattern of squares and circles.

Social geometry, and space and structure

Like the Woodland Chapel by Asplund (*Case Study 8*) the internal shapes of both the chapel and the meeting room recognise and establish the social circle, even though the way the seating is usually placed facing the altar tends to contradict this.

This social circle is contained by the principal structural elements of the chapel – the frame of the aedicule and the flank walls – which are also the principal space defining elements. In the crypt the space is defined by the four structural piers. The space is also defined by the curved walls of the three sets of stairs, which are not roof supporting.

Ideal geometry

Although it is sometimes difficult to establish exactly which ideal geometric shapes and volumes an architect used in determining the form and disposition of a building, it is clear that the Fitzwilliam Chapel is organised on a conceptual armature of circles and squares, cylinders and cubes (rather like *Il Tempietto*, whose stratification this building shares). The aedicule is a central cube, which is extended by half a cube towards the tree and a full cube to the rear, making the organ-place. In plan, the central square of the aedicule (which laterally is measured to the centre-lines of the columns, and longitudinally to their outer faces) sits within another square, one-third larger, which determines the radius of the curved walls; and a circle subscribed within it seems to determine the positions of the four outer columns of the aedicule and the radius of the seating and rail behind the altar.

The geometry of the section, as in the Villa Rotonda, is not as clear and simple as that of the plan. The central cube of the aedicule is there, but it is not a purely spatial cube – its height is measured from the platform floor to the top of the upstands around the flat roof. The square of the aedicule in section is extended downwards as half a square to determine the height of the crypt, though again this includes the depth of its roof – the platform.

There appear to be some other alignments: the angles of the batters on the piers in the crypt seem to align with the tops of the outer columns in the chapel above; the angle of the slope of the capstones on the side walls seems to derive from a long diagonal line through the section, from the notional bottom corner, through the base of the inner aedicule columns on one side, and through the top of the aedicule columns on the other.

The geometric arrangement of the section is not simple, but you can extract lines that appear to regulate the shapes and positions of elements.

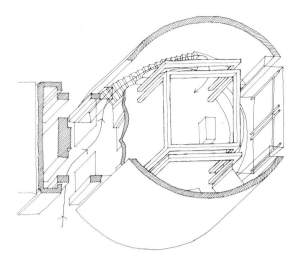

Transition, hierarchy, heart and parallel walls

For such a small building the transition from outside to inside is elaborate. This accords with the idea that holy spaces should be reached through 'layers of access' (as suggested by Christopher Alexander in 'Pattern 66' of *A Pattern Language*).

The route follows an architectural promenade through a hierarchical arrangement of spaces, culminating in the chapel itself, where there is a view of the outside from which one has come (comparable with the 'window' on the upper roof terrace that terminates the architectural promenade through the Villa Savoye).

To get into the chapel one first goes under the link between it and the existing wing of college accommodation. Thus the way in is provided with an integral protective 'porch'. (This was intended to have been part of a covered walkway, following the line of the innermost pathway on the site plan, creating an inner courtyard garden for the college. The walkway has not been built.) Through the entrance there is a vestibule with the door to the meeting room opposite. One rises into the chapel up either of the two stairways that run just inside the curved walls. In this way one emerges into the chapel, not on its main axis, but at either side.

Notwithstanding the circular plan and the related arcs of the side walls, the chapel – like the Ruskin Archive building by the same architects – has some of the characteristics of the architecture of parallel walls. A comparison has already been made with the Student Chapel by Siren and Siren at Otaniemi. In both it is the side walls that identify and protect the place of the chapel; in both, these act like blinkers blocking the lateral directions and framing a particular view; in both, one's passage through and into the chapel transforms one's view of the outside world. But whereas in the Otaniemi chapel (where the chapel is not lifted on a significant platform) the drift of movement runs longitudinally along one of the walls, here the dynamic is an upward spiral – or rather a pair of spirals running in counter directions, up each of the staircases onto the raised platform.

The Fitzwilliam College Chapel is an exercise in geometry, poetic intent and reference to previous works of architecture. One might even draw a parallel between it and Bramante's Tempietto. Each is set in an enclosed courtyard or quadrangle. Each is circular in plan and ordered according to a framework of geometry. Each is 'stratified' into three vertical layers: an above; a below; and an in-between, which is the main level.

The chapel defines a route that takes the worshipper from the lower level of the outside world up to the level of the altar.

241

Case Study 6 – THE SCHMINKE HOUSE

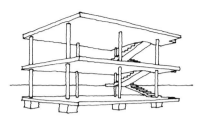

T he Schminke House was designed by Hans Scharoun and built for the German industrialist Fritz Schminke in 1933. Schminke owned a noodle factory in Löbau, close to the border with Czechoslovakia. The house was built on land to the north of his factory.

The Schminke House sits against a slope (above). Spatially it uses ideas expressed by Le Corbusier in his 'Dom-Ino' (above left).

Conditions

The site available for the house was generous in size. The adjacent factory lay to the south, and the best views were to the north and north-east. (This of course set up a conflict between sun and views.) The land had a slope, though not a dramatic one, from the south-west down to the north-east.

Scharoun was designing at a time when the new architecture promoted by Le Corbusier and others in the aftermath of the First World War was an exciting prospect. In 1923 Le Corbusier had published *Vers Une Architecture*, in which he celebrated (amongst other things) the beauty and adventure associated with ocean-going liners. Scharoun had been a contributor to the *Weissenhof* housing exhibition in Stuttgart in 1927, alongside Le Corbusier, Mies van der Rohe, Walter Gropius and others.

By this time, the use of large areas of glass and of steel as a structural material was well-established, and some architects – Le Corbusier in particular – had been experimenting with the free-planning that framed structures made possible (for example in the 'Dom-Ino' idea of 1914, above left, and in the Villa Savoye of 1929), and the reduced division between inside and outside that large areas of glass allowed. The development of central heating had also made planning less centred on the hearth, while electric lighting had been available for some years. Scharoun had an adventurous and wealthy client who seemed to want a house that manifested his forward-looking, 'modern' mentality. Mr Schminke would have had one or two resident servants.

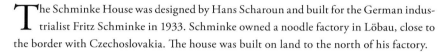

The house has a tricky site. The client's own (ugly) factory is to the south, so the usual southern orientation is not attractive. The best views are to the north.

Identification of place and basic elements

Scharoun's task was to identify places for all the mixed activities of dwelling: eating, sleeping, sitting being sociable, bathing, cooking, playing, growing plants, and so on.

The basic elements Scharoun employed were, primarily: the platform, the roof, the wall, the glass wall and the column. Most important of these are the two horizontal platforms and the roof, between which all the internal spaces of the house are contained, and which also form the terraces at the eastern end.

Reference for the Schminke House:
Peter Blundell Jones – *Hans Scharoun*, 1995, pp. 74-81.

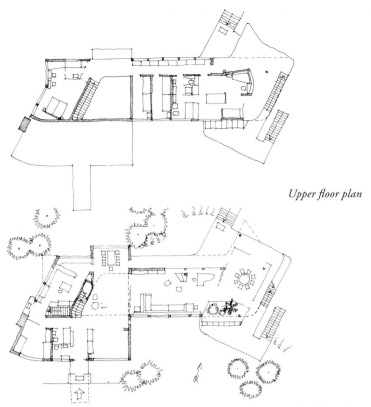

Upper floor plan

Entrance level floor plan

Other basic elements used include: the path, clearly defined only when in the form of staircases, and in the landing on the upper floor; the pit, which identifies the area of the conservatory; and the canopy, which identifies the place of the main entrance. There is a hearth that is a focus, though not a particularly imposing one, in the living area. Also, the chimney stack to the central heating boiler, at the western end of the house, acts as something of a marker, though possibly Scharoun wanted to play down this vertical element, against the prevailing horizontality of the platforms and roof.

Although these basic elements compose the house in its setting, Scharoun tried, for the most part, to avoid the traditional combined elements of enclosure and cell. These are found only where unavoidable: in the maid's bedroom, the sanitary provisions and in the children's bedrooms. Elsewhere, in the main living spaces and in the master bedroom at the eastern end of the house, the cell is not used, such enclosure being negated by the use of glass walls.

Modifying elements

The most important modifying element in the Schminke House is light. It has been carefully planned with sunlight and views uppermost in the mind of the designer. Also, the provision of electric light has been very carefully thought about, and used precisely to identify different places in the house.

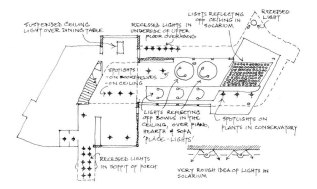

The views and the sunlight exert opposing forces on the house. To the south of the site, in the direction from which the sun shines, is the less attractive prospect – the factory. The better views are to the north and north-east. Scharoun tackled this dilemma by allowing the sun's light into the building through the south-facing walls, part of which is formed into a conservatory, but also by orienting the living spaces towards the views, through glass walls on the northern face of the house. On both of the main living levels of the house he projected decks out to the north (the pointed deck on the upper level is particularly distinctive), designed to catch the summer evening sun from the west.

The lighting plan above shows the care with which Scharoun used different kinds of electric light to help identify different places within the house. He designed light fittings especially to achieve a variety of effects; some of them he actually called *Platzleuchte* – place-lights. (Two photographs, reproduced in the book on Scharoun by Peter Blundell Jones, show the great difference in the character of the living spaces in sunlight and at night, and the dramatic effect of the different kinds of electric light used by Scharoun.)

Elements doing more than one thing

The house contains the living places, but it also acts to divide the site. Its angle creates an entrance area off the access road, and its mass separates and screens the factory from its garden.

Inside, the main internal stair and the hearth in the living space illustrate two distinctive examples of elements used by Scharoun to do more than one thing at once.

The stair between the entrance level and the upper level of the house is situated just opposite the main entrance (right, upper). It has a slight change of direction, curving on the bottom three steps. The primary purpose of the stair is obviously to make a pathway, a link for moving between the two levels. It is also used as the main part of the physical separation between the service end of the house (1) and the living parts of the house (2). The stair also does a third, more subtle, thing: its position and its angle on plan (which follows the angling of the kitchen window away from the factory) serve to 'nudge' people entering the house to the right – i.e. towards the dining space and the living places.

The hearth in the living space performs its timeless purpose as a focus, but it also acts as a divider between the piano place (2) and the living area (1). It too is angled towards the settee, which itself, like in other houses by Scharoun discussed earlier in this book, is positioned to make the most of the view across open countryside to the north.

Scharoun identified different parts of the main living floor by means of different sorts of lighting.

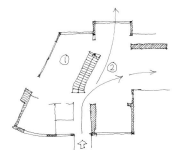

As you enter the house the stair deflects you to the right, towards the living space.

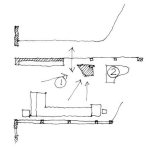

The hearth performs its traditional role as focus, but also acts as a spatial divider.

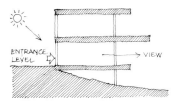

Although you enter the house at ground level, you find yourself a level above the garden. It is like going on board a ship.

Using things that are there

Scharoun used the views to the north and north-east to help in the organisation of his plan. But probably the most effective thing he used that was already there was the slope of the land. The effect of this is most apparent at the important east end, which accommodates the principal living spaces. The slope allowed entrance into the house not at the lowest level (the traditional ground floor), but at the intermediate level, rather like boarding a boat. It also meant that, although one enters at ground level without rising up steps or a ramp, one finds oneself, upon reaching the eastern end of the house, a storey above ground. This effect is further exaggerated on the upper level – on the 'prow' outside the master bedroom, where one may survey the rolling landscape from a commanding height. Many photographs of this house show it like a small modern pleasure boat at its moorings.

Primitive place types

The house contains, but does not seem to celebrate in traditional fashion, the usual primitive place types one finds in a dwelling. There is a hearth in the living area (which plays the various roles mentioned above); there are beds and places to wash upstairs; there is a place to cook in the kitchen; there is even a prow, which might on occasion be used (probably in jest) as a pulpit. But none of these seem to be the *raison d'être* of the living spaces; there are other, more interesting things going on.

Architecture as making frames

Like any house, the Schminke House frames the lives of its inhabitants. It does this in particular ways. It emphasises the horizontality of those lives, with its division into three pronounced horizontal levels which relate to the landscape around. It does not enclose those lives in a protective carapace; its platforms and roof protect them from the sky, but the transparent sides make them open to the horizon, the views and the sun.

And the Schminke House's allusion to ships and sailing seems to suggest that the house is a vessel rather than a cell. It looks as if it might be possible to cast of the ropes from the mooring and sail away. The house accommodates adventure and change through time and space, rather than security in enclosure and stasis. This is a conscious component of the poetry of Scharoun's design.

245

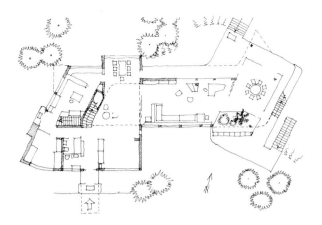

Temples and cottages

Three characteristics of the Schminke House belong to the 'temple': its separation of the living spaces from the ground level at the eastern end of the house; its use of highly finished materials; and its apparent arrogance in the face of climatic forces (Scharoun was no doubt depending on the central heating to make up for the heat lost through the large areas of glass, and on modern materials to prevent the flat roof from leaking).

Otherwise the house exhibits some 'cottage' characteristics: its responsiveness to site – sun and ground; and its thorough relation of planning to purposes.

Although in this house there is an underlying armature of orthogonal geometry (a 'temple' characteristic) it is Scharoun's responsive attitude – to sun, to site, to views, to function – that twists this geometry into an irregular plan form. Though this results in a sculptural form, particularly at the picturesque east end of the house, Scharoun was not motivated solely by a desire to make form or paint pictures with his architecture. Thus Scharoun's plans exhibit subtle conflicts between different kinds of geometry.

Geometry

First, there appear to be no instances where Scharoun has allowed the shapes of his spaces to be determined by ideal geometric figures, no circles, no squares, no rectangles with particular harmonic proportions. Dismissing ideal geometry as a way of making decisions about the positions of things, his conflicts seem to have been between the geometries of being and of making. To these were added his perception that the site had within it two different grains. One of the most obvious characteristics of the house is that it is not a simple, orthogonal form. The geometry of making is not given the highest priority, but is allowed to be distorted by other pressures. These other pressures begin with the circles of presence, distorted as they are in most instances into rectangles, and with the social geometries that constitute the various places in the house: the dining place; the place around the hearth; the place around the table in the solarium (at the extreme east end of the main living floor).

Next there are the lines of sight, within the building and also from the inside to the outside. Scharoun seems to have seen the latter – the views – as being at an angle to the lie of the land that set the datum for the general grain of the house. This overlaying of

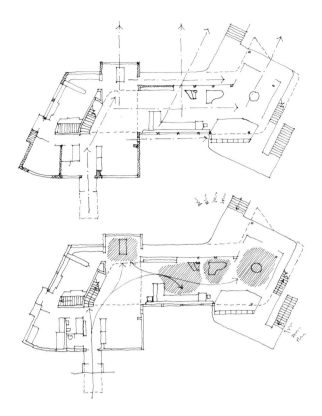

In the lower drawing (left) you can see (reading from left to right) the distorted circles of presence of the dining table, the hearth, the piano and the table in the solarium. It also shows the lines of passage that thread between and through them. The upper drawing shows the principal lines of sight in the plan. Notice that they follow three principal directions: one set up by the main entrance; another by the living area; and a third, at an angle, by the main stair and the solarium.

the different geometries, with a refusal to submit to the geometry of making, produced a distinctive response to the six-directions-plus-centre. The house has two overlapping grains. The up and the down directions are, at most positions, contained by the horizontal platforms and the roof. But with the four horizontal directions, the situation is more complex.

Taking the entrance as the starting point one is aware of the forward and of the rearward; one is also, as one enters, very much aware of the right, but the left is diminished, being replaced by the deflection of the stair, (in the way already mentioned) to reinforce the direction right.

At the other end of the house, at the solarium, something different happens with the four horizontal directions. Here it is the forward (roughly to the north) that is deflected, to focus the space more on the better views.

The house has no one centre but a number: the hearth, the dining table, the table in the solarium, for examples. It seems that for Scharoun the most important centre was the mobile person.

Space and structure

The structure of the house is a skeleton of steel frame. Its columns are not laid out on a regular grid, but respond to the complex attitude to the six-directions mentioned above. At the east end of the house the vertical structure – the columns – are reduced to a minimum to increase the openness of the spaces. Even so they still contribute to the identification of

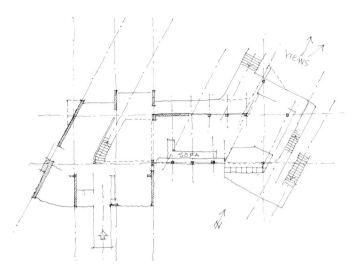

In this drawing you can see the complementary grains of the house. They distort the simple geometry of making to take account of the alternative grains suggested by the lie of the land, the views and the direction of the sun.

places. There is a column in the solarium that seems to help identify its extreme corner; there is another on the deck outside that supports the prow above and that also makes a 'doorway' between the deck at the top of the steps down to the garden and the narrower deck outside the solarium; and there is a third column in the conservatory, about which Scharoun seems perhaps to have been less happy – he tried to camouflage its structural identity by painting it with small squares of different colours, making it into an elemental sculpture (as distinct from a place identifier) amongst the cacti.

At the other end of the plan the spaces are more definitely enclosed by walls and windows. The boiler chimney stack at the extreme west end of the house is built of brick – a weighty contrast to the apparent levitation of the decks at the other end of the house.

The static places in the plan tend to be at the extremities: the dining area; the solarium; the conservatory; the bedroom and the prow of the deck on the upper floor. The heart of the house is probably the living area, with its static focus the hearth.

In some circumstances however, this heart also works as a dynamic space, a route from the hallway, which is the datum place of the house, to the solarium. Other, clearer dynamic spaces are the stairs, the deck outside the piano place and the corridor landing on the upper floor.

The canopy over the main entrance begins a process of transition from outside to inside the building. This process of fairly abrupt enclosure is reversed by the progressive openness of the rest of the house.

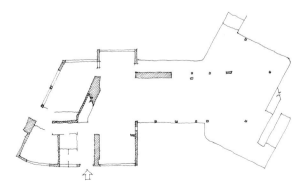

The steel columns do not obey the usual discipline of a regular grid. In most of his buildings, Scharoun avoided regular geometry. He certainly avoided the ideal geometry of perfect squares and circles etc. But he also refused to accept the authority of the geometry of making. He preferred to follow more complex and subtle geometries.

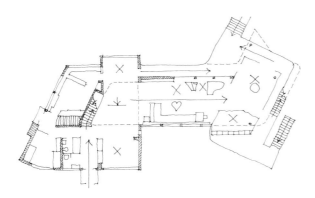

The crosses on this plan idenfy the principle places of the entrance level. The house does seem to have a 'heart', around the hearth.

Scharoun was adept at making zones between the inside and outside. There are the various decks on both levels, which create an intermediate zone that is neither inside nor wholly outside. There is the conservatory too, an inside space that, unlike the majority of spaces in the house, also has contact with the sky. And there is the solarium itself, which is a space more open than the living room but less so than the decks – a zone between the two. The dining area, not quite a zone between, is defined by the overhang of the landing above. It is at one end of what looks to be the remnants of a parallel wall space, which sets up an axis into the countryside through the broad window over the dining table.

On the upper floor the layout is more cellular, until one comes to the master bedroom. This insinuates itself amongst a composition of planar walls, mostly arranged orthogonally, but with one wall slightly skewed to broaden the view to the north-east. This one piece of wall obeys neither of the two grains set up on the main living floor beneath; its freedom is due to the independence of the two floors allowed by the Dom-Ino idea.

The house is clearly stratified. There is an undercroft dedicated to the services of the house – the boiler room, etc. The entrance floor, in the middle, is at one end a *piano nobile*. The upper living floor, further from the ground, is the sleeping floor, its contact with the sky manifest in the deck prow outside the master bedroom that in the summer basks in evening sun.

The Schminke House is as divorced as was possible at the time from history. In its design Scharoun celebrates the possibilities of materials that had not long been available to architects. He also celebrates openness and the sun. He explores the potential of steel structure and large panes of glass. He avoids regular geometries based on ideal shapes such as squares and proportional rectangles (such as one would find in neoclassical architecture). He subdues the roles played by primitive places in the house, in favour of openness to the horizon and beyond. He even divorces the house, as much as he can, from the ground. This is a house which, through its architecture, tries to reinvent life itself and provide it with a setting that owes as little as possible to the past.

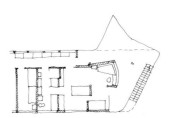

The prow on the bedroom level projects from the north facing elevation of the house far enough to catch the evening sun in the west. In this way the house benefits from a sun terrace facing away from the factory to the south.

Case Study 7 – VANNA VENTURI HOUSE

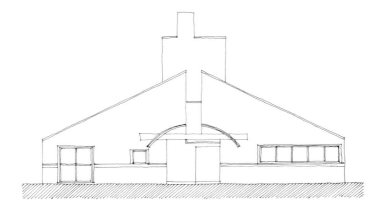

Robert Venturi designed this house for his mother. It was built at Chestnut Hill, Pennsylvania, in 1962. At about the same time, he was writing a book called *Complexity and Contradiction in Architecture*, which was published in 1966. The design of the house is related to the argument of the book.

Conditions

At the time of both the house and the book the teaching and practice of architecture were dominated by Modernism. Venturi, rather than accepting the prevailing orthodoxies, questioned and rebelled against them. His arguments are set out in detail in his book. He rejected the quest for simplicity and resolution associated with Modernism (arguments for which are found particularly in the writings and works of Frank Lloyd Wright, Mies van der Rohe and Louis Kahn), in favour of complexity and contradiction, which he argued made products of architecture more witty and less boring; more appropriate (poetic) reflections of the complexities and contradictions of life, and more stimulating, intellectually and aesthetically.

Venturi used the design of his mother's house to express his reaction against the orthodoxies and seriousness of Modernism. In it he consciously avoided what might be considered 'right answers', and contrived conflicts in the arrangement of forms and the organisation of space.

Basic elements

Even in his choice of basic elements Venturi expressed his reaction against Modernism.

The distinctive palette of elements used by orthodox Modernist architects included: the flat roof; emphasis (externally) of the horizontal floor; the column (*piloti*), allowing the opening up of the ground level and free planning; and the glass wall, which reduced (visually) the cellular division of space internally and between inside and outside. Modernist architects also tended to play down the formal importance of the hearth, and of its external expression in the chimney stack. (Scharoun used this palette in the Schminke House.)

The site of the Vanna Venturi House is flat. Around its boundaries it is enclosed by trees and fences. It is entered through a neck of land, and the house is positioned to present its gable elevation to the approach.

Reference for Vanna Venturi House:
(Venturi) – *Venturi Scott Brown & Associates, on houses and housing (Architectural Monographs No. 21)*, 1992, pp. 24-9.
Robert Venturi – *Complexity and Contradiction in Architecture*, 1966.

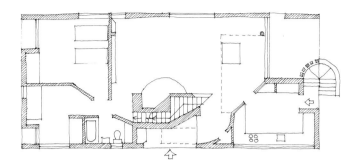

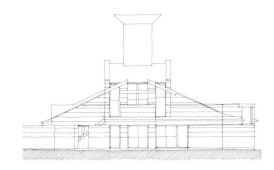

In his mother's house Venturi directly contravened every one of these 'rules' of Modernism. The roof is pitched; the horizontality of the floors is not expressed externally; there are no columns (except one – an expedient to hold up the roof over the dining area, which is omitted in some published plans of the house), and the house is firmly set on the ground; there is a glass wall (between the dining area and a covered terrace) but in the main elevations Venturi prefers to make windows (almost caricatures of traditional windows) in the walls; he also gives emphasis internally to the central hearth and externally to its chimney.

In this early version of the Vanna Venturi House, the chimney stack is even more prominent than in the built version. In his architecture Venturi borrowed ideas from historical examples; he took the idea of prominent chimneys from British domestic architecture (of the Arts and Crafts and Edwardian period, and from the eighteenth-century work of John Vanbrugh) and similar houses in the United States. Venturi was also interested in conflicts of scale: in this version the chimney is 'too big' for the house; in the final version (on the previous page) the chimney appears to be both 'too big' and 'too small'.

Space organisation and geometry

There are quirks in Venturi's design that are well discussed elsewhere in critiques of this house: his 'mannerist' touches (the broken pediment of the front elevation for example); his (counter-Modern) use of ornament (the appliqué arch superimposed on the clearly structural lintel over the entrance); the 'ingrowing' bay-windows in the downstairs bedrooms and verandah off the dining area; the stair going up to nowhere from the upstairs bedroom; and so on. But Venturi's attitude of complicating and contradicting orthodox ways of doing things is perhaps most architectural (in the terms set out in this book) in his spatial organisation of the house and in the ways he deals with the various kinds of geometry.

The design of the house 'begins' with two parallel walls, which define the area of ground inside of the house. As discussed in the *Parallel Walls* chapter, these tend to establish a longitudinal axis that sets up a dominant direction within the plan and also begins to order relationships between inside and outside. But Venturi contradicts the orthodox architecture

The plan of Venturi's design 'begins' with a pair of parallel walls.

251

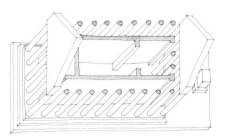

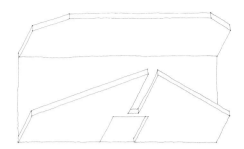

of parallel walls in a number of ways. First he positions the walls perpendicular to, rather than parallel with, the principal axis of the site, which is the axis of entrance (right). Then he contradicts the arrangement of gables found in ancient parallel-wall buildings (temples) by placing the gables of his complex roof on the long sides of the rectangular plan (above right). In ancient temples it was the geometry of making that influenced the three-dimensional geometry of the roof, resulting in triangular pediments at each end. Venturi's contradictory arrangement, together with his avoidance of columns, results in the front of his mother's house being like a pediment on one of the 'wrong' sides of the rectangular plan, and resting directly on the ground.

As can be seen in the sections (below), the geometry of Venturi's roof is complex: there are slopes in three different directions; it does not always reach the walls that should be its support. (This happens over the entrance and at the 'ingrown' balcony outside the upstairs bedroom, and reinforces the sense that these very two-dimensional walls are masks, screening rather than expressing the inside – another counter to the Modernist suggestion that barriers between inside and outside should be broken down.)

Venturi's contradiction of orthodoxy informs his plan too.

In his own explanation of the house in *Complexity and Contradiction in Architecture*, Venturi describes his plan as deriving from, but a distortion of, 'Palladian rigidity and symmetry'. As Rudolf Wittkower has shown in *Architectural Principles in the Age of Humanism*, Palladio's villa plans, whether square or rectangular, were generally arranged

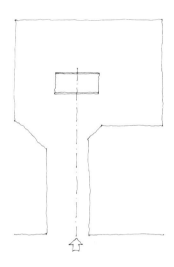

In positioning the house, Venturi lays the parallel walls across the main axis of the site.

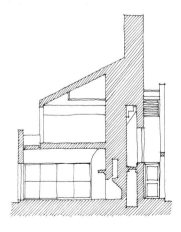

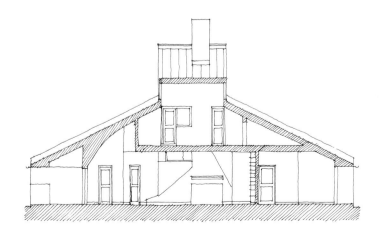

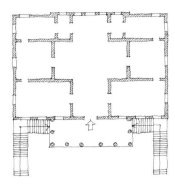

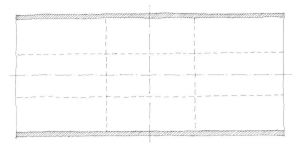

The plan of Venturi's house is based on a geometric grid somewhat similar to a Palladian house.

according to a division into three in both directions; they were given a dominant central space, surrounded by subsidiary rooms. (Above, for example, is Palladio's Villa Foscari.)

If Venturi's design had followed these Palladian arrangements, it might have turned out something like this (upper middle right): with a large room in the middle and secondary rooms arranged symmetrically at the sides. There might have been a portico protruding at the front. Windows would, as far as possible, have been arranged symmetrically within rooms. The staircase and fireplace might have occupied equivalent positions in the two halves of the plan. Venturi broke this Palladian discipline in various ways, establishing and then destroying symmetry; creating then denying axes. The contradictory move he appears to make first (lower middle right), is to bring the stair and the fireplace together, and to position them centrally so that they block the axis of entrance. In the Palladian plan that axis would be open, as a line of passage leading into the main central space (and maybe also as a line of sight out into the surroundings). Venturi, having set up the axis, denies it with a closed and opaque solidity. This move does other things too. It creates a porch, but one that recedes into the building rather than projecting out from it. It also gives Venturi another opportunity for complexity by setting up a situation in

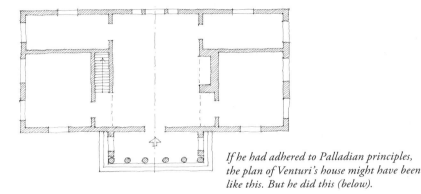

If he had adhered to Palladian principles, the plan of Venturi's house might have been like this. But he did this (below).

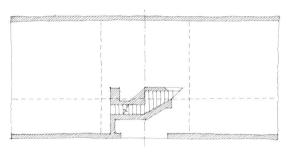

The fireplace and the stair compete for space with the entrance...

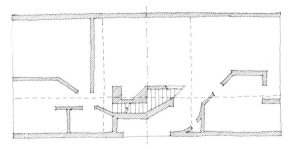

... and the walls distort Palladian geometry to accommodate different sized spaces.

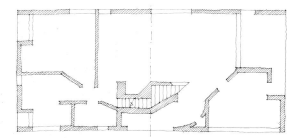

Venturi breaks a classical rule of architecture by positioning a window so that its edge, rather than its centre-line, aligns with the axis of the house. Another window has the end of a partition wall intruding into it.

which entrance, stair and fire all vie to occupy the same part of the plan. The orthodox form of each is changed in some way in response to this (contrived) competition for space: the fireplace is moved off axis to allow room for the stair; the stair is narrowed half-way up conceding to the chimney stack; and the entrance doorway, which itself has been usurped from its axial position, 'pushes' the adjacent wall to an angle that nudges into the stair.

The angle of this wall seems intended to acknowledge the line of passage into the house, now made diagonal, mitigating slightly the blocking effect of the stair and fireplace. The line of passage is further managed by the quadrant curve of the closet wall, turning an axial Palladian line of entry, into a chicane.

Elsewhere in the plan (above) partition walls are positioned both to accord with and to distort Palladian orthogonality. The wall between the living room and the bedroom (to the left on the plan) is at a right angle to the parallel walls, whereas the walls that run across the plan, which help delineate the small bedroom, the bathroom, entrance and kitchen, are afflicted by a spatial warp, seemingly caused by the position of the stair and fireplace.

Finally, the positioning and nature of the window and door openings presents Venturi with more opportunities for architectural contradiction. Venturi refuses clarity in differentiating the ends and the sides, putting a mix of types of opening in each elevation of the house.

All architecture is to some extent philosophical, in that it makes sense of the world for us in spatial rather than verbal terms. But Venturi's architecture, particularly in the Vanna Venturi House, is philosophical and polemic. It illustrates how architecture can contain cultural commentary. Where the Schminke House expressed a vision of a new way of life, open to the countryside and sunshine, unimpeded in the horizontal directions, the house Venturi built for his mother uses architecture dialectically, to put forward an argument against the puritanism of modernist architecture. Venturi 'writes' his house like a philosopher might construct an argument, taking each of his antagonist's arguments in turn and contradicting it explicitly in his own.

Case Study 8 – THE WOODLAND CHAPEL

The Woodland Chapel stands in the extensive grounds of the Woodland Crematorium, on the outskirts of Stockholm. Designed by Erik Gunnar Asplund just after the First World War, it was intended for the funerals of children. At first sight the chapel appears simple and without pretensions to being anything more than a rudimentary hut in the woods. But Asplund managed to imbue this unassuming, elemental building with a remarkable range of apt poetic ideas. The subject of the 'poem' is, of course, death.

Conditions and identification of place

Asplund designed the Woodland Chapel at a time before Modernism had become the dominant movement in Swedish architecture. The prevailing interest was in the power of traditional forms and methods of building – a movement which has been called National Romanticism.

The chapel is reached through the grounds of the Woodland Crematorium. Around the main crematorium – a later building also by Asplund – the landscape is open, undulating and with a big sky. By contrast, the Woodland Chapel is hidden away in a dark wood of pine trees.

Asplund's task was to identify a place for funeral services: where family and friends could come together to mourn. The steep hipped roof acts as a marker in the woods.

Basic and modifying elements

Basic elements are used in clear and straightforward ways. There are defined areas of ground, columns, walls and a roof. There is a pathway leading to the building, a platform on which the coffin is placed and another used as the lectern. The floor, walls and roof form a simple cell, in which there is a doorway on the line of the approach and a small domestic window in one corner. The floor around the perimeter of the inside of the chapel is raised by two steps, suggesting that the main place is a shallow pit.

The chapel stands in the dappled light of the wood. There is the faint smell of pine. Walking towards the building, one's footsteps are muffled by the carpet of pine needles, except on the stone paving that defines the area of the chapel floor, inside and under the porch.

Inside, the main place is lit by a roof-light at the highest part of its domed ceiling. Sounds are reflected by the hard surfaces.

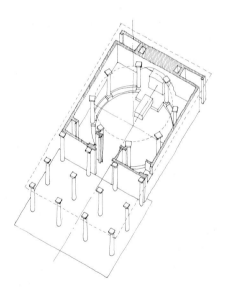

References for The Woodland Chapel:
Caroline Constant – *The Woodland Cemetery: Towards a Spiritual Landscape*, 1994.
Peter Blundell Jones – *Gunnar Asplund*, 2006.

Elements doing more than one thing

As one approaches, the roof appears as a pyramid and acts as a marker. The porch columns support the roof, but also channel the route into the building, creating a transition between the woods and the interior. The returns of the walls alongside the entrance help to create small subsidiary places off the main chapel space, but they also make the cell walls appear much thicker than they are, increasing its cave-like quality. This 'thick wall' effect is reinforced by the deep reveals of the small window and the niche in which the lectern stands. The internal columns appear to support the dome above, but also define the main place, like a clearing in the forest.

Using things that are there

Asplund uses the woods to give the chapel a particular setting. The pathway to the building, which begins at a gateway some distance from it, strikes a straight line through the irregularly spaced trees. The porch columns are themselves like trees, though regularly positioned, bringing something of the character of the surrounding woods in under the roof.

Primitive place types and architecture as making frames

The niche in which the lectern stands is not a hearth, but like one. (Externally there is a chimney stack in the same position, but this leads from the basement.) The lectern itself is like an altar. The catafalque on which the coffin rests is both a bed and an altar. It is also the focus of the performance place – like a clearing in the woods – defined by the shallow pit, surrounding columns and domed ceiling.

The building is a temporary frame for the body of a dead child and for the ceremony associated with its funeral.

In its outer form the chapel is like a house, framed by the surrounding woods. The porch frames the gathering mourners, who mingle with the columns (which have a presence like ancestors come to the funeral).

Under the roof there is also the cell that separates the special place of the ceremony from everywhere else, and inside that cell there is the pit and the ring of columns like a primitive henge. This circle, lit from the sky above, frames the catafalque that frames the coffin, which is itself a frame for the body. The lectern is framed in its own niche. The henge,

catafalque, lectern, coffin and the mourners are all framed, pictorially, by the entrance doorway, but architecturally by the womb-like interior.

Temples and cottages, and geometry

The chapel is a 'temple' in 'cottage' clothing; the unquestionable authority of death is cloaked in the appearance of domestic simplicity. The building, though not raised on a platform, is formal and symmetrical. It has no pragmatic irregularity, though its materials are simple and natural. Its scale is small; it is a building for human beings.

Asplund employs many of the various kinds of architectural geometry.

The circle of columns – again like ancestors standing around the shallow pit – define, literally, the circle of presence of the catafalque and coffin; it is within the social geometry of this circle that the mourners sit.

The line of passage and the line of sight from the entrance gateway coincide. In experience and symbolically the building – the pyramid – terminates this axis. It establishes two of the six directions inherent in the chapel – stretching from the symbolic hearth to the western horizon and the setting sun.

The circle of eight columns set up the cross axis – the other two horizontal directions blocked by the side walls – and thus establish a centre. Below is the basement, above is light coming through the 'sky' of the dome, (the ideal geometry of which disrupts the geometry of making of the roof). Through the centre is the vertical axis – the *axis mundi* (axis of the earth).

The catafalque is positioned, not at the centre of the circle on the *axis mundi*, but between the symbolic hearth and that vertical axis – suspended for the duration of the ceremony between home and eternity.

Where Venturi's mother's house is polemic, Asplund's Woodland Chapel is poetic. He uses architecture to evoke an ancient, timeless place for a funeral. In this he uses resonance, between the columns and the trees, and reference to ancient precedents – the stone circle with an altar near its centre. He employs symbolism too, in the pyramid form of the roof.

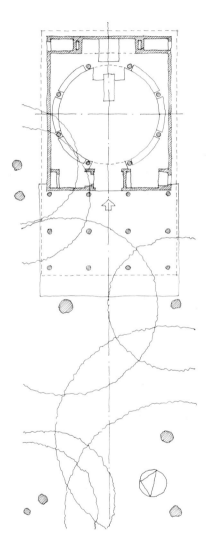

Case Study 9 – HOUSE VI

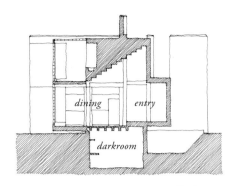

Section

If an architect is a 'god' – in that he or she makes a 'world' for us to live in – then the architect of House VI is generally acknowledged to have been a jealous 'god', indifferent (and unapologetically so) to the needs and comforts of the 'Adam and Eve' who were to live in the small 'world' he made for them.

House VI was designed by Peter Eisenman and built in Cornwall, Connecticut, in the first half of the 1970s (and largely reconstructed in 1990 by Will Calhoun with advice from Madison Spencer of Eisenman's practice). It was, as the name implies, his sixth house design, and the fourth to be built. The 'Adam and Eve' – the clients of this weekend house – were Suzanne and Dick Frank, who, because of their experiences trying to inhabit it and because of its notoriety, have written about and photographed the house (see the reference below). They also paid for its reconstruction.

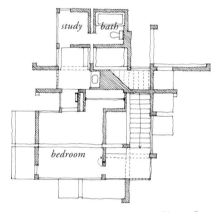

Upper floor

Temples and cottages

House VI is a 'temple'. It is even nearer to the 'temple' extreme of the 'temple–cottage' spectrum (discussed earlier in this book) than an ancient Greek temple. Its naming as a 'house' implies that the building identifies a place to live, which to some extent it does. But any intention to accommodate places for inhabitation was eclipsed by the priority Eisenman gave to its complex geometric composition. Eisenman's attitude has been described by Suzanne Frank (in her book) as 'arrogant', though she also seems to have come to accept that it was a principled arrogance. The features of this house usually cited as evidence of Eisenman's arrogance are: a glazed strip down the centre of the bedroom floor that prevented use of a double bed and provided a view from the living room below into the privacy of the bedroom above; a column in the dining area that made it difficult to insert a dining table, and which stands as an extra guest at any meal; kitchen cupboards which because of the need to obey the geometric discipline of the house are too high to reach without a step-ladder; and a number of single high steps, particularly on the ground floor, that make moving around awkward. Also, much of the fabric suffered deterioration due to the weather, necessitating the reconstruction within twenty years.

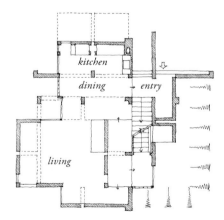

Entrance floor

Apart from this indifference to the physical and psychological comfort of its human occupants, the chief 'temple' characteristics of this house are: its ideal geometric discipline, which transcends any geometry of making; the concealment of visible evidence of the way in which it was constructed (it is actually a timber frame clad with plywood panels that have been rendered and painted to hide the joints); its denial of the orthodox 'rules' of structural

Reference for House VI:
Suzanne Frank – *Peter Eisenman's House VI: the Client's Response*, 1994.

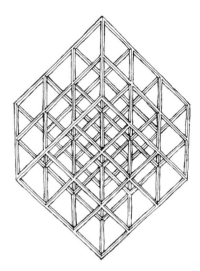

The drawings opposite (left) illustrate the house broadly in the form it was built as measured around the time of the reconstruction in 1990. Eisenman's original idea – which is illustrated in Suzanne Frank's book – was to have a double-height (almost cubic) living space with the bed consigned to an alcove (the present study) on the upper floor.

order (the house has a famous external column that does not reach the ground); and its conceptual detachment from the earth (Dick Frank's darkroom makes a basement but this is recessed to make the house seem to float above a ground surface that slopes down steeply under it). Nevertheless, the house does follow a rigorously orthogonal geometry, which accords with the verticality of gravity and the geometry of the stock timbers used, and which counterpoints the intrinsic 'six-directions-plus-centre' of its human and canine occupants. But this too is subverted by the inclusion of an upside-down staircase in the ceiling over the dining area, suggesting that the house, like an etching by M.C. Escher, could be turned over and still retain its validity as a work of architecture.

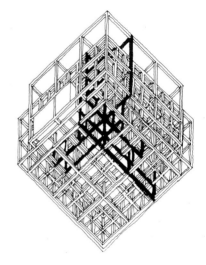

Ideal geometry

To analyse the geometry of House VI it is perhaps most appropriate to look at the platonic drawings that Eisenman produced and which he would probably accept are the purest representation of the architecture of the house, uncorrupted by the inconveniences of gravity, weather and human occupation, and the unavoidable imperfections of construction with real materials. Eisenman's own drawings are meticulous in their attempt at precision. They are reproduced in Suzanne Frank's book.

    Near the beginning of the present book, in the chapter *How Analysis Helps Design*, I suggested having a piece of squared paper available as an underlay when drawing in a notebook, analytically and conceptually. This graph paper is particularly useful idea to have in mind when studying Eisenman's House VI, though the house is so complex that neither the plans nor sections easily yield to simple geometric analysis. The house is designed on a conceptual spatial framework that is a three-dimensional cubic grid, or rather a number of overlapped cubic grids. The generative process appears to begin with a 'crate' of 3 x 3 x 2 cubes of space defined by square section ribs (top right). By repeating, superimposing and shifting this grid a complex armature is produced (middle right). This complex armature is then taken as the starting point for the excisions, completions and transformations that will turn it into the house. Many of the ribs are amputated, but the complex armature of cubes remains as a ghost (bottom right). Some of the interstitial spaces of the armature are turned into the rooms of the house – the living room, bedroom, kitchen, etc. Some of the surviving ribs become structure – though Eisenman, by his column that does not touch the ground, is keen to send the message that this is a primarily an intellectual structure, and only secondarily a physical structure. Some of the faces of the armature are glazed to

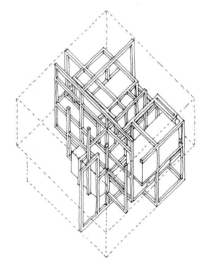

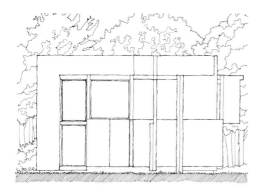

The elevations of House VI are reminiscent of the early twentieth century 'Neoplasticist' paintings of Piet Mondrian. In a similar way to Eisenman's resistance to allowing life to hold sway over architecture, Mondrian suggested painting should not attempt to portray reality.

become windows whilst others are filled to become screen walls. Finally, and perhaps most interestingly, whilst some of the ribs are left solid others are treated as 'absences' and become slots of light – the glazed strip in the bedroom floor is one example. In his drawings and in the house itself Eisenman colour-codes the various 'layers' of this complex composition. The outside is in shades of grey; the stair to the upper floor is green; the upside-down stair over the dining space is red, and so on.

Eisenman submitted his PhD* dissertation at Cambridge University in 1963. Its subject was 'The Formal Basis of Modern Architecture'. House VI is informed by this work. Its complex armature may be interpreted as a development, in the direction of complexity and multi-dimensionality, of those used by architects such as Gerrit Rietveld, Mies van der Rohe, Le Corbusier, Giuseppe Terragni and others, which were themselves developments from the formal frameworks of neoclassical architecture (e.g. Alberti, Bramante, Palladio) and further back to the classical architecture of ancient Rome and Greece, and the precepts of Vitruvius. In this way, Eisenman's work can be positioned relative to a very long historical continuum of architectural ideas related to ideal geometry.

An acerbic critic might conclude, 'In the final analysis we can easily identify the "god" in whose honour the "temple" House VI was created', or even that its architect was more the 'serpent' in this particular 'Eden'. ('Eve' first met Eisenman by a photocopier in the Avery Library at Columbia University rather than by the 'Tree of Knowledge of Good and Evil'.) But Eisenman might defend himself by suggesting that his House VI is rather a 'temple' to the religion of architecture, which through geometry in its 'purest' form transcends the mundane and occupies a middle 'being' – that which John Dee identified as (see the chapter on *Ideal Geometry*) in-between the natural and the supernatural, above the earth but lower than paradise. In striving for the divine it is a drag to be shackled by earthly needs.

In the reconstruction, the clients managed to find an accommodation with their house, which is what most of us do with the conditions – life situations – in which we find ourselves. Architecture is usually considered one of the prime means of finding an accommodation with natural conditions that can be challenging; but in this case it was the architecture that set some of the challenges the clients had to cope with. For example, 'Eve' reconciled herself to using a step-ladder to reach the apples in the kitchen cupboard; and 'Adam' contrived a double bed that would straddle the glazed strip in the bedroom floor.

* Peter Eisenman – *The Formal Basis of Modern Architecture*, 2006.

Case Study 10 – THE BOX

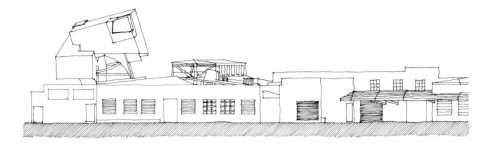

The Box was designed by Eric Owen Moss and built in 1994. It is part of a refurbishment scheme in Culver City, California. The Box comprises a small self-contained composition of fractured or abstracted geometric forms inserted into an existing industrial building. The main space – the box itself – is a conference room (initially it was intended as a party room for a restaurant), supported above the roof of the existing shed, reached by a contorted stair from below. The complex geometry and uniform grey material of the Box contrasts with, and seems an alien intrusion into, the ordinariness of the original building.

Identification of place

The Box identifies itself as a place, not so much by the way it accommodates or frames a particular use, but by 'standing out' from its surroundings: by the oddness of its appearance within its context. It is a 'temple' that exists in its own world, separate from mundane reality. It hovers as a strange sculptural ornament above the roof of the boring, earth-bound shed below. It has its own distorted structure that intrudes into, and breaks, the shed's standard orthogonal structure. The Box is a cell that floats above and apart from the world, a place to which one ascends to see the world around from an abnormal vantage point. The Box stands aloof from the world in space. It also distinguishes itself as strange by its attitude to pragmatic use, by the way it is made and by the way in which it has been composed architecturally. In each of these the design of the Box challenges many aspects of what in this book have been called the *Geometries of Being*, and plays the game of fracturing and drawing abstractions from *Ideal Geometry*.

Geometries of being

In designing the Box, Moss made few concessions to utility. This is, seemingly intentionally, not a building for 'dwelling' in the sense implied by Martin Heidegger when he wrote (in his essay 'Building Dwelling Thinking') that 'We do not dwell because we have built, but we build and have built because we dwell, that is, because we are *dwellers*'. This is architecture as abstract form. It has a horizontal floor, on which it is possible to walk, to stand, to place furniture; it has a stair of dimensions sufficient for a human being, giving access from below; it has openings that allow in light sufficient to see what one might be doing, and views to the surroundings; it keeps out the weather. But these few concessions to dwelling are eclipsed by other concerns.

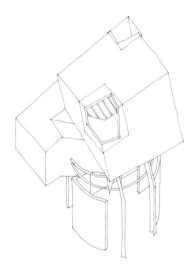

Reference for The Box:
Brad Collins and Anthony Vidler – *Eric Owen Moss: Buildings and Projects 2*, 1996.

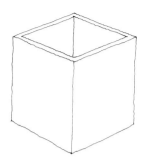

The way the Box is constructed, and its materials treated, challenges the geometry of making. Its irregular geometry presents difficulty in assembling standard materials, and its uniform grey finish gives the false appearance that the building is all made of one, indeterminate, material. Construction joints are concealed, except where simple sheets of glass cover openings in the corners of the cell. Some necessary structure is evident, but this too breaks the usual discipline of structural geometry.

Also, the six-directions-plus-centre, which resonate with those of the human form and which are evident in most orthodox four-walled rooms, are unsettled by the disturbed geometry of the Box. The building's composition is based on ideal geometry, but in a disturbed and fractured form.

Ideal geometry

The diagrams on this page and the next illustrate the underlying geometric composition of the Box. The composition begins, conceptually, with a cylinder, a hemisphere and a cube (above). These are fundamental geometric forms in architecture and could have been composed as a domed circular chamber set in a cubic building (rather like the Villa Rotonda). But Moss assembles them in a different, unusual, way. The dome (hemisphere) sits above the cylinder, as usual, but the cube is balanced on top of them.

The next stage in Moss's conceptual process is to fragment, distort, or unsettle these simple geometric forms (opposite page). Sections of the cylinder are removed. The hemisphere is reduced to a structural armature, which suggests the space occupied by a dome rather than being a dome itself. (This armature provides the structural support for the floor of the cube.) And, most significantly, the cube, which would ordinarily be aligned with the horizontal and vertical dimensions of the world, is canted unequally in two of those dimensions, disrupting its resonance with its context and content (the building on which it sits and the world around it, as well as the people who might occupy it). To complicate the geometry further, part of the cube is missing, the part that would have been below the horizontal floor. A complicated irregular staircase, which starts from within the cylinder, finds its way up to the space of the cube. It passes through the roof, and is for a short stretch open to the outside air before being enclosed again and finally reaching the floor of the cube. The breach in the roof of the original building, through which the staircase and the structure supporting the Box pass, is covered by a simple glass platform supported by a simple timber structure.

The Box is composed of simple geometric forms, the cylinder, hemisphere, and cube...

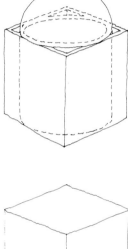

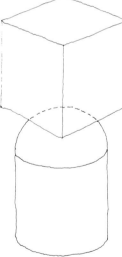

These forms could have been assembled in a traditional way, but they have been put together oddly, with the cube balanced on top of the cylinder and hemisphere.

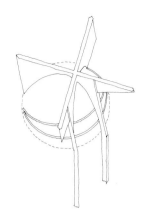

The last touch of the design is that two 'negative' cubes are cut from the corners of the Box, to give light. These openings are made weatherproof with the simple tacked-on glass covers mentioned above.

As a work of architecture, the Box is an exercise in fragmented and re-assembled geometric forms. This approach contradicts many of the orthodox ways of doing architecture, and gains attention because of its difference. The result is a sculptural object that is noticed because its irregular form contrasts with the orthodox geometries of the surrounding buildings. This is a seductive form of architecture, stimulating because of its games with geometry and aesthetic complexity. But it is a form of architecture that is hermetically sealed from its users who, even when they are inside, are excluded. They are not considered or engaged by the architecture but asked to stand as admirers of its sculptural form.

... have been fragmented, distorted and disrupted.

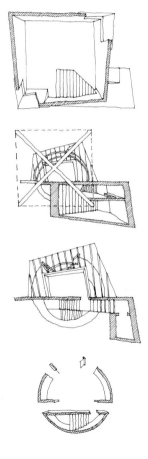

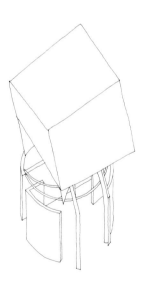

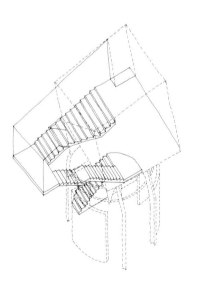

An irregular stair starts from within the cylinder, and winds its way up to the cube.

The plans show the difficulty of conveying the complex composition of the building using conventional architectural drawings.

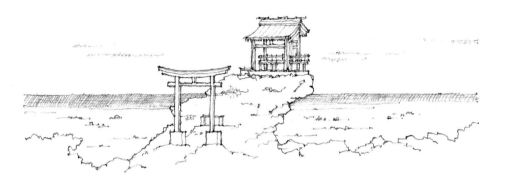

ACKNOWLEDGEMENTS

FIRST EDITION

Many people have contributed, knowingly or unwittingly, to the preparation of this book, not least the numerous student architects who have been subjected to various forms of teaching related to its development. Some of them have said things or done things in their designs that have prompted thoughts that are included here.

The same is true of my colleagues in architectural education, in particular those I work with week by week in the Welsh School of Architecture. Some of the examples were suggested by Kieren Morgan, Colin Hockley, Rose Clements, John Carter, Claire Gibbons, Geoff Cheason and Jeremy Dain.

I have benefitted from many discussions with Charles MacCallum, Head of the Mackintosh School of Architecture in Glasgow, and from the encouragement of Patrick Hodgkinson of the Bath School.

I am also grateful to the Head of Department at the Welsh School, Richard Silverman; and to various visitors to the school who have, unknowingly, stimulated ideas that are included in the preceding pages.

Some of my colleagues in architectural education have contributed to the evolution of this book by asserting things with which I found I could not agree. My attempts to determine why I did not agree have affected my thinking greatly; so, although I shall not name them, I must also thank my theoretical antagonists as well as my friends.

Some ideas have come from far afield, from friends and opponents I rarely or never see, but with whom I sometimes indulge in discussion across the Internet: in particular, Howard Lawrence, together with other contributors to the 'listserv' group –

DESIGN-L@psuvm.psu.edu

Thanks are due too to Gerallt Nash and Eurwyn Wiliam at the Museum of Welsh Life at St Fagans for kindly providing me with a survey of the cottage Llainfadyn, which is the subject of *Case Study 3*, and on which the drawings at the beginning of the chapter *Space and Structure* are based.

I am especially grateful to Dean Hawkes, Professor of Design at the Welsh School, who was kind enough to read the material while in preparation and who made a number of useful comments.

And finally, as always, one must thank those who are close and who put up with having someone around who is writing a book. In my case these long-suffering people are Gill, Mary, David and James.

Simon Unwin, Cardiff, December 1996

SECOND EDITION

In my 'acknowledgements' for the first edition I should also have mentioned Tristan Palmer and Sarah Lloyd, who were my first editors at Routledge, and without whose midwifery this book would never have emerged. To both I owe sincere thanks.

In preparing the second edition, I am grateful for the support and encouragement of Caroline Mallinder and Helen Ibbotson of Routledge, and of Peter Willis, who, in reading through every word never failed in offering advice which was sound.

I must also thank many more colleagues in architectural education, including: Tony Aldrich, Baruch Baruch, Michael Brawne, Peter Carolin, Andy Carr, Wayne Forster, David Gray, Richard Haslam, Juliet Odgers, Richard Padovan, Malcolm Parry, Sophia Psarra, Flora Samuel, David Shalev, Liora bar am Shahal, Adam Sharr, Roger Stonehouse, Andy Roberts, Irit Tsaraf-Netanyahu, Jeff Turnbull, Richard Weston... as well as a few more generations of student architects.

Simon Unwin, Cardiff, March 2003

THIRD EDITION

One of the joys of producing a book like this is that one receives e-mails from people who have taken interest enough to read it, and maybe found it of use. Some of these have made significant contributions to the development of the work.

I would particularly like to thank architect Liza Raju Subhadra for prompting my first trip to India and for her kindness in taking me to see some extremely interesting places, including the small mud-built house outside Trivandrum included in the chapter on *Architecture as Making Frames*, and her own Ramesh House, included in the chapter on *Stratification*. I would like to thank the staff of Trivandrum School of Architecture, especially Professor Shaji T.L. for inviting me to contribute to their seminar on architectural education. I wish them all the very best in the continued success of their school.

I should thank Armin Yeganeh too, for being motivated to translate *Analysing Architecture* into Persian for students in Iran. I wish him success in his career. Also, Masuhiro Agari for his translation into Japanese. I am afraid I have had no contact with the translators of the Spanish, Korean and Chinese versions, but I thank them too.

This third edition has been prepared in the context of the School of Architecture in the University of Dundee rather than that of the Welsh School of Architecture in Cardiff University, so I have a different set of colleagues to thank for their good humoured tolerance of my wanderings in architecture, especially Graeme Hutton the Dean of the School. I would also like to thank Peter Richardson of the School of Media Arts and Imaging in Dundee for his continued interest in the broader dimensions and relevance of the themes explored in this book.

Thanks too go to Fran Ford at Routledge for suggesting this third edition and to Katherine Morton for seeing it through production.

Finally, it seems appropriate to thank my friends, especially Alan Paddison who has always been ready to share discoveries from his own eclectic wanderings, and again my 'long-suffering' family, especially Gill, as the rest of them have fled (more or less) in the dozen years since the appearance of the first edition of *Analysing Architecture*.

Simon Unwin, Dundee, September 2008

SELECT BIBLIOGRAPHY
AND REFERENCES

The following may seem at first sight a disparate set of books, but the principles by which they have been selected are consistent. All contain discussion of architecture either as (what I have termed) *identification of place*, or put forward ways of analysing architecture according to conceptual themes, or discuss related theoretical issues. As such they deal with architecture in ways to which architects, concerned with design generation, can relate. No particular one can however be said to be the authority for the present book. Some of the authors cited have produced other related works; only those most immediately pertinent to the arguments in this book are included here.

Abin, Rob and de Wit, Saskia – *The Enclosed Garden: History and Development of the Hortus Conclusus and its Reintroduction into the Present-day Urban Landscape*, 010 Publishers, Rotterdam, 1999.

Alexander, Christopher and others – *A Pattern Language: Towns, Buildings, Construction*, Oxford UP, New York, 1977.

Alexander, Christopher – *The Timeless Way of Building*, Oxford UP, New York, 1979.

Atkinson, Robert and Bagenal, Hope – *Theory and Elements of Architecture*, Ernest Benn, London, 1926.

Bachelard, Gaston, translated by Maria Jolas – *The Poetics of Space* (1958), Beacon Press, Boston, 1964.

Baker, Geoffrey H. – *Design Strategies in Architecture*, Van Nostrand Reinhold, New York, 1989.

Baker, Geoffrey H. – *Le Corbusier: an Analysis of Form*, Van Nostrand Reinhold, New York, 1984.

Benedikt, Michael – *For an Architecture of Reality*, Lumen Books, Santa Fe, NM, 1988.

Benzel, Katherine – *The Room in Context: Design Beyond Boundaries*, McGraw-Hill, New York, 1998.

Brand, Stewart – *How Buildings Learn*, Phoenix Illustrated, London, 1997.

Ching, Francis D.K. – *Architecture: Form, Space and Order*, Van Nostrand Reinhold, New York, 1979.

Clark, Roger H. and Pause, Michael – *Analysis of Precedent: an Investigation of Elements, Relationships, and Ordering Ideas in the Work of Eight Architects*, North Carolina State University, Raleigh, 1979.

Crowe, Norman and Laseau, Paul – *Visual Notes for Architects and Designers*, John Wiley & Sons, New York, 1984.

Deplazes, Andrea, editor – *Constructing Architecture: Materials, Processes, Structure*, Birkhäuser, Basel, 2005.

Durand, J.N.L. – *Precis des Leçons d'Architecture*, Paris, 1819.

Eliade, Mircea, translated by Sheed – *Patterns in Comparative Religion*, Sheed and Ward, London, 1958.

Eliade, Mircea, translated by Trask – *The Sacred and the Profane: the Nature of Religion*, Harcourt Brace and Company, San Diego, 1957.

Evans, Robin – *The Projective Cast: Architecture and its Three Geometries*, MIT Press, Cambridge, Mass., 1995.

Evans, Robin – *Translations from Drawing to Building*, and Other Essays, Architectural Association, London, 1997.

Farrelly, Lorraine – *The Fundamentals of Architecture*, AVA Publishing SA, Switzerland, 2007.

Frankl, Paul, translated by O'Gorman – *Principles of Architectural History* (1914), MIT Press, Cambridge, Mass., 1968.

Guadet, Julien – *Éléments et Théorie de L'Architecture*, Librairie de la Construction Moderne, Paris, 1894.

Hawkes, Dean – *The Environmental Imagination*, Routledge, Abingdon, 2008.

Heidegger, Martin, translated by Hofstader – 'Building Dwelling Thinking' and '… poetically man dwells…', in *Poetry Language and Thought* (1971), Harper and Row, London and New York, 1975.

Hertzberger, Herman – *Lessons for Students in Architecture*, Uitgeverij Publishers, Amsterdam, 1991.

Hertzberger, Herman – *Lessons in Architecture 2: Space and the Architect*,
    010 Publishers, Rotterdam, 2000.

Hussey, Christopher – *The Picturesque, Studies in a Point of View*,
    G.P. Putnam's Sons, London and New York, 1927.

Kent, Susan, editor – *Domestic Architecture and the Use of Space*,
    Cambridge University Press, Cambridge, 1990.

Lawlor, Anthony – *The Temple in the House*,
    G.P. Putnam's Sons, London and New York, 1994.

Le Corbusier, translated by de Francia and Bostock – *The Modulor, a Harmonious
    Measure to the Human Scale Universally Applicable to Architecture and Mechanics*,
    Faber and Faber, London, 1961.

Lethaby, William Richard – *Architecture: an Introduction to the History and Theory of
    the Art of Building*, Williams and Norgate, London, 1911.

Lynch, Kevin – *The Image of the City*, MIT Press, Cambridge, Mass., 1960.

Martienssen, R.D. – *The Idea of Space in Greek Architecture*,
    Witwatersrand UP, Johannesburg, 1968.

Moore, Charles and others – *The Place of Houses*,
    Holt Rinehart and Winston, New York, 1974.

Moshé, Salomon – *Urban Anatomy in Jerusalem*, Technion, Haifa, 1996.

Nitschke, Günther – *From Shinto to Ando: Studies in Architectural Anthropology in
    Japan*, Academy Editions, London, 1993.

Norberg-Schulz, Christian – *Existence, Space and Architecture*,
    Studio Vista, London, 1971.

Padovan, Richard – *Proportion: Science, Philosophy, Architecture*,
    E. & F.N. Spon, London, 1999.

Pallasmaa, Juhani – *The Eyes of the Skin: Architecture and the Senses* (1996),
    John Wiley & Sons, Chichester, 2005.

Parker, Barry and Unwin, Raymond – *The Art of Building a Home*, Longman, London, New York and Bombay, 1901.

Pearce, Martin and Toy, Maggie, editors – *Educating Architects*, Academy Editions, London, 1995.

Perec, Georges, translated by Sturrock – *Species of Spaces and Other Essays*, Penguin, London, 1997.

Robbins, Edward – *Why Architects Draw*, MIT Press, Cambridge, Mass., 1994.

Rapoport, Amos – *House Form and Culture*, Prentice Hall, New Jersey, 1969.

Rasmussen, Steen Eiler – *Experiencing Architecture*, MIT Press, Cambridge, Mass., 1959.

Relph, Edward – *Place and Placelessness*, Pion, London, 1976.

Rowe, Colin – 'The Mathematics of the Ideal Villa' (1947), in *The Mathematics of the Ideal Villa and Other Essays*, MIT Press, Cambridge, Mass., 1976.

Ruskin, John – *The Poetry of Architecture*, George Allen, London, 1893.

Schmarsow, August, translated by Mallgrave and Ikonomou – 'The Essence of Architectural Creation' (1893), in Mallgrave and Ikonomou (editors) - *Empathy, Form, and Space*, The Getty Center for the History of Art and the Humanities, Santa Monica, Calif., 1994.

Schumacher, Thomas – *The Danteum*, Triangle Bookshop, London, 1993.

Scott, Geoffrey – *The Architecture of Humanism*, Constable, London, 1924.

Scully, Vincent – *The Earth, the Temple, and the Gods; Greek Sacred Architecture*, Yale UP, New Haven and London, 1962.

Semper, Gottfried, translated by Mallgrave and Hermann – *The Four Elements of Architecture* (1851), MIT Press, Cambridge, Mass., 1989.

Sharr, Adam – *Heidegger's Hut*, MIT Press, Cambridge, Mass., 2006.

Smithson, Alison, editor – *Team 10 Primer*, MIT Press, Cambridge, Mass., 1968.

Spengler, Oswald, translated by Atkinson – *The Decline of the West* (1918), Allen and Unwin, London, 1934.

Sucher, David – *City Comforts*, City Comforts Press, Seattle, 1995.

Tanizaki, Junichiro, translated by Harper and Seidensticker – *In Praise of Shadows* (1934), Vintage, London, 2001.

Unwin, Simon – *An Architecture Notebook: Wall*, Routledge, London, 2000.

Unwin, Simon – 'Constructing Place on the Beach', in Menin, editor – *Constructing Place: Mind and Matter*, Routledge, London, 2003, pp. 77-86.

Unwin, Simon – 'Analysing Architecture Through Drawing', in *Building Research and Information*, Volume 35 Number 1, 2007, pp. 101-110.

Unwin, Simon – *Doorway*, Routledge, Abingdon, 2007.

van der Laan, Dom H., translated by Padovan – *Architectonic Space: Fifteen Lessons on the Disposition of the Human Habitat*, E.J. Brill, Leiden, 1983.

van Eyck, Aldo – 'Labyrinthian Clarity', in Donat (editor) - *World Architecture 3*, Studio Vista, London, 1966.

van Eyck, Aldo – 'Place and Occasion' (1962), in Hertzberger and others - *Aldo van Eyck*, Stichting Wonen, Amsterdam, 1982.

Venturi, Robert – *Complexity and Contradiction in Architecture*, Museum of Modern Art, New York, 1966.

Venturi, Robert, Scott Brown, Denise and Izenour, Steven – *Learning from Las Vegas*, (second edition), MIT Press, Cambridge, Mass., 1977.

Vitruvius, translated by Hickey-Morgan – *The Ten Books on Architecture* (first century BC), Dover, New York, 1960.

von Meiss, Pierre – *Elements of Architecture: from Form to Place*, Van Nostrand Reinholt, London, 1986.

Wittkower, Rudolf – *Architectural Principles in the Age of Humanism*, Tiranti, London, 1952.

Zevi, Bruno, translated by Gendel – *Architecture as Space: How to Look at Architecture*, Horizon, New York, 1957.

Zevi, Bruno – 'History as a Method of Teaching Architecture', in Whiffen (editor) - *The History, Theory and Criticism of Architecture*, MIT Press, Cambridge, Mass., 1965.

Zevi, Bruno – *The Modern Language of Architecture*,
University of Washington Press, Seattle and London, 1978.

Zumthor, Peter – *Thinking Architecture*, Birkhäuser, Basel, 1998.

Zumthor, Peter – *Atmospheres*, Birkhäuser, Basel, 2006.

The following is a list of the references given in the main text of this book and in the margins. Most of these are references to publications where more information can be found on the particular examples used. More general texts cited are included in the *Select Bibliography*. I have not included non-architecture books, novels etc.

Ahlin, Janne – *Sigurd Lewerentz, architect 1885-1975*, MIT Press, Cambridge, Mass., 1987.

Alberti, Leon Battista, translated by Rykwert and others – *On the Art of Building in Ten Books* (c1450), MIT Press, Cambridge, Mass., 1988.

Asplund, Erik Gunnar, – 'Var arkitoniska rumsuppfattning', in *Byggmästeren: Arkitektup-plagan*, pp. 203-19, translated by Unwin, Simon and Johnsson, Christina as 'Our Architectural Conception of Space', in *ARQ* (*Architecture Research Quarterly*), Volume 5, Number 2, 2001, pp. 151-60.

Betsky, Aaron – *Zaha Hadid: Complete Buildings and Projects*,
Thames and Hudson, 1998.

Blaser, Werner – *The Rock is My Home*, WEMA, Zurich, 1976.

Blundell Jones, Peter – 'Dreams in Light', in *The Architectural Review*, April 1992, p. 26.

Blundell Jones, Peter – 'Holy Vessel', in *The Architects' Journal*, 1 July 1992, p. 25.

Blundell Jones, Peter – *Hans Scharoun*, Phaidon, London, 1995.

Blundell Jones, Peter – *Gunnar Asplund*, Phaidon, London, 2006.

Bosley, Edward – *First Church of Christ, Scientist, Berkeley*, Phaidon, London, 1994.

Brawne, Michael – *Jørgen Bo, Vilhelm Wohlert, Louisiana Museum, Humlebaek*,
Wasmuth, Tubingen, 1993.

Brown, Jane – *A Garden and Three Houses*, Garden Art Press, Woodbridge, Suffolk, 1999.

Christ-Janer, Albert and Mix Foley, Mary – *Modern Church Architecture*,
McGraw Hill, New York, 1962.

Collins, Brad and Vidler, Anthony – *Eric Owen Moss: Buildings and Projects 2*,
Rizzoli, New York, 1996.

Collins, Peter – *Concrete, the Vision of a New Architecture*, Faber and Faber, London, 1959.

Collymore, Peter – *The Architecture of Ralph Erskine*, Architext, London, 1985.

Constant, Caroline – *The Woodland Cemetery: Towards a Spiritual Landscape*,
Byggforlaget, Stockholm, 1994.

(Coop Himmelb(l)au) – (Cinema, Dresden), *Architectural Review*, July 1998.

Crook, John Mordaunt – *William Burges and the High Victorian Dream*,
John Murray, London, 1981.

Daniels, Glyn – *Megaliths in History*, Thames and Hudson, London, 1972.

Dee, John – *Mathematicall Praeface to the Elements of Geometrie of Euclid of Megara* (1570),
facsimile edition, Kessinger Publishing, Whitefish, MT., undated

(Dewes and Puente) – 'Maison à Santiago Tepetlapa',
in *L'Architecture d'Aujourd'hui*, June 1991, p. 86.

Drange, Tore, Aanensen, Hans Olaf and Brænne, Jon – *Gamle Trehus*,
Universitetsforlaget, Oslo, 1980.

Edwards, I.E.S. – *The Pyramids of Egypt*, Penguin, London, 1971.

Eisenman, Peter – *The Formal Basis of Modern Architecture*,
Lars Müller Publishers, Switzerland, 2006.

(Endo, Shuhei) – (Lavatories, Japan), *Architectural Review*, December 2000.

(Foster, Norman) – 'Foster Associates, BBC Radio Centre',
in *Architectural Design 8*, 1986, pp. 20-27.

273

Frank, Suzanne – *Peter Eisenman's House VI: the Client's Response*,
Whitney Library of Design, New York, 1994.

(Gigon and Guyer) – 'Kalkriese Historical Park', in *Architectural Review*, July, 2002.

Greene, Herb – *Mind and Image*, Granada, London, 1976.

Gregotti, Vittorio – 'Address to the Architectural League, New York, October 1982', in
Section A, Volume 1, Number 1, February/March 1983, p. 8.

Goldberger, Paul and others – *Richard Meier Houses*, Thames and Hudson, London, 1996.

Gropius, Walter – *Scope of Total Architecture*, George Allen & Unwin, London, 1956.

(Hadid, Zaha) – 'Vitra Fire Station', in *Lotus 85*, 1995, p.94.

Harbeson, John F. – *The Study of Architectural Design*,
Pencil Points Press, New York, 1927.

Hawkes, Dean – *The Environmental Tradition*, Spon, London, 1996.

Heaney, Seamus – *The Redress of Poetry*, Faber and Faber, London, 1995.

(Hecker, Zvi) – (Apartments in Tel Aviv), in *L'Architecture d'Aujourd'hui*, June 1991, p. 12.

Heidegger, Martin – 'Art and Space', in Leach, editor – *Rethinking Architecture*,
Routledge, London, 1997.

Hewett, Cecil – *English Cathedral and Monastic Carpentry*, Phillimore, Chichester, 1985.

Institut de Théorie et d'Histoire de l'Architecture – *Matiere d'Art: Architecture
Contemporaine en Suisse*, Birkhäuser, Basel, 2001.

(Imafugi, Akira) – (Wall House), in *Japan Architect '92 Annual*, pp. 24-5.

Johnson, Philip – *Mies van der Rohe*, Secker and Warburg, London, 1978.

(Kaplicky, Jan) – (House, Islington), *Progressive Architecture*, July 1995.

(Kocher and Frey) – (House on Long Island), in Yorke, F.R.S. – *The Modern House*,
Architectural Press, London, 1948.

(Konstantinidis, Aris) – (Summer House), in Donat, John (editor) – *World Architecture 2*,
Studio Vista, London, 1965, p. 128.

Lawrence, A.W. – *Greek Architecture*, Penguin Books, London, 1957.

Le Corbusier, translated by F. Etchells – *Towards a New Architecture* (1923),
John Rodker, London, 1927.

Lethaby, W.R. and others – *Ernest Gimson, his Life and Work*,
Ernest Benn Ltd, London, 1924.

Lim Jee Yuan – *The Malay House*, Institut Masyarakat, Malaysia, 1987.

(MacCormac, Richard) – (Ruskin Library), in *Royal Institute of British Architects
Journal*, January 1994, pp. 24-29.

(Mackintosh, Charles Rennie) – *Charles Rennie Mackintosh and Glasgow School of Art: 2,
Furniture in the School Collection*, Glasgow School of Art, Glasgow, 1978.

Macleod, Robert – *Charles Rennie Mackintosh, Architect and Artist*,
Collins, London, 1968.

Mallgrave, Harry Francis, and Ikonomou, Eleftherios, translators and editors – *Empathy,
Form and Space*, Getty Center for the History of Art and the Humanities, Santa
Monica, Ca., 1994.

March, Lionel and Scheine, Judith – *R.M. Schindler*, Academy Editions, London, 1993.

(Masieri, Angelo) – (Casa Romanelli), in *Architectural Review*, August 1983, p. 64.

McLees, David – *Castell Coch*, Cadw: Welsh Historic Monuments, Cardiff, 2001.

Melhuish, Clare – *Modern House 2*, Phaidon, London, 2000.

(Moss, Eric Owen) – (The Box), *Eric Owen Moss: Buildings and Project 2*,
Rizzoli, New York, 1996.

Murphy, Richard – *Carlo Scarpa and the Castelvecchio*,
Butterworth Architecture, London, 1990.

Muthesius, Stefan – *The English Terraced House*, Yale UP, New Haven and London, 1982.

(MVRDV) – (VPRO Building), *Architectural Review*, March 1999.

(MVRDV) – (Dutch Pavilion), *Architectural Review*, September, 2000.

Neumeyer, Fritz – 'Space for Reflection: Block versus Pavilion', in Schulze, Franz – *Mies van der Rohe: Critical Essays*, Museum of Modern Art, New York, 1989, pp. 148-171.

Nicolin, Pierluigi – *Mario Botta: Buildings and Projects 1961-1982*, Architectural Press, London, 1984.

Norberg-Schulz, Christian and Postiglione, Gennara – *Sverre Fehn: Works, Projects, Writings, 1949-1996*, The Monacelli Press, New York, 1997.

Papadakis, Andreas and others – *Venturi, Scott Brown and Associates, on Houses and Housing*, Academy Editions, London, 1992.

Pendlebury, J.D.S. – *A Handbook to the Palace of Minos at Knossos*, MacMillan & Co., London, 1935.

Pevsner, Nikolaus – *A History of Building Types*, Thames and Hudson, London, 1976.

Pevsner, Nikolaus – *An Outline of European Architecture*, Penguin, London, 1945.

(Piano, Renzo) – (Beyeler Art Gallery), *Architectural Review*, December 1997.

Quinn, P., editor – *Temple Bar: the Power of an Idea*, Gandon Editions, Dublin, 1996.

Rattenbury, Kester – (Baggy House swimming pool), in *Royal Institute of British Architects Journal*, November 1997, pp. 56-61.

Robertson, D.S. – *Greek and Roman Architecture*, Cambridge UP, Cambridge, 1971.

Royal Commission on Ancient and Historical Monuments in Wales – *An Inventory of the Ancient Monuments in Glamorgan, Volume IV: Domestic Architecture from the Reformation to the Industrial Revolution, Part II: Farmhouses and Cottages*, H.M.S.O., London, 1988.

Rudofsky, Bernard – *Architecture Without Architects*, Academy Editions, London, 1964.

Rudofsky, Bernard – *The Prodigious Builders*, Secker and Warburg, London, 1977.

Rykwert, Joseph (Introduction) – *Richard Meier Architect 1964/84*, Rizzoli, New York, 1984.

Schinkel, Karl Friedrich – *Collection of Architectural Designs* (1866), Butterworth, Guildford, 1989.

(Schnebli, Dolf) – (Lichtenhan House), in Donat, John (editor) - *World Architecture 3*,
    Studio Vista, London, 1966, p. 112.

(Scott, Michael) – (Knockanure Church), in Donat, John (editor) - *World Architecture 2*,
    Studio Vista, London, 1965, p. 74.

Semenzato, Camillo – *The Rotonda of Andrea Palladio*,
    Pennsylvania State UP, University Park, Penn.,1968.

Sigel, Paul – *Zaha Hadid: Nebern*, William Stout, San Francisco, CA., 1995.

Smith, Peter – *Houses of the Welsh Countryside*, H.M.S.O., London, 1975.

Sudjic, Deyan – *Home: the Twentieth Century House*, Laurence King, London, 1999.

Summerson, John and others – *John Soane* (Architectural Monographs),
    Academy Editions, London, 1983.

(Sundberg, Olson) – ('Renewal' museum), *Architectural Review*, August 1998, p.82.

Tempel, Egon – *Finnish Architecture Today*, Otava, Helsinki, 1968.

(van Postel, Dirk) – (Glass Pavilion), *Architectural Review*, September 2002.

Warren, John and Fethi, Ihsan – *Traditional Houses in Baghdad*,
    Coach Publishing House, Horsham, 1982.

Weaver, Lawrence – *Small Country Houses of To-day*, Country Life, London, 1912.

Weschler, Lawrence – *Seeing is Forgetting the Name of the Thing One Sees: a Life of Contemporary Artist Robert Irwin*, University of California Press, Berkeley, 1982.

Weston, Richard – *Alvar Aalto*, Phaidon, London, 1995.

Weston, Richard – *Villa Mairea* (in the Buildings in Detail Series), Phaidon, London, 1992.

Wrede, Stuart – *The Architecture of Erik Gunnar Asplund*, MIT Press, Cambridge, Mass.,
    1983.

Yorke, F.R.S. – *The Modern House*, Architectural Press, London, 1948.

(Zumthor, Peter) – 'Peter Zumthor', *Architecture and Urbanism*, February, 1998.

INDEX

*'Study the past if you would define
the future.'*

Confucius (551-479 B.C.)